THE CROSS & THE GAVEL

THE DRAMATIC COURTROOM OF HEAVEN: A LEGAL INTERPRETATION

JUANITA SANDERS THOMAS

The Cross & The Gavel

Trilogy Christian Publishers
A Wholly Owned Subsidiary of Trinity Broadcasting Network
2442 Michelle Drive Tustin, CA 92780

Copyright © 2022 by Juanita Sanders Thomas

- Scripture quotations marked ABPE are taken from the Aramaic Bible in Plain English, 2010 Copyright©, Rev. David Bauscher, Lulu Enterprises Incorporated, 2010.
- Scripture quotations marked AMP are taken from the Amplified® Bible (AMP), Copyright © 2015 by The Lockman Foundation. Used by permission. www.Lockman.org.
- Scripture quotations marked ASV are taken from the American® Standard Bible (ASV), Copyright © 2015 by The Lockman Foundation. Used by permission. www.Lockman.org.
- Scripture quotations marked BLB are taken from The Holy Bible, Berean Literal Bible, BLB. Copyright ©2016, 2018 by Bible Hub. Used by Permission. All Rights Reserved Worldwide. www.berean.bible.
- Scripture quotations marked BSB are taken from The Holy Bible, Berean Study Bible, BSB. Copyright ©2016, 2018 by Bible Hub. Used by Permission. All Rights Reserved Worldwide. www.berean.bible.
- Scripture quotations marked CEV are taken from the Contemporary English Version®. Copyright © 1995 American Bible Society. All rights reserved.
- Scripture quotations marked CSB are taken from the Christian Standard Bible®, Copyright © 2017 by Holman Bible Publishers. Used by permission. Christian Standard Bible, and CSB®, are federally registered trademarks of Holman Bible Publishers.
- Scripture quotations marked ESV are taken from the ESV® Bible (The Holy Bible, English Standard Version®), copyright © 2001 by Crossway Bibles, a publishing ministry of Good News Publishers. Used by permission. All rights reserved.
- Scripture quotations marked GNT are taken from the Good News Translation® (Today's English Version, Second Edition). Copyright © 1982 American Bible Society. All rights reserved.
- Scripture quotations marked GW are taken from God's Word®, © 1995 God's Word to the Nations. Used by permission of God's Word Mission Society.
- Scripture quotations marked ISV are taken from the International Standard Version, Copyright© 1996-2008 by the ISV Foundation. All rights reserved internationally.
- Scripture quotations marked KJV are taken from the King James Version of the Bible. Public domain.
- Scripture quotations marked NASB are taken from the New American Standard Bible® (NASB), Copyright © 1960, 1962, 1963, 1968, 1971, 1972, 1973, 1975, 1977, 1995 by The Lockman Foundation. Used by permission. www.Lockman.org. Scripture quoted by permission.
- Quotations designated NET are from the NET Bible® copyright ©1996, 2019 by Biblical Studies Press, L.L.C. http://netbible.com All rights reserved.
- Scripture quotations marked NIV are taken from the Holy Bible, New International Version®, NIV®. Copyright © 1973, 1978, 1984, 2011 by Biblica, Inc.™ Used by permission of Zondervan. All rights reserved worldwide. www.zondervan.com. The "NIV" and "New International Version" are trademarks registered in the United States Patent and Trademark Office by Biblica, Inc.™
- Scripture quotations marked NKJV are taken from the New King James Version®. Copyright © 1982 by Thomas Nelson. Used by permission. All rights reserved.
- Scripture quotations marked NLT are taken from the Holy Bible, New Living Translation, copyright © 1996, 2004, 2015 by Tyndale House Foundation. Used by permission of Tyndale House Publishers, Inc., Carol Stream, Illinois 60188. All rights reserved.
- Scripture quotations marked WEB are taken from the World English Bible. Public domain.
- Scripture quotations marked YLT are taken from the 1898 Young's Literal Translation of the Holy Bible by J.N. Young, (Author of the Young's Analytical Concordance), public domain.

No part of this book may be reproduced, stored in a retrieval system, or transmitted by any means without written permission from the author. All rights reserved. Printed in the USA. Rights Department, 2442 Michelle Drive, Tustin, CA 92780.

Trilogy Christian Publishing/TBN and colophon are trademarks of Trinity Broadcasting Network.

For information about special discounts for bulk purchases, please contact Trilogy Christian Publishing.

Trilogy Disclaimer: The views and content expressed in this book are those of the author and may not necessarily reflect the views and doctrine of Trilogy Christian Publishing or the Trinity Broadcasting Network.

Manufactured in the United States of America
10 9 8 7 6 5 4 3 2 1
Library of Congress Cataloging-in-Publication Data is available.

ISBN: 978-1-68556-336-3
E-ISBN: 978-1-68556-337-0

DEDICATION

Deum Laudo! Father God, I ascribe total dedication, surrender, glory, and praise to you. Your Highness, *In Excelsis Deo*!
Jesus, my redeeming lamb, *Agnus Dei*, I behold you! I revere you!
Holy Spirit, *Paracletos*—"Helper in a court of law"—I adore you!
All exalted worship be to the most Holy Trinity—Your Highnesses!

I honor my excellent husband and groom, Trent, my co-laborer in Christ, superlative supporter, furthermost gentleman, and very best friend. I owe homage to my noble mother, Ethel, *Mater Magnifica, Mater Nobilis*—you bore the torch of the fiercest, sweetest, and godliest flame of motherhood that I've ever witnessed! Dad Foster, you taught me to smile while I praise!

ACKNOWLEDGMENTS

Special thanks to *all* of my prayerful pillars!

FOREWORD

I met Juanita Sanders Thomas over twenty years ago. My first impression of her was that of a bold, clear-voiced, and kind spokesperson for believing and faithful Christians. It is obvious that her years of familiarity with the court have caused her to develop a knowledge that she is able to impart in such an easy manner that even the non-legally trained person can assimilate. Her style of writing and communicating in this book will allow the reader to easily construct their own high level of communications beyond their normal exposure. Juanita has a talent that she shares in this book of making the reader feel smart about the law, and any student, Bible teacher, or pastor will feel and sound more scholarly with her dynamic tool in their hands.

I enjoy the way Juanita spreads wide those curtains of mystery hiding the High Court, not the Supreme Court as we know it, but the Divine Court of Heaven, which she introduces us to.

She will take the reader on a *voyage*, explaining things about the priestly lawyer, *Yeshua*, and His representation of sinners. It is a *voyage* you don't want to end.

One of the precious things about *The Cross & The Gavel* is that it empowers the reader with divine enlightenment of how heaven's laws function around God's earthly cast. Juanita introduces us to a "judicial bookshelf" of Christ which surely must have shaken an unsuspecting Satan (Hebrew 7:14, CWSB). She understands this master move on heaven's part. The reader will not want to miss the deft way she compares the earthly courts' protection of the accused with God's celestial protection.

Juanita gets it—Jesus of Nazareth is a law library standing on two legs. This book is heaven-sent because of the arduous research Juanita has clearly done for her readers, and because it discloses court procedures in such a welcome and teachable way that the reader may finish the book delightfully feeling like he went to law school. I highly recommend this book because it powerfully helps believers to understand our rights in heavenly places.

— Bishop Demetrics Roscoe
Living Church Ministries International

DISCLAIMER

The information contained in this publication is meant as an instructional tool of valuable information for the reader; however, it is not meant to serve or to be a substitute for industry, professional legal counsel or direct or indirect legal advice.

TABLE OF CONTENTS

Dedication iii

Acknowledgments v

Foreword vii

Disclaimer ix

Preface 17

Introduction 19

Prologue 23

Chapter 1—Redemptive and Legal Artistry 27
    Judgment Per Angelic Melody: The Legal Arts 29
    A Judgment within a Judgment 31
    Legal Sounds of Praise and Worship. 33
    A Glorious Doxology: A Legal Ode to Christ. 35

Chapter 2—Heavenly Court Is in Session 39
    The Lord's Prayer: A Legal Approach 41
    Open Court: A Lawyerly Perspective of the Book of Job . . 43
    From the Throne Room to the Courtroom. 47
    God Came Down: The Legal Rewind 50
    The Day God Attended A Funeral: An Aerial Viewing
        of Christ's Body 52
    He Got Up!: A Legal Analysis of Jesus' Resurrection 53
    The Illegal Body Snatcher: Biblical Angelology 56

Chapter 3—Legal Crossology: The Swag of the Cross! 61
    Oh, that man would behold Him post the cross!. 61
        CHRIST *61*
        CROSS *62*

xi

Legal Crossology: The Legal Immensity of the Cross 62
A Day in the Life of God: The Immense Building
    Blocks of Crossology. 63
Legal Crossology: The Cross—Was It a Gift, Contract,
    or Covenant?. 64
Crossology: The Legal Gift of the Cross. 64
Crossology: The Legal Contract of the Cross 65
Crossology: The Legal Covenant of the Cross 69
Crossology: Covenantal Resurrection 73
Crossology: The Legal Fluidity of the Cross. 74
    C = *Cross Examination of the Lamb of God* 74
    R = *Resurrection Authority* 75
    O = *Obvious Demonstration of God's Love* 76
    S = *Summons to Salvation* 76
    S = *Studies of Forensics Confirm Jesus' Death*. 76
Crossology: Treason & the Legal Progression of the Cross . 80
Crossology: Garden v. Garden 84
Crossology: Real Estate Law Meets Legal Redemption. . . 86
Crossology: A Lawful Revolution & an Illegal Revolt. . . . 87
Crossology: God's Legal Strategy of Double Jeopardy. . . . 90

Chapter 4—Brilliant Attorney Jesus: A Legal Fight-Fest! 93
A Courtyard Becomes a Court: What Did Jesus Write
    and Why? 93
The Fire and the Finger 97
Gender Representation and Legal Loopholes 99
The Trial Venue: The Chosen Courtyard 100
Jesus, Champion of Women 105

Chapter 5—Jesus: Enfranchisement, the Sixth Amendment,
and Women 109
Sixth Amendment & The Bible 111
The Esther Effect: Dare to Touch Me 113
God's Heart Coloration: A Lesson in Diversity 117

Chapter 6—The Legal Instrument by Which God Gets
   Things Done 121
   Religiosity Collides with the Legal Supernatural:
      Lightholes 121
   The Human Rights Legacy of God 124
   Weighing the Bible with a Legal Scale. 129
   Weighed in the Balance 131
   God's Power of Attorney, Angelic Agents & Celestial
      Legalities 131

Chapter 7—Nine Fascinating Trials: God's Legal Response
   to Sin 133
   Four Trials of Christ Jesus 133
      1. *A Trial by the Jewish Council of Elders*. *134*
      2. *A Trial by Prefect Pontius Pilate* *134*
      3. *A Trial by Herod Antipas* *135*
      4. *A Second Trial by Governor Pilate* *136*
      5. *The Inner Trial of Jesus' Faith* *139*
      6. *The Temptation of a Baker's Delight* *140*
      7. *The Temptation of a Quenching Drink* *141*
      8. *Temptation of Self-Regard* *142*
      9. *The Temptation of Enticement* *143*
   The Trial of Humankind 145
   The Trial of Satan: The Condemnation of Satan 145
   Trial by Fire: Jesus' and Peter's Friendship 149
   God on Trial: The Trial of God's Heart 152
   The Mistrials of Jesus. 154
   Prosecutorial Misconduct & Grounds for Mistrial. 157

Chapter 8—The Shalom Breach and Its Legal Repair. 163
   Joshua Goes to Court 171
   The Bodywork of the Gospel: A Legal Mechanic 173
   Jesus' Posture, Shame, or Shameless Victory? 174

The Shame Exchange: The Weight of Justice Meets the
   Nails of the Cross 177
The Five Postures of Christ: Standing, Standing
   Ovation, Stooping, Sitting, Sleeping 178
   Standing Still *178*
   Standing Ovation *178*
   Stooping *179*
   Sitting *179*
   Sleeping *180*
The Gatekeeper 180
Operation Invention & God's Legal Trademark of the
   Church 182

Chapter 9—God, Justice, Bloody Murder, and Double Jeopardy 185
Loving Justice, Doing Justice, Appreciating Justice 185
The Legal Equitableness, Equality & Equableness of God 186
Double Jeopardy and Other Constitutional Violations . . 188
God, Murder & Blood 191
Jesus Takes the Witness Stand!: The Mistrial that Never
   Was Declared 197

Chapter 10—Legally Perfect: The Power of One, The Fire of
Two 205
A Wedding Covenant: The Bride and the Lamb 210

Chapter 11—A Bottle of Grace & a Keg of Kindness 219
Good Grace: The Facts of the Gracious Gospel 219
Do You Own What's in Your Prayer Closet? Your Legal
   Possessory Rights 220
The Will 224

Chapter 12—What's in the Legal Name of Jesus 235
The Legality of Jesus' Name 239
God and His Legal Adoption Process 241

The Legal Parameters of Love: Making a Case for the
　　　　　Father's Love 244
　　　Illegal Religiosity Collides with the Legal Supernatural . . 245
　　　Mysteries of God. 246

Chapter 13—The Warrior: A Legal-Prone God 249
　　　Jesus: Author of Adversarial Redemption 251
　　　Jesus, the Legal Advocate: Criminality in Need of a
　　　　　Defense. 253
　　　Criminality on the Cross: Will the Real Jesus Please
　　　　　Stand Up? 254
　　　The Legal Agility of Christ the Lawyer: The Law v. the
　　　　　Lawyers. 255
　　　Jesus, the Greatest Attorney Who Ever…Died 257
　　　The Mystery of a Mysterious God 259
　　　The Legal Pardon of God: Waymaker 261
　　　Why God Allowed Jesus to Go to Trial: Why God
　　　　　Allows the Believer's Trial 263
　　　Silence Is Ruby. 265

Chapter 14—God's Judgeship 267
　　　A Judge Throws the Book 267
　　　BEMA Judgment 268
　　　The Crowning 269
　　　Establishing Jesus' Judgeship 272
　　　Great White Throne Judgment. 274
　　　Diversity: The Straight and Narrow of It? 276
　　　Diversity and God's Round Table, Here & in the Hereafter 277

Chapter 15—The Devil Is A Liar! Legally Shut Him Up! 279
　　　Christ Inside the Courtroom: Rules of Evidence 281
　　　Hearsay Evidence 282
　　　The Testimony of JESUS CHRIST 283
　　　Witness-Corroboration 287
　　　Acquittal Evidence Here: The Blood Goes to Court . . . 289

Chapter 16—Good Grace and Good Law 291
    GRACE: The Facts of the Gospel 293
    The Work of the Cross 294

Chapter 17—Theology of Law 297
    The Law of Faith 299
    Law of Faith & Healing 300
    The Law of Faith II 302
    Logos V. Logic: Collision with the Law of Faith 303
    Law of Love: Lawyer to Lawyer 305
    The Law of the Mind 306
    Law of Divine Healing. 307
    Self-Care Law: Laws of the Heart 308
    Law of Spiritual Warfare 311

Chapter 18—The Christian's Bill of Rights 313
    The Christian Bill of Rights: My Version 315
    God's Patriot 320
    Legal Compensation: Pay Day in God's Court 322

Chapter 19—Satan's "Legal" Defense 327
    Hide & Seek: Game Over!. 331

Chapter 20—Making It Legal: The Gospel in a Nutshell 335
    All Souls Rise 339
    Be It Resolved: All Souls Matter 340

Chapter 21—The First of Noels: Execute the Challenge! 345

Afterword 349
Bible Versions 351
About the Author 353
Endnotes 355

PREFACE

I have discovered a conjoining of the American legal system with God's biblical theocratic system; when the two meet, it evokes the life-changing dynamism, love, and brilliance of God! I wrote this book to reveal the merging of those two systems. This book is archeological in nature in that its focus is discovery and treasure-hunting-driven. It is a shovel-friendly read because there is lots of digging for exciting, buried biblical truths. As a tireless life coach, a gratified attorney retiree, and a former energetic associate pastor, I've come to vastly appreciate the rewarding mix of law and ministry and have experienced the power of the concentric fusion of foundational faith with the law.

Within the United States pre-trial process, before a case makes its way to court for trial, it undergoes the discovery phase. During that discovery phase, supporting documents for potential litigation are dug up, information relating to the trial, such as admissions, are sought out, and sworn testimony and statements are ferreted out through depositions or affidavits. This complex process involves a deep-digging expedition and scrupulous examination.

Similarly, God's awesome Word lends itself to this type of micro-examination of its hidden nuggets. In this book, that explosive legal mode of discovery is paired with "The Christ Experiment," and sparks fly! The Christ Experiment is the real-life, tangible salvation experience; it is experimental because you have to "try Christ" by trying on His promises by faith. In this book, you are bid to God's action-packed Court for a personal audience with Him. Along the way, you can excavate His Word down to its core of legal gems, all the while seeking Him intimately and continuously with bated breath. This book will take you on an excursion and immersion into God's holy territory. It is a visual progression in law and order, with the cross at the center of the Holy One's love. Expect combustion of simultaneous progression and satisfying fiery revelation!

INTRODUCTION

> *"They read from the book of God's law,*
> *explaining it and imparting insight.*
> *Thus the people gained understanding from what was read."*
>
> NEHEMIAH 8:8 (NET)

Did you know that Jesus walked the earth as an astute lawyer? Did you know that God is a powerful Judge who attended a funeral He dare not miss? These are just some of the relevant concepts you will explore in reading the legal realities of this book. This book is a legal interpretation of the Bible, and its real-life content concentrates on the road of necessity that Jesus traveled to "legally" get to His crucifixion and His resurrection. On a cross at a place called Calvary, Jesus made a decision to redeem humankind's soul, which had rolled away from Him because of a bad decision He had made. God made good on His own decision of redemption because He is a good God, *par-excellence*, and three days later He rolled away two stones: One from the mouth of the useless grave of His Son and the other from the mouth of bondage so that it could no longer repress His creation. Jesus was bodily raised from the dead, and today, He is incontestably alive! The legal protocol that paved the way for God's beloved emissary to get to the cross and to legally secure the redemption of lost humankind is heavily judicial, noticeably transactional, and hoisted by true grit and raw passion, all of which have been set forth in this book.

Breaking news! Every believer has legal rights which God will back up!

If you know your rights, you can win in God's court of law. *"Open my eyes to see the wonderful truths in your law"* (Psalm 119:18, NLT). The Bible *is* a legal document, which is very different from it merely containing legal supplementation within it. The Bible, itself, constitutes a legal, authorizing document as well as supplies portions, which excerpted, can stand alone as legal provisions also. The Bible is the sum total of its existence. It has a multi-revelational, multi-featured, multicultural, and multigenerational existence. It exists for several purposes, one of which is to be a legal transactional record of the interaction and exchange between heavenly and earthly events. Also, within its multi-capacity, it exists to memorialize legal provisions of contracts and covenants between God and His creation, all of which are entirely enforceable before God's high bench. Moreover, the Bible exists as the repository of rights and privileges for the believer. Ultimately, it exists as the inspired, written exhale of God and the exalted articulation of God's love. Put another way, the Bible functions as the *"is"* of the great *"I AM."* It houses excavatable layers of God's legal manifestos which He wants to reveal; these manifestos are illustrative of God's redemptive love and are provable in God's Court of law. He set it up that way. Intriguingly, America's courts of law mirror God's Court of law in large part; hence, this book embarks on a legal journey of exploration: Case study in Americana law meets Bible study in theology. *"…But God has revealed it to us by the Spirit. The Spirit searches all things, even the deep things of God"* (1 Corinthians 2:10, BSB).

> *"I rejoice at Your word as one who finds great treasure… I love your law."*
>
> PSALM 119:162–163 (NKJV)

I love the heft of justice. I love the Word of God and am enamored of the study of law. For me, the exploration of these three side by side has resulted in a differentiation of ideas and compounded argumentation that freshly elucidates familiar passages in the Bible. The pages of this book are a reflection of that grouping and the voyaging of the legal reasoning behind the hand of God, calling for what I term as "divine scoping." It may not be instantly perceivable, but the Bible unfolds like a legal arena. With a microscopic tight zoom, I explore the legalities of Bible passages until it becomes obvious that its content greatly reflects one big, exciting courtroom. Behind many of its storied constructions and events, there lies the juxtaposition between the courtly charitable and the harsh adversarial. A closer examination reveals legal sparring between its printed type and its chapters brim with buried, legal proclamations; in fact, the New Testament unfurls like a whopping court scene surrounding the crucifixion and the resurrection of Jesus. Both the Old and New Testaments bear theatricality and have story drops of unwinding twists and colossal turns of revelations, all culminating in a gavelled verdict from God. Lean in!

PROLOGUE

"The foolishness of God is wiser than man,
the weakness of God is stronger than man...
God chose the foolish things of this world to put the wise to
shame. He chose the weak things of this world to put the
powerful to shame."

1 CORINTHIANS 1:25, 27; CEV

Irrespective of the fact that the Bible is the greatest book ever written, cheap shots are taken at it for its perceived lack of analytic value and erudition. The inspired Word of God, however, is the exact opposite. Contextually, it is "chock-full" of robust, analytic patterns and application; and it certainly has widespread, intellectual depth. Its composed chapters are God-breathed and, as such, are imprinted with His scholarship. To detractors everywhere, I have this message—God is smart!—supremely so. I submit that rather than viewing God's Word as amorphous and nebulous, as it has been pegged in many polemic circles, it should be seen as scholarly-worthy, with clear and defensible legal form. I am certain that closer scrutiny of God's inscripturated waters will allow the reader to pearl-dive: *"O the depth of the richness both of the wisdom and knowledge of God..."* (Romans 11:33, KJV). This book sums up the gospel by answering some of its most grappling questions about the cross. It will look at the meaning of the gospel through the eyes of the cross with different calibrations of the cross, within different scenarios involving the cross, and from different vistas surrounding the cross. In a few words, this book is cross-conscious! If you love the cross, oppose the cross, not sure how you feel about the cross, are confused by the cross, or just want to understand the cross better, this book will open up new and helpful ways to look at the landscapes of the cross. It introduces easy-access, legal analysis about the cross and correlating biblical events for both the initiated and the uninitiated novice in law.

There is a saying, "guilty as sin;" well, that's exactly what humankind was. This book presents a number of ways humankind's guilt of sin is seen through an American court's eyes while exploring various legal paths by which that guilt is maneuverably undone or otherwise overridden so that, in the end, humankind is legally restored to its Maker.

> *God used the law to save His world!*

There is an American legal expression known as "the long arm of the law" that describes the expansive reach of the law; actually, God has an even longer arm of the law: *"To whom has the LORD revealed his powerful arm?"* (Isaiah 53:1, NLT). Both the long and short of the matter is that God used the law to save His world! This book is an un-watered down, close-up inspection of the overlapping of the American legal scales of justice and God's sword of justice. Look for Jesus in cameo appearances as an attorney and look for allusions of Him as a star witness. At the book's core is this affirmation: Surely, God's arm is not so short that it cannot save.

A friendly warning to those who are spiritual trend followers or religious avant-garde groupies. One would do well to be aware of the following caveat: God's issued challenge of the Christ Experiment goes against some emerging trends of societal and neo-spiritual tanks of thought. America now finds itself in an era of counterculture post-Christianity and in what I term as "post-ecclesia," that is, an era where the "called-out ones" are no longer prized or even applicable. Those two counter thoughts have become twin nemesis of not only the Christ Experiment but also of the "Cross Experiment." There has been a genuine disconnect; instead of a dependence on God's suitable truth and interdependence within the body of Christ, there has been a growth of separatist, *inapropos* independence. Put succinctly, there has been a measurable falling away. Trending well is the anti-church concept that proselytizing Christians are the problem, and further, that the solution to true, sanguine inner peace is the proselytizing of those Christians into secularism. In other words, promoting the "saving of the Christian from salvation" as the means to rectify what's wrong and bad in the world today. Truly, the problem with that concept syllogistically is that relativism is relevant, so the marker of authentic comparison must be relevant to Jesus, Jesus' salvation, and the emblematic cross out of which God birthed His church because God is the only valid standard of absolutism. Salvation, then, is the just solution to the world's problem and is, indeed, both the traditional means and the modern end to true, inner peace. This book is built on God's aerial view of truth. Salvation is not a countervailing truth; it is the prevailing truth, and the only legal avenue to God—per God's law: *"Salvation is found in no one else, for there is no other name under heaven given to mankind by which we must be saved"* (Acts 4:12, NIV).

CHAPTER 1

Redemptive and Legal Artistry

"But they delight in the law of the LORD, *meditating on it day and night."*

PSALM 1:2 (NLT)

What is the gospel? I perceive the gospel as a tripartite story because it has a sequence that can be told in three phases and should be viewed through trifocal lenses. The gospel is this:

1. Adam, God's first created son and the representative of humankind, is overtaken by sin and dies a consequential, spiritual death. Sequentially, the immortal Spirit God makes an unstealthy entrance into the earth as a flesh-blanketed, divinely-human baby known as Immanuel and the begotten second Adam.
2. The man-child, the baby-man who is no longer a flesh-coated infant, becomes a middle-aged redeemer. The Redeemer Christ then completes His mission as the Donor Christ by donating His life as the God-sacrifice for lost humanity; He takes His place on a pre-planned, un-benevolent cross where He willingly succumbs to death.
3. After dying like a powerless lamb, He is resurrected as the all-encompassing, all-powerful Lord and King of His eternal, spiritual kingdom, but not before vanquish-

ing both Satan's stronghold of sin and his deathly stranglehold over jailed humanity.

That triple-tiered litany of events was completed not only by God's seen celebratory hand but was also completed by the long arm of legal, spiritual laws which were behind the scenes; it all was governed by a set of God-created, planned statutes, and ordinances. Pragmatically speaking, municipalities have their feasibility plans, businesses have their business plans, and God has His kingdom plans. In the natural world, it is easy to see that each of these visionary, developmental plans set forth God's legislative aims of governance, economy, ideology, and the judicial means by which to actuate them. So, too, did God activate His kingdom plan in the earth with its goals and revealed it to Moses and His prophets, then codified it in the Bible. Importantly, God doesn't do anything by improvisation. God's supernatural was artfully launched by strokes of His systematic; that is, God would cause His spiritual laws to be propelled in the earth to accomplish His beauteous end. The choreography of God's law and natural law in the land produced that miraculous trio of events for the redemption of humankind. The beauty of the spiritual artistry of the cross combined with the force of the legal merit of Jesus' death created an unrivaled masterpiece by God. It is that sacred metanarrative and poetic orchestration that was angelically heralded as the Good News.

Judgment Per Angelic Melody:
The Legal Arts

"... Let all the angels of God worship Him."

HEBREWS 1:6 (NKJV)

The angels were engrossed. It was rare that this angelic retinue encountered a half-sized hush on this side of heaven. Pondering this day of *nuit,* they looked on as jurors, semi-jurors, because they did not get to vote. As they waited for an explanation as to why God had draped the day in king-sized black, they peered backward in time. The year was roughly 4 BC. The divine trio was immersed in the Son's departure. They had been present there, too, the night of the nascence. The veil that separated the activities of heaven and earth was parted at the Savior's birth as the rounded terra hosted a glimpse of their high-wattage, angelic caroling. Peace on earth, the choristers piped. They hastened to and fro through the earth, alighting with marathon precision, chiming that wonder of peace in melodic virtuosity, only to still themselves long enough for a band of nightly shepherds to spy them as they delightfully looked upon the small Mighty One. Now it was roughly 30 AD. They had not enjoyed seeing the body of their Lord-in-Chief unroyally handled and decrowned. Bewildered, they were ordered to stand still again, strangely flightless this time, not for shepherds in a field, but for throngs in front of puzzling cross-shaped beams. Their angel wings now swaying as laurels of ribbons as they nestled close to hear the verdict about the hallowed Lamb. Their gazes fixed on the Divine One. They heard these reverberating words as they floated above God's legal echo chamber: "The material facts of the blood-clad contract between Father and Son were not in contention. No breach of contract to be found anywhere in this civil case. Jesus, He came and He conquered—*Venit et Vicit!*" There was no prolonged judicial deliberation, no judicial abeyance, and no announcement of taking the matter under judicial advisement before summarily issuing a judgment favorable to the blood-drenched Lamb. Their captain's conclusive death erased all meritless "ifs," "ands," or "buts" of dispute, and as a matter of law,

> *God brought the blood-tainted gavel down!*

had hurled an explanation point after *Amen!* They sensed the King of heaven, a lone-paneled judge, their God, would render judgment quickly. Indeed the decision was given, the adjudication was swift. "Not Guilty." Behold, God brought the blood-tainted gavel down! Turning their darting eyes and gaping mouths to the second case, now a criminal one before heaven's bar. They were visionless in fathoming this perplexing charge—"Guilty As Sin." The Judge's directed verdict rang out in the celestial colonnades of cascading timelessness, atop the whistling bells of justice. Their supernal wings hummed as they clustered closer, for they had waited for boundless ions to hear the Lamb's message, and now they were huddled messengers aflame, engulfed with fiery readiness, about to minister to humankind. Then they heard it—that one polysyllabic word that jettisoned from the mouth of God, "*Guilty!*" Incredulous, the stunned mellifluous flutter of their aesthetic wings could barely be composed until they heard the barraging sequel…"but not *found* guilty!!" Cherishing that barreling tiding of the acquittal of their peerless wonder, the throne's messengers took to kinetic flight.

A Judgment within a Judgment

"... When they spoke of the things that have now been told to you by those who have preached the gospel to you by the Holy Spirit sent from heaven. Even angels long to look into these things."

1 PETER 1:12 (NIV)

The enigmatic mystery of the special judgment of God concerning Jesus' redemptive work can be likened to a multi-foci riddle. It is a true fact that the guilt of the world was transferred to Jesus, which made Him guilty in a legal sense, but truth be told, in character and in His Holy essence, He was guiltless because no fault was found with Him. Riddle this:

The perfect sacrifice, although guilty, was not found guilty; how?—because Jesus absorbed the sin but remained forever sinless. The Adamic Jesus was guilty, but the second person of the Godhead, Jesus, was guilt-averse.

The great judgment rendered above in the case which I have entitled *Sin v. Superiority of Love* occurred before watchful angels who biblically look into the affairs of men with heightened curiosity. Although angels have watchful capacity, these heavenly sentinels could not fulfill the role of true jurors, so they watched in virtual capacity because, legally, jurors are to be peers of the accused and Jesus is peerless; therefore, in exceptional essence, God was both Judge and Jury in a very literal sense. The heavenly Court proceeding, which overwhelmingly would decide the case of humankind's guilt or innocence, was directly hinged to that of its Savior. There were two cases in one since the outcome of Jesus' verdict would impact humankind's verdict; judicially, humankind's tethered salvation depended on Jesus "taking the guilty fall" for him, that is, depended upon Jesus being a guilty scapegoat for him. The Eternal Judge's adjudicatory judgment of Jesus being "guilty" simultaneously transformed humankind's legal status from guilty to "not guilty" because Jesus technically exchanged places with Him on the cross, becoming the guilty party instead. I submit that the memorable judgment resulted in two purposeful and powerful messages that resound even unto this day. The pivotal determination of the guilt of the Lamb of Grace was the overarching reason that God's Court was convened, but the determination of the guilt of humankind's soul was intertwined with it. That judgment of guilt led to the other judgment that was contained within it—and arose out of it—which was a declaratory judgment. There, the Court of God's legal ruling was declaratory in that it translated into a statement of humankind's redeemed status, declaring the right to salvation under God's "insurance plan." In a legal sense, zooming in, every believer was also a claimant in an underlying "class action suit" against sin's injurious dominion over them. A class-action suit is a lawsuit in which the court authorizes one individual who has been injured to stand for a whole class of persons who have been similarly injured. Adam would have been that single individual, and humankind would have been the group which he stood for.

It is extremely interesting that God's ethereal spirits have only an inquisitive understanding and not a visceral understanding of the salvation plan; they cannot experience salvation because they are essentially soul-less—Angels have no souls to be saved: "*The Son did not come to help angels; he came to help the descendants of Abraham*" (Hebrew 2:16, NLT). Sitting "courtside," therefore, the angels' indirect grasp of grace's redemption is greater than their direct grasp of Jesus' highest calling. That investigative assembly only has a divinely academic perception of salvation, although they were gleefully present for the verdict.

Sin v. Superiority of Love involved a double proceeding that set a legal precedent that would be relied upon for the outcome of *every* future soul before God's Court. This case revealed that God's love overcame the evil of sin's chokehold over humankind. God's Court determined that Grace's Lamb was guilty of the sin placed on Him; thus, God's outflowing, loving grace would be placed upon the soul of man, rendering him innocent upon receiving the Christ-Lamb. This precedent would affect every child of God; thereafter, *"Tear your heart, and not merely your clothes, and return to the Lord, your God; for He is gracious and compassionate... Then everyone who calls on the name of the* LORD *will be saved..."* (Joel 2:13, 32; NASB).

Legal Sounds of Praise and Worship

"To the end that my glory may sing praise to You."

PSALM 30:12 (NKJV)

I am strongly convinced that there is a legal element to sonorous praise and worship. It follows that God has made the voice a legal instrument of praise; therefore, when a voice of praise is released into the atmosphere, it demonstrates that it has legal license to soundly augment a desirable atmosphere or disrupt an undesirable one. For example, such licensed authority is seen when believers cry, "Holy, Holy, Holy is the Lord;" God's power explodes in the atmosphere, and anything opposed to it implodes. The praise instrument is either fortifying or shattering everything around it because we, His vocal messengers, are crying out in holy anthem, pointing to the renown of a Holy God, and contained within that sound of praise and worship, is the outflowing and recurring reality of fixed victory. Praise allows ascendancy! Through it, we get to "come up" to where God is; it is a stair-stepping righteous escapade. A biblical analysis shows that an audience with God is legally supported when it is preceded by narrated sounds of praise;

> *Our prayers dance on His praise.*

that is, Scripture points out that thanksgiving and praise are both preconditions and precursors to legally hosting God's presence: *"Enter into His gates with thanksgiving and into His courts with praise"* (Psalm 100:4, KJV). In a real sense, our prayers dance on His praise. Prayer accompanied by a ripple of Hallelujah is a legal, causative turning point in the Spirit realm.

A move of God is often preceded by a sound: The visitation of the Holy Spirit on the Day of Pentecost was preceded by a mighty rushing wind. Also, Jesus cried with a loud voice on the cross prior to His death; and a *shofar*, the heavenly trumpet, is to be blown prior to the triumphant, earthly return of Jesus just "yocto-seconds" before He raptures His church. These sounds signal a type of legal notice to the believer, known in the earth known as "Due Process of Law." Under this due process, which was so important to get right that it appears in our Constitution twice, the Fourteenth and Fifth Amendments to the United States Constitution require that notice, among other protections, be given by a federal or state governing power before it takes certain types of action in the private lives and liberties of its citizens—primarily to prevent it from acting arbitrarily.[1] God, as the omnipotent governor of our lives, gives believers that same spiritual, procedural legal notice. Specifically, sounds that originate from God give the believer notice of God's intended, unarbitrary presence and action in our lives. Another example through which God affords humankind due process is His" knocking" before entering a heart. He allows the believer the liberty of saying "yes, come in" or "no, do not disturb:" *"Listen, I am standing at the door and knocking! If anyone hears my voice and opens the door, I will come into his home and share a meal with him, and he with me"* (Revelation 3:20, CEV).

Interestingly, however, sounds offered to God give God reciprocal notice of the believer's desired and intended audience *with Him* as well. God waits for the sound of a creaky, open door of the believer's heart which may be represented by a blasted, harmonic scream, "Yes, Lord! " or a soft, off-key, "Just as I am," or a tearfully muttered, "Use me." The account of Joshua's camp surrounding the walls of Jericho exemplifies another sound exchange that went forth between God and the vociferous Israelites. On the seventh day of the battle, the Israelites shouted praises unto God, and simultaneously, God noisily pulverized the crashing walls of Jericho with a miraculous, acoustical demolition. In the sounds of worship, there is "warship!" There, God illustrated the legal practice of sonorous exchange. *Laus Deo!*—Praise God!

> *In sounds of worship is warship.*

A Glorious Doxology: A Legal Ode to Christ

> *"And when Christ, who is your life, is revealed to the whole world, you will share in all his glory."*
>
> COLOSSIANS 3:4 (NLT)

The cross not only produced Jesus' finest hour both on the earth and under the earth, the cross was legally fashioned by God to be Jesus' doxology. God glorified Christ on the cross. A glorified Christ then glorified His church. The cross testified of that glory when Christ was risen as the "Lord of Glory." The cross is, therefore, Jesus' doxology since a doxology has become known as an anthem of praise and glory. There, at the site of the cross, God set up His new covenantal precedent and sealed it by instituting its principle as supernatural law—that earthly suffering cedes to glory! A legal precedent is an established principle or decision in a case that influences the outcome of future cases like it, so how did God's precedent affect the believer? Following Jesus' glorious work at the cross, a believer's outcome would indeed be tailored by that precedent. God extended the glory provision! Since

Jesus was the first fruit of God's glory, God made it legal that to incur earthly suffering in His Son's name would produce for all believers the same automatic, heavenly reward of glory that Jesus received.

Doxa is the Greek word for glory. Doxology, thus, means the study of glory. If you truly want to study glory, you need to look no further than the cross. It is ironic that the ill-reputed, barbaric cross that housed human symbols of cruel disrepute and historically served as the conveyor of ignobility would propel Jesus to the other side of scandal into soundful glory. *"Oh LORD, our Lord, how majestic is your name in all the earth! You have set your glory above the heavens"* (Psalm 8:1, ESV). The Bible says that God has made His body to be kings and priests, so it is apparent that God has imbued all of His children with a kingly hunger for priestly searchability: *"It is the glory of God to conceal a thing, but the honor of kings is to search out a matter"* (Proverbs 25:2, KJ21). Humankind is constantly immersed in a searchfest for everything, whether it's knowledge, fame, or fortune. The object of that God-derived hunger, however, was meant to be God Himself, for God says in His Word, if you hunger for Him, you will be filled with Him. Imagine that!...being filled from your toes up to your hairline with God. It is a bold honor to find God amidst His glorious concealment, which is encryptic by its nature. That encryption is not meant to be an obstacle but a welcome challenge; it is the means of getting to know the deeper canyons of God. God wants to be known by humankind in all of His collective glory, and really if truth be known, that is what we all want at our cores. All along, humankind has been searching for its High Priest and its King of Kings, the one that we were meant to be most like. In my estimation, God's glory has a circulatory effect in that it travels from God's heart to ours and back to His. Moses wisely said, *"Show me your glory"* (Exodus 33:18, NIV). God wants to elaborately reveal His glory to all of us. It is most clear that God went through great lengths to ensure that we could access His glory, which, in part, is chiseled in His face, as well as in His back. With Moses concealed in a rock, God showed him His glory as His back—or glory train—

passed; however, today, we can face His glory head-on. Why? It is possible because of what I term "The Great Rocky Exchange." You see, God hid His facial glory from the marred *face* of Jesus, the "Rock of Ages," and that one act ensured that legally culpable humankind could come boldly before His haloed throne and be *face to face* with His eye-catching glory. Jesus' death legally corrected what I call the case of *The Hidden Face*. Isaiah 59:2–4 (NIV) puts it this way: *"…Your iniquities have separated you from your God; your sins have hidden his face from you, so that he will not hear…no one calls for justice; no one pleads his case with integrity. They rely on empty arguments."* Jesus is due reams of praise because, there on the cross, His sinlessness and copious trail of blood gloriously pleaded with integrity for the saving justice of God: *"Father the hour has come; glorify your Son so he can give glory back to you"* (John 17:1, NLT). *"Oh LORD, our Lord, how majestic is your name in all the earth! You have set your glory above the heavens"* (Psalm 8:1, NIV).

God inspired hymnody throughout the ages. We sing Thomas Ken's four hundred century-old doxology, "Praise Father, Son, and Holy Ghost," or we relish Handel's nearly three-century-old Christmas doxological oratorio, "Messiah," but I propose that these musical relics were inspired by God in infinity's past to glorify Christ; that is, through God's time-sequenced lens, these songs were inspired to help us heap glory on Jesus. God spied the end from the beginning, had already glorified His Son in the futuristic-past, and had inspired a holy musical ode through Ken, and a Christmas doxology through Handel, both of whom composed these rhapsodic hymns for timeless eras. Through that couplet of the inspired poetic, God used the listening arts genre to extend lyrical glory and lasting renown upon His Son who is the full reflection of God's glory and the Godhead: *"Sing to the LORD, all the earth; Proclaim good tidings of His salvation from day to day. Tell of His glory among the nations"* (1 Chronicles 16:23–25, NASB1995).

CHAPTER 2

Heavenly Court Is in Session

"Then you will come and pray to me and I will listen…"
JEREMIAH 29:12 (NIV)

At the federal level, the United States Attorney General is America's leading law officer and foremost attorney who represents it at trials. Following second in rank is the United States Solicitor General, who is the chief legal officer of the executive branch that solicits—or petitions—on behalf of the United States as its lawyer. Both of their roles usually require them to

> *Jesus serves as a divine Attorney General & Solicitor.*

deploy skills of legal reasoning. In a similar fashion, Jesus serves as a type of divine Attorney General and Solicitor on behalf of the people of God, and God is easily solicited in His Court of law by legal reasoning: *"Come now, let us reason together, says the LORD"* (Isaiah 1:18). *"But the wisdom that is from above is first pure, then peaceable…easy to be entreated"* (James 3:17, KJV). The American judicial system provides a setting where a petitioner, whether appearing on her own without counsel (*pro se*) or perhaps through her lawyer, may appear before a judge to bring a petition. Analogous to that, a believer who brings prayers before God's Court, similarly solicits—or prays—for the legal attention of God in that particular matter. To emphasize the legal-forward nature of praying, I point to archaic English court terminology: Your Honor, I "pray" thee...! This eighteenth-century English speech was part of an attorney's oral presentation and the corresponding "Prayer for Relief" was a formal written request of desired outcomes that was addressed to the court. In fact, the Anglo-American rooted Prayer of Relief still accompanies the American civil lawsuit today, typically appearing at the end of a submitted legal complaint before the court. There, one can make a "special prayer" for specified, entitled relief or make a "general prayer" of unspecified relief, which the court can appropriately determine.[2] This mode of legal petitioning makes it clearer that the "pray-er," in a true legal and spiritual sense, means a *petitioner*—known also as a "claimant"—is making an appearance before God and asserting her legal claims and requests: *"Do not be anxious about anything, but in everything by prayer and petition with thanksgiving, let your requests be known to God"* (Philippians 4:6, BSB). Understanding this legal history of the word "pray" and the conduct associated with this word cements the Apostle Paul's clarion call to prayer. There is undeniably a depth of legal potency found in entreating God in His Court: *"Present your case, says the LORD. Submit your arguments..."* (Isaiah 41:21, KJV).

The Bible is illustrative of the fact that God has an open court policy for these petitions and that His forum is quite accessible. One who brings prayers before God as He sits on heaven's regal throne is, in fact, a courtroom petitioner: *"And another angel came and stood at the altar, having a golden censer... that he should offer it with the prayers of all saints upon the golden altar which was before the throne"* (Revelation 8:3, KJV). The Bible says prayers are a memorial to God, basically meaning they stay in God's memory. Our judicial system uses the practice of stenographic memorialization to record important trial content and also uses a court "docket" to record scheduled court appearances and proceedings. It uses this formal, punctilious system because having a memorialized record is extremely crucial in the court world; apparently, this standard of record-keeping is a tool found within God's judicial system too: "Your prayers ...have come up before God as a memorial..." (Acts 10:3, NIV).

> *The Lord's prayer is filled with legal inference.*

The Lord's Prayer: A Legal Approach

"Then you will call upon me and come and pray to me, and I will hear you."

JEREMIAH 29:12 (BSB)

In the American court of law, a petitioner petitions the court for a specific action or a specific ruling from the Judge. God, too, formally hears the petitions—or prayers—of His people, and unknown to many, the Lord's prayer is filled with legal inference. I, therefore, encourage the following dissection:

- "Our Father"—The one who is the founding Father of the earth and its supreme Judge.
- "Who are in *heaven*"—The upper forum for all judicial cases which come up before God.
- "*Hallowed* be your name." On earth, a judge's name is honored, which is why he is called "Your Honor." Likewise, we honor God by referring to Him as the Holy One, which can be extended to "Your Holiness."
- "Let your kingdom come. Let your *will* be done." On earth, when a judge expresses his will for an outcome, it is written in the form of a judge's order. In God's kingdom, when He expresses His will to be done, it is also expressed as His judge's order with one word, *Amen*! Revelation

3:14 expresses that Jesus is God's Amen! Amen in the Hebrew means so be it! Or so ordered!—both signifying its use in God's judicial protocol.

- "Also in the earth, just *as it is* in Heaven"—On earth, lawyers approach a judicial bench which consists of a seat. In heaven, there is also a judicial bench which is the seat of mercy. It is before this seat that personified mercy and justice present their cases before God in the person of the Advocate Jesus Christ.

- "Give us our necessary bread *today*"—This part of the prayer alludes to the believer's daily expectations of daily provision from God and daily interaction with the Bread of Life. Jesus taught the disciples to pray, or to present themselves before God each day, by modeling it with His own presence before the Father daily. Likewise, in America's court system, there is a daily calendar that is known as the "docket," as mentioned previously, which daily records the parties that will come before a judge.

- "Forgive us of our sins as we have *forgiven* those who sin against us"—This part of the prayer refers to a certain standard of the Spirit—who is the standard-bearer—by which one must lift up the standard of forgiveness, so as not to grieve Holy Spirit and allow Him to have full free reign in the believer's life: *"And do not grieve the Holy Spirit of God…"* (Ephesians 4:30, NIV). This carriage of forgiveness is important because, true to court form, a judge looks for a certain posture of order in the court so that proceedings move smoothly. Similarly, all witnesses are to conduct themselves with an acceptable standard in order not to offend the judge or risk being removed from the court. The Bible likewise says, *"Let all things be done decently and in order by His Spirit"* (1 Corinthians 14:40, KJV).

- "And lead us not into *temptation*, but deliver us from evil"—This section is both a petition and a warning. It is a petition in which the pray-er asks for leadership to resist temptation. It is also an admonition for the "pray-er about the adversary," lest the pray-er become the prey. Likewise, in our judicial system, petitioners and witnesses are warned of the temptation of perjuring themselves or lying under oath.
- "For Yours is the kingdom, and the *power*, and the glory, forever. Amen" It is true that as part of judicial Americanism, a judge wields a measurable amount of curtailable power and commensurate authority within the judicial branch, and therefore can be reigned in by appellate courts; but this added section to the original Lord's prayer refers to God, alone, and makes it clear that He is subject to no one. He is the only omnipotent judge that reigns over His kingdom with absolute, non-adjustable power and undilutable authority.

Open Court: A Lawyerly Perspective of the Book of Job

"I remember the law you gave us long ago, Lord."
PSALM 119:52 (ERV)

The Devil always has a lie behind his words, even when his ventriloquist act appears true; I call it "the rear mirror reality" because he's closer than you think with a lie. Without a doubt, the Bible creates the setting found in a marvelous amphitheater, a place known for its legendary ancient battles and conquests. Its pages combine to form architectonic frames of verbal and visual spectacles of spiritual combat.

No need for legal fiction because its true stories and legal commentary stir with tough tumble and adversarial tones, as in the book of Job.

Heaven contains the throne of God, and Scripture depicts it as the venue where the Court of God convenes. *"I am the LORD, the King of Israel! Come argue your case with me. Present your evidence"* (Isaiah 41:21, ESV). A lawyer is sometimes referred to as counsel, and God established that His counsel is supreme: *"The counsel of the Lord Stands forever…"* (Psalm 33:11, BSB). The Bible also informs us that followers of Christ sit in heavenly places as law-abiding citizens with Him (See 1 Corinthians 15:12–19). I submit that it is heavenly citizenry, which entitles us to appear before the Court of heaven because legally, we have what is called residential rights *in absentia*, meaning those of us who are not physically present in heaven can still have all of our legal cases brought there because of our heavenly status. In our American court of law, upon entering the courtroom, the complainant who has brought the complaint usually sits down with his lawyer at the counsel's table. I propose that is one reason why the scriptural text has us seated with our Lord, our Counsel, in heaven.

When the book of Job begins, there is drama in the heavenlies, and we get to peek into the precise nature of the link between God's laws and angelic activity. A crooked angel reappears before his boss, having been kicked out, but allowed to keep his entry pass to the Court. Scripture photographs that God's Court is open to not only human believers but also to non-human supernatural beings—holy and unholy—who have an appointed day for their Court appearances. Clearly, even the disgruntled fallen angel, that inhuman and inhumane Satan, is also allowed access: *"When the day came for heavenly beings to appear before the LORD, Satan was there among them"* (Job 1:6, GNT). This contextual reference to Satan's "appearance" is important to note because, in the American court system, lawyers make what is referred to as procedural "appearances" in court matters; similarly, slotted appearances in legal matters are obviously central to God's own organizational flow in heaven. Tracking with God's open accessibility is God's predilection for fairness in hearing a good court case that comes before Him. God's untainted angels appeared before Him, along with that soiled Devil who managed his evil enthu-

> *Satan cannot rant against believers in God's Court.*

siasts. Although an enemy of the children of God and an ousted foe of God, Satan was not banned unjustly from the Court of God because God conducts His judiciary justly: *"A God of truth and without injustice"* (Deuteronomy 32:4, NKJV). In the Greek, Satan means accuser, and the accuser lives up to his name, for he is often seen in the Scriptures wrangling and clawing for overtime: *"For the accuser of the brothers and sisters, who accuses them before our God day and night, has been hurled down"* (Revelation 12:10, NIV). To give a comparative application here, within the legal circles of the American judiciary, Satan would be tantamount to the prosecutorial counsel against the brethren of God. Many believers underestimate Satan's legal IQ and are underwhelmed by him, but although the believer should not be overwhelmed by him, "that old serpent" is shrewd: *"Be wise as a serpent and harmless as a dove"* (Matthew 10:16, Revelation 20:2, KJV). Satan cannot rant against believers in God's Court of law just because he hates them; surely, for all that wicked Satan is not worth, he shows an identifiable worth of his litigious, shrewd knowledge of God's laws, and that is how he is able to have some productive appearances in God's Court. His accusations are actionable because, contextually, he knows the Word of God although he distorts it out of context for the uninformed mind of the believer, and he steals it from the un-acknowledging heart of the Christ-follower: *"Study to show thyself approved, a workman who does not need to be ashamed"* (2 Timothy 2:15, KJV). Every believer, then, should heed this warning to become a wise litigant who is a clever and armed participant in the Court of God with the word of God!

Honing in on the drama, Satan heard God say, *"Have you considered my servant Job?"* (Job 1:8, BSB). Satan was able to enter the Court of God because he had a case to pursue against Job, and wanted legal "injunctive relief" to get it done. In other words, conceivably he sought a judicial remedy like an interim search order which would allow him to search Job's home, family, and cattle assets. Having done his search, he was ready for court and the determinate point for his permitted access was that he had an underlying legal claim to his viable lawsuit which God did not deem frivolous. In other words, his lawsuit had pinpointable worth; he had arguments of good legal merit that could be rightfully decided under God's law concerning his launched destruction against Job, his household, and possessions. One of the serpent's crafty, meritorious arguments was grounded upon Job's fear which he had searched out; arguably, Job's admitted fear became a claim-worthy basis for Satan's legal operation in Jobs affairs because God's law prohibits fear: Jesus said *"Fear not"* (Luke 12:32, KJV), but Job said, *"The thing that I have feared most has come upon me"* (Job 3:25, KJV). Job had meant well but clearly had given in to fear: *"Set a guard over my mouth, LORD; keep watch over the door of my lips"* (Psalm 141:3, NIV). God had articulated, "Fear not," 365 times in the Bible, one of which is: *"Haven't I commanded you? Be strong and courageous. Don't be afraid, neither be dismayed: for Yahweh your God is with you wherever you go"* (Joshua 1:9, NIV). Satan had shrewdly found the open door to begin his legal interference into the affairs of Job's life. What was Job's fear? What did he believe that could be used against him in God's Court of law? Job feared that his children would curse God and that they would lose their lives due to their excessive partying. Job, by his own fearful admission, had given way to the very peg on which Satan hung his court case. Under God's Law of Confession, one gets what he confesses, and Satan, who is an opportunistic legalist, knows this law, for the Bible explicitly says that *"Death and life are in the power of the tongue, And those who love it and indulge it will eat its fruit and bear the consequences of their words"* (Proverbs 18:2, NIV). In the scriptural account of Job's ponderings and confessions, he actually initiated that law of confession, and his fear gave Satan a master key to the door through which he walked to lawfully accuse him before God. Culpable fear was the precipitating trigger for Satan to marshall Job's words against him; it was Job's *mea culpa* moment, and he regretted it later. Satan was allowed access to God because of God's three unchanging traits: God's spiritual rectitude, God's perfect fairness, and God's eternal justice. Given that God is so predisposed to hearing a worthy legal presentation, even from the arch-nemesis of His children, God is even more predisposed to hearing fearless and worthy petitioning from His children whom He encourages to come boldly before His throne (Philippians 4:6; Hebrews 4:16). It should be nutritious and spiritual fodder for the believer to remember that God is so appreciative of a believer's courtroom audacity and preparation, that He promises to answer that deserved petitioner before he evens petitions: *"Even before they call, I will answer, and while they are still speaking, I hear"* (Isaiah 65:24, BSB). At the drama's end, Job brought his own lawsuit for "legal redress" (compensation for loss and harm) before God's Court and recovered twice as much as he lost: *"Though He slay me, I will hope in Him. Nevertheless I will argue my ways before Him"* (Job 13:15, NASB). *"After Job had **prayed**… the* LORD *restored his prosperity and doubled his former possessions"* (Job 42:10, BSB).

From the Throne Room to the Courtroom

"…When He had by Himself purged our sins, sat down at the right hand of the majesty on high."

HEBREWS 1:3 (KJV)

Jesus left heaven on a legal assignment, and it took Him thirty-three years to issue His attorney's three-word closing statement on the earth: *"It is finished!"* (John 19:30, NLT). Jesus' three ministerial years on planet earth shaped a nation, but three words from Jesus shaped an eternity. Before that, the pre-existent, pre-millennia Jesus had spoken in unison with the Father with His *first* opening statement: "Let us make man..." It is key that the multi-dimensionality of Jesus required that He have two opening statements because of His coupled divinity and humanity; Jesus launched that pre-incarnate divine statement above, but He also initiated His earthly incarnate statement: *"The Spirit of the Lord GOD is on Me, because the LORD has anointed Me to preach the good news..."* (Isaiah 61:1, BSB). Seven hundred years before Jesus actually walked the earth to fulfill His legal pursuit of reconciling us to God with that good news, the prophet Isaiah had prophesied through that verse that Jesus would be anointed for that pursuit. Profoundly, even earlier than that, the patriarch Jacob experienced that same prophecy in motion. To explain, in Genesis 28:18, Jacob is seen pouring oil on a rock after he had a vision of angels climbing kinetically on a ladder between heaven and earth. I believe that expositional dream foreshadowed that Jesus, the heavenly Rock and the ladder between humankind and God, would be anointed for His earthly ministry: *"I assure you: You will see heaven opened and the angels of God ascending and descending on the Son of man"* (John 1:51, HCSB).

It is significant that both Jesus' opening statement and His closing statement ended with His sitting down, especially because that is what an attorney typically does after he makes his opening statement, and also after he makes his final statement at trial. In Luke 4:18–20 (CEV), Jesus took the scroll that was handed to Him and read: *"... The Lord has sent me to announce freedom for prisoners, to give sight to the blind, to free everyone who suffers, and to say 'this is the year the Lord has chosen'... then ... sat down."* This intensely dramatic, jaw-dropping moment not only activated Jesus' monumental ministry on the earth by letting the world know what His job description was, but it also started the time clock on the invisible, legal trial of humankind's soul that was to follow after His death. In the spirit world, Jesus had just assumed His dual role as

Advocate General for the State of Heaven and Lamb Advocate-Litigator for the state of humankind: *"… If anyone does sin, we have an advocate with the Father, Jesus Christ the righteous"* (1 John 2:1, HCSB).

Jesus is no stranger to scrolls. I find it thrilling that Jesus' opening statement on earth began with a scroll, and in the book of Revelation, it is stenciled that He again takes a scroll from the hand of God and worthily opens that heavenly scroll, signifying another opening statement of earthly judgment to come (Revelation 5:1–7). Jesus' closing statement was made on the cross at the slopes of Golgotha during the "trial of His life," which I submit was separate from His "life trial" that had already taken place the night before. During His Roman life trial, Jesus had been sentenced by man to death by crucifixion, but during the trial of His life, only Jesus could determine its end, for it was a trial of obedience unto the Father. Jesus' life decision was made at what I title "Calvary's Crossing" because it is where the crossroads of free will and commandment came together. I further propose that the greatest trial that Jesus confronted was whether He would subordinate His power to God's commandment. By His own admission, He had the power to come off the cross with angelic pomp and fireworks; indeed as Captain of heaven's military messengers, in a most spectacular move, He could have ushered in at a minimum twelve legions of heaven's finest armed forces, but it wasn't a soldierly defense that Jesus needed to win there. Intent that His last words were to reflect that He had passed the Father's trial of faith and had conquered sin and evil, He horned, "Tetelestai!—Greek for "It is finished!" At Calvary, Jesus finished His case and gave that rousing, dramatic three-word summation. It was Jesus' way of saying in legal jargon—trial over! Case closed! I rest my case! Yes, Jesus had rested His case and now signaled with His second *communique* to the Father that He was ready to enter into rest with Him by committing His Spirit to Him: *"Father, I entrust my spirit into your hands!"* (Luke 23:46, NLT). In the Spirit realm, after making that concluding statement of victory, Jesus then sat down: *"The one who conquers, I will grant him to sit with me on my throne, as I also conquered and sat down with my Father on His throne"* (Revelation 3:21, ESV). Thus, as Jesus began, so He would finish... seated.

God Came Down: The Legal Rewind

"Who has gone into heaven and is at the right hand of God, with angels, authorities, and powers having been subjected to him."

1 PETER 3:22 (ESV)

The end result of Jesus' finished work on the cross was His re-enthronement on the right hand of the Father, but let's take a look back at His pre-ascension itinerary, specifically on Good Friday. Jesus was pretty "occupied." The Herodian temple's veil was ripped vertically, rendering it unrecognizable as the pristine, luxurious wonder of the ancient world. It now stood devoid of the intact covering of its most holy splendor. Something irreversible and incontrovertible had happened that day on earth and in heaven. The holiness of God swirled with the wrath of God, creating a vortex, and the cross was its legal entry point! The separateness of God, aided by the pure anger of God, cycloned until it met its cataclysmic tip on an unsuspecting cross. A proliferation of sin upon the divinely human sacrifice caused a Holy God to unleash condemnatory justice upon Jesus, and He was consumed unto death. The climactic killing of one prevented the just and eternal mass killing of all humankind because the lamb-man, the child-king, the bereaved-lion who held back its ferocity, came face to back with the ever-living, wrothful God. Because of Jesus' holy atonement for humankind's guilty commission of crime-filled sin, it received a vacated judgment of its guilt and sentencing, one that is legally canceled upon God's judicial review. It was a historic day where the whirling Word of God boomed with such a right fury as to herald these words about the Beneficent One: *"His mercy endures forever!"*

(Psalm 136:1, NKJV). The rage of each jot and the jolt of each tittle rumbled throughout the heavens as each letter was ferried across a sea of His blood. Such a sight; it was on earth as it was in heaven—the veil on earth was split because heaven's veil had been patently split by God's presence. Explosively, there was a clap-less silence in heaven when the divine fissure occurred because scripture says, *"Let all the world be silent-the* LORD *is present in his holy temple"* (Habakkuk 2:20, CEV).

I submit there was a synchronization of the veil cutting ceremony on earth at the precise time it was in heaven when the LORD stood in His own temple to come down. At the moment of Christ's death, God descended from His temple on high and beheld the blood-shrouded temple of His Son. It was a divine reckoning on earth when God, Creator of the mighty heavenly militia, embraced the spear-ridden side of His Son and declared a treaty of peace with the soul of man! And so, God bolted out of His fronted gold streets and descended into the Second Temple where He split the sacred, thickly-aged veil from top to bottom as if it were merely minced royal threads in order to behold the greater temple—His own Son—that was now blood-gouged. Undeterred by His averted glance just moments ago, God could interminably stare at Him now because of the blood-bought armistice, for the adjudged debt had been satisfied by the fluid geysers of Jesus' willing, claret blood. *"For a brief moment I abandoned you, but with deep compassion I will bring you back. In a surge of anger I hid my face from you for a moment, but with everlasting kindness I will have compassion on you, says the* LORD *your redeemer"* (Isaiah 54:7–8, NIV).

The Day God Attended A Funeral: An Aerial Viewing of Christ's Body

> *"The LORD said to my Lord: 'Sit here until I make your enemies your footstool.'"*
>
> PSALM 110:1 (NIV)

It was God's own personal viewing.

There lay His Son on top of a wooden, perpendicular coffin. Although nailed there with bloodied wrists, it was nail-less love that inarguably kept Him there. As God glided down for a closer world survey, He shook the sandy earth beneath His drooping Son's crowned locks. It was a curious funeral for heaven's angels to behold. Their captain's encasing lay starkly still. A serpent's head for His jagged footstool. That day the Almighty would reflect on His pre-planned Eulogy. It was brief. It would read something like this:

> *He was a man of sorrows. He was sinless. He was obedient to the cross because I asked Him to be. I promised not to leave His soul in the grave. He believed me.*
>
> *He is worthy of all power, so now, by His name, He shall command all other powers.*

With a scheduled meeting to keep, God ascended to meet the Prince of Life, for He had commended His Spirit to Him. Theirs would be a meeting of the heavenly House of Lords: The *Lord* with the Lord of Lords. A re-coronation was to immediately follow.

He Got Up!: A Legal Analysis of Jesus' Resurrection

"For the law of the Spirit of life in Christ Jesus has set you free from the law of sin and of death."

ROMANS 8:2 (NASB)

It is extremely important to establish the legal logistics that made it possible for Jesus, the sent envoy of God, to be raised from the dead. I propose that to accomplish this resurrection, the ingenuity of God was front and center as He used a legal method involving His own *"Habeas Corpus"* Writ. One of my favorite legal terminologies is *Habeas Corpus*. *Habeas Corpus,* which comes from two Latin terms, habere and corpus, means to hold or to have, and corpus means body; therefore, *Habeas Corpus* means you hold, or you have the body. In sum, A *Habeas Corpus* Writ is an authorization and a formal command to release the body which "you hold." Since the Writ is a command, linguistically, the phrase alternatively means "you must have the body produced." God tremendously used such a legal mechanism. To begin, let's look at the Writ's use in the American legal sphere. The flexible *Habeas Corpus* Writ petition can proceed as a civil action against a state agent, such as a warden of a prison, a government official of military alien detainees, or even a custodian of a state mental hospital, who holds a defendant in unlawful custody, and that Writ forces him to produce the body before the court. The Writ has a real application spiritually to Christ's physical body and His resurrection. Of note, the Bible gives insight into the fact that Satan left his first estate as a

> *Satan cannot legally share God's sole parental authority over the soul.*

godly being and is now a type of evil warden over the "state" of the unbeliever's soul, which, without Christ, is incarcerated in a type of spiritual prison-house: *"I am the Lord your God who took you out of the …prison-house"* (Exodus 20:2, GNT). It is important, however, for the believer to firmly know this truism—that Satan has no automatic legal authority over God's people's souls; Satan cannot legally share God's sole parental authority over the soul which God brought into existence. There is a biblical analogy for the constitutionality of this awesome truth. The Tenth Amendment to the Constitution of the United States emphasizes our type of specified government by establishing that certain powers not specifically granted to the federal government are not to be shared between the federal government and the state government; these powers are called Reserved Powers because they are reserved for the people (of the State only).[3] Likewise, in God's legal domain, He has constitutionally specified the breadth of Jesus' divine government by establishing His designated power to curate the *believer's* soul. It is a reserved power under Jesus' legal scope only and is not to be shared with Satan; so it is the *unbeliever* who *invite*s the endangerment of a satanically imprisoned soul: *"…And the government shall be on his [Jesus] shoulder"* (Isaiah 9:6, ESV).

Who does not like a good ending to a movie or a novel? A good ending thrills audiences everywhere. Well… the great end to the Christian's story is that Christ got up! The efficacy of the *Habeas Corpus* Writ is seen with the bodily resurrection of Christ Jesus. Since this constitutionally protected Writ orders the immediate release of a detained body absent legal grounds for its detention, it preserves an individual's lawful liberty. In other words, the Writ, upon review of a detainee's rights, acts to restore a person's freedom and to prevent wrongdoing if there is abusive power, no sufficient jurisdiction, or no authority for that unlawful custody.[4] With respect to Jesus, the Devil was up to wrongdoing when he tried to unlawfully hold Jesus' body in the grave. The Devil was the warden, and the grave was the detention cell, but neither could detain Jesus' body lawfully. Just like the Habeas

Corpus Writ, which is known as "the Great Writ," affords the detainee a judicial review, the Holy Writ of God's Word—the Greatest Writ—afforded Jesus a judicial review from the High Justice of Heaven, Himself. God reviewed the lawfulness of Jesus being kept in that grave and took note of the fact that the enemy's earthly ambassadors had doubly obstructed the exit of His Son's grave with a two-ton boulder that acted as a seal of detention. Perusing the legal provisions of His lawful Word, the Holy Judge saw the following:

1. *"A body you have prepared for me"* (Hebrews 10:5, NKJV).
2. *"For You will not leave my soul among the dead or allow your holy one to rot in the grave"* (Psalm 16:10, NLT).
3. *"But God raised him from death, setting him free from its power, because it was impossible that death should hold him prisoner"* (Acts 2:24, GNT).

Based on that law, God found jurisdictional defects in the devil's abusive authority and ruled that he was acting beyond his legal grasp and jurisdictional territory, and therefore, was illegally detaining Jesus. He determined that there was an unlawful interference of Jesus's personal freedom by the Devil and his evil emissaries, both of whom had no legal power to hold His body! Conclusively, upholding His rule of law, God held that Jesus had a divine constitutionally protected right to Habeas Corpus; the grave, therefore, must loose the body, for not even death could defy His judicial order. God commanded death, the devilish warden of hell, and his demonic patrol to produce the body of Christ Jesus, and so ordered: *"By the judicial mandate of MY Holy Writ, Release His Body! Court Adjourned!"* The corporeal Christ was resurrected immediately. Death could not legally have nor hold the risen Christ because God's Writ had authorized death's stinger to be pulled and grave's victory to be spoiled! (1 Corinthians 15:55–57). What does that mean for the believer? Jesus bashed the lock and confiscated the keys of attempted shared authority from the Devil before rising from the dead, and on that "great resurrection day," he could no longer legally hold our bodies down either! Jesus saves in life and in death! The Bible waives the victory flag like this: *"But God raised him from the dead, releasing Him from the agony of death, because it was impossible for Him to be held in its clutches"* (Acts 2:24, BSB). The Writ also had to be honored because of who God is and because of who Jesus is. Jesus said He was hidden in the Father and further said that He came from the bosom of the Father (See John 1:18). In the Bible, the bosom spiritually represents that "heart" place of ultimate richness and safety; thus, if Jesus was begotten of the Father in His bosom, then at His resurrection, He would go back into the heart of God. Jesus is the heart of God's Heart; There was no way that God would not reunite His Heart with His heart of hearts-Writ Large*!* *"…God had already promised through His Prophets in Holy Writ concerning His Son…"* (Romans 1:2, WNT).

The Illegal Body Snatcher: Biblical Angelology

"The battle doesn't belong to you, but to God."

2 CHRONICLES 20:15 (ISV)

"This is not a wrestling match against a human opponent."

EPHESIANS 6:12 (GW)

Beyond the cosmos, in the spiritual stratosphere, there were two battles going on for the apprehension of humankind. In one battle, Satan was vying for the body of humankind, and in another, he was tussling for the soul of humankind. As if the conquest of the eternal soul would not have been enough of a devilish grand slam, the arch-rival of humankind wanted to crown himself "snatcher and destroyer-in-chief" and "evil abductor-in chief" of God's created physical specimen—the body. *"The thief cometh not but to steal, kill and destroy"* (John 10:10, KJV). True to the Devil's nature, lying in wicked wait for Jesus' corpse was seemingly not the first time he tried to restrain a dead body. Not only did he try to illegally defy the ascension of Jesus' grave-cradled body, as expounded above, but Scripture says the Devil had earlier "disputed" with the archangel Michael over the body of Moses.[5] I believe that the contention involved the Devil's attempt to unlawfully take the body away by force—to snatch Moses' corpse. Body snatching is the illicit removal of or theft of a body from a grave or resting place, also known as "illegal disinterment."[6] I submit that devilish bandit was trying to steal the patriarch's body to preclude its personal burial by God, Himself. Stealing and detention is the Devil's *modus operandi*; according to the Bible, he operates like a bandit toward the human body all the time: *"The thief cometh not but to steal, kill and destroy"* (John 10:10, KJV). I propose the Devil especially wanted to wipe out all intelligible references to Moses' because he was a prophetic exemplification of Jesus. Later, and similarly, the Devil would attempt to steal the identity of Jesus' dead body by trying to manipulate the identifying inscription above Jesus' cross. Moreover there, I suggest he wanted to alter any associated appearance of Jesus by causing him to have a mutilated body. Fearing Jesus would rise from the dead as He said He would, the Devil influenced officials to pay off guards to say that Jesus' body was stolen (See Matthew 28:12). How ironic, but how predictable, that the father of lies would engineer a pricey lie about stealing a body.

Analytically, it seems God's bodily creation garnered a special fixation for the Devil because he was a created being like man but revered his own body and function to a fault. The book of Genesis paints the pre-rebellious Devil with heightened beauty, for he had been created with astounding pulchritude and was a sonorous wonder as a one-angel orchestra (See Ezekiel 28:12–15). Back then, Lucifer was his name, and his lucent, jewel-encrusted body belonged to a lovely thinking angel. The book of Genesis paints the pre-rebellious devil with a heightened beauty, for he had been given an astounding pulchritude and was a sonorous wonder as a one-angel orchestra. He became narcissistic about his looks, about his " in house" otherworldly fame among his angelic cohorts, and about his bodily fortune of coated gold, diamonds, and emeralds. Regrettably, he became perverted and unrighteously prideful of his staggering beauty and would eventually rue the day he caused his ruin. That perversion caused him to be disowned by His Divine Designer, God, and caused him his "residency permit" in heaven. Satan wanted to be the beauty in charge of all of heaven—the beauteous one wanted to be The Divine One. Lucifer was his name then, and the lucent, jewel-encrusted body of his angelic form would not be able to halt his pride-induced fall. After trying to commandeer God's throne and usurp God's resplendent glory, he was banished from heaven, and his body, which was a fabricated extravaganza that reflected the splendid and colorful glory of God, was altered forever: *"How you have fallen from heaven, O Lucifer"* (Isaiah 14:2, KJV). As a dissatisfied beneficiary who lost the exquisite beauty and worshipful function of his own body, he clearly wanted to deny the spiritual body of Christ the eminence of its beautiful, sparkling worship. Hating Christ's church, therefore, He wanted to deny humankind's beautifully created physical properties so much that his obsession with the theft and destruction of its flesh is streamed throughout the Bible, including where he afflicted believers' bodies with illnesses: *"When the evil approached me to consume my flesh, my enemies and my haters stumbled together and fell"* (Psalm 27:2, ABPE).

Satan's obsession with the conquest of the physical body is streamed throughout the Bible, especially where godly angels had to act as sentinels, actually guarding the body of Moses against bodily interference, even after he died. It is somewhat perceptible that Satan would have a preoccupation with the destruction of the living body, particularly since God let the world know that He would produce a Savior through the human body, and He that would be Satan's downfall and nemesis. Satan, however, attempted to steal Moses' dead body, to carry it away illegally, which is also kidnapping—whether the person was alive or not according to American federal law.[7] I believe that Satan hates the body also because, after death, it will ultimately be reunited with the soul through the Spirit and the power of God: *"The sea gave up the dead that were in it, and death and Hell gave up the dead that were in them"* (Revelation 20:13, NIV). The Devil would very much like to preclude this. The soul is immortal and will live forever, and to the extent that Satan can cause man to lose his soul by worshipping him, he is semi-content, but not totally. The Devil yearns for a package deal of man's fallen soul and fallen body—just like his.

Jesus was aware of Satan's malicious intent to destroy the body and to take its well-being, but Jesus turned this idea on its head when confronting the Pharisees who did not want Him to heal the bodies of the sick and feeble, nor raise dead bodies. Their natural inhibitions collided head-on with His supernatural permissiveness, and He proved that His Super was greater than their natural.

The book of Jude gives us insight into two very high-tiered angels, Michael, a chief warrior angel who was known to enforce God's law and judgment, and the Devil; both of these angelic dignitaries were openly involved in a heated scuffle over the body of Moses. In verse 9, Jude—reputed to be the brother of Jesus—was frankly clear that Michael did not bring "railing accusations" against the Devil; that is to say, there was no indictment or blistering charge brought against him by Michael regardless of Michael's inclusion in God's superior order of angels. Importantly, one definition for "rail" is to hold in contempt. To hold one "in contempt" is a legal measure, such as in contempt of court, which a *judge* may apply for punishable disrespectful or disobedient conduct. Such punishable actions by a judge, and not an angelic dignitary, is the main reason why Michael declined to rail against the Devil. To "rail" alternatively means to bring slanderous judgment, which Michael also declined to do; he simply made a fact-based interjection saying, *"The Lord rebuke you!"* (Jude 1:9, NIV). Michael purposely refrained from using denigrating, condemning oral speech. Why is that? I firmly believe that Michael was aware that he would be operating outside of his legal authority. In fact, rebuking Satan was entirely within the Lord's—the divine Judge's—dominion. Zechariah 3:2 (NLT) points this out: *"And the LORD said to Satan, 'I, the LORD, reject your accusations, Satan.'"* This Lordship and dominant language point to that same "God authority" that Michael knew was reserved and dared not to appropriate for himself. Since to "rail" is to hold in contempt, Scripture implies that Michael would have risked being in contempt in God's court; so, it would have been contemptuous for him to judge the rogue angel, as that is within the realm of the Godhead's authority. Michael, instead, reminded him that the "Lord rebuke you," which includes the definition of contempt because it also means: the Lord "pushes against you or punishes you."

As we know, the Devil and all his forces of hell could not interfere with the resurrected body of Christ because Jesus successfully overcame the thief and His ascension-bound body eluded the grave. As it turns out, the Devil also did not prevail over Michael nor over Moses' body either.

In the end, like in the beginning, God's superior *modus operandi* prevailed: *"Then there was war in heaven. Michael and his angels fought against the dragon. And the dragon lost the battle and he and his angels were forced out of heaven"* (Revelation 12:8, KJV).

CHAPTER 3

Legal Crossology: The Swag of the Cross!

Oh, that man would behold Him post the cross!

I define Legal Crossology as the legal role of the cross that is dovetailed with the Christ of the cross. Each of the subchapters below is what I dub as "cross-scapes," that explore the purpose and effect of the cross from a unique legal vantage point through the legal executions and orchestrations of God. Every section is misted with the cross and gives a sketch about what the Christ of the cross accomplished legally for the believer. In the end, it is evident that Jesus' cross is a universal symbol that is dichotomy-centric to the onlooker because either one welcomes it or opposes it. There is no in-between. God, Himself, prefers a decisive, not a sleepy, lukewarm response to it: *"So because you are lukewarm, and neither hot nor cold, I will spit you out of my mouth"* (Revelation 3:16, NASB1995).

CHRIST

The following " Christ Chapters" are a cross-stitching of ideas that point to Christ; they deliberately incorporate Christ and are intentionally deluged with what I label as "Christ-scapes." This Christ-centric theme is not mere superfluity; it is necessary because Christ is the embodiment of the Bible. In Him is the fullness of the Godhead, the fullness of the entire Gospel, and most certainly the full assemblage of God's legal prescription for doing things.

> *The cross is the grit and the muscle of salvation.*

CROSS

One of the greatest mysteries of the Bible can be summed up in two words—the cross.

Its strength is summed up in ten words—the cross is the grit and the muscle of salvation.

I cannot boast enough about the cross. It is the swag and the sway of God! Universally recognizable, the cross is both a puzzling symbol and an easily comprehended one. At its core, it is both basic and erudite at the same time. It is amazingly complex in its simplicity; it has both breath and breadth. Only the cross could bull-horn so sweetly the profundity of the simple message of God's heart: *He loves you!* Solely by God's omnipresence was He seated in the heavens, while at the same time dying on an earthly cross (See Psalm 139:7-12). Because of His quintessential duality of existence, He was both the onlooker as well as the action figure.

Legal Crossology: The Legal Immensity of the Cross

> *"For God so loved the world that He gave His one and only Son, that everyone who believes in Him shall not perish but have eternal life."*
>
> JOHN 3:16 (BSB)

A Day in the Life of God: The Immense Building Blocks of Crossology

The cross event was a plethora of phenomena; it was an avalanche of heaven's best with earth's worst. To its rawest core, it allowed the exposition of the Father's heart. On that unforgettable day, God's heart ran a marathon as it chased after humanity. He had a non-stop agenda of miracles to catalyze: Hiding His face, bearing His heart, and His agenda included recreating the Passover on the cross. On the cross, Jesus interposed His body between the wrath of God and humankind, becoming a divine "bodyguard" for us. Because of Christ's male lamb's blood that extended above the door post of the believer's heart, eternal damnation would be ordered to leave humankind alone! In a real legal sense, humankind would receive a restraining order from God's Court, so although Jesus endured insufferable pain and hobbled in pooling blood, His giving in and folding in the towel before the cross's end was not an option. It pleased God to bruise Him, which caused a juxtaposition of a pleasant outpour of sappy redemption from His open flesh along with the salty rife of an atmospheric effluvium that made the noses of observers recoil and their senses cringe. Looking back, Jesus' temple-body was grossly ripped apart from top to bottom. The top of his head was contused from the barbed garland masking as a crown. The stinging flesh of His back was essentially butterflied by the bone of the cat o'nine tails whip. His welted, nailed feet joined the disfiguration of His marred face. Splintered and unrecognizable, Christ, nevertheless, was *not* unidentifiable. There was a distinctive "Jesus factor" which was very much recognizable—it was His law enforcement status; Jesus was God's High Priest and a literal law enforcement officer of God's highest court. Yes, Jesus' martyrization was seen, but so was His enforcement prowess. What awe to behold. At first glance, one might think of Him as a lifeless martyr, but upon second glance, one can see the bold mantle of life-changing power and indomitable authority that rested upon His defaced flesh. "*…We have confi-*

dence to enter the holy place by the blood of Jesus, by a new and living way which he inaugurated for us, through the veil, that is, His flesh" (Hebrews 10:20). In Isaiah 54:8, the Jewish prophet prophesied that daily event of the cross, mainly that God the Father would remove His face out of Jesus' sight momentarily when His Son's canopy of inflammatory sin ignited the Father's Holy rage. At the end of the day, God consumed the lamb-laden sacrifice of the redeemer and lavished compassion on a saved world. In doing so, God initiated the human race into the kingdom race.

Legal Crossology: The Cross—Was It a Gift, Contract, or Covenant?

The fulsome triumph of the cross is the thesis of God's love and possesses three legal dimensions. God chooses to involve man in His orb of execution through gift-giving, contractual relationship, and covenantal interfacing. The redemption of man's soul involved the legal execution of these processes. They are the proof of God's love three ways, and they explain "the legal how" of the cross.

Crossology: The Legal Gift of the Cross

Redemption by the cross legally qualified as a gift because it was given gratuitously. In order to be a gift, legally, there needed to have been a transfer of property to another voluntarily and an acceptance of that property without the requirement or transference of any compensation whatsoever for it.[8] The word property refers to something that you can own, use and enjoy, such as salvation; God voluntarily gave us the free gift of salvation to accept as our own, to utilize, and by all means, to enjoy: *"God saved you by his grace when you believed. And you can't take credit for this; it is a gift of God"* (Ephesians 2:8, NLT). There was no *Quid Pro Quo*—literally meaning "what for what" in Latin. In other words, God did not require any preconditions from us or set up any "must be" or "must have" contingencies *prior* to its implementation: *"But God has shown us how much he loves us—it was while we were still sinners that Christ died for us!"* (Romans 5:8, GNT). The stark truth is that not only did empty, sinful humankind have nothing to give toward its redemption, nothing to barter with that was of desirable worth to God, it was not even a party to the discussion of its own rescue. Humankind's soul, which had been lethally kidnapped by sin, was oblivious to God's mission to ransom it. God had prepared a rescue—without its solicitation—which had been in the making with the Son since earth's pre-era because humankind could not mortgage its soul to pay its ransom due to its enslavement by sin. The reality was humankind's soul was in debt to sin, and its dormant spirit was equally bankrupt. We were in debt and could not possibly have paid our way clear; however, Jesus paid a debt He could not possibly have owed! Humankind needed a gift. God gave the gift; greater said, God gave the most valuable thing He had, His greatest treasure—His only begotten Son. Now that He had been gifted, humankind could either accept or decline the greatness of all gifts.

Crossology: The Legal Contract of the Cross

The demand for our salvation cost Jesus His life, so we were bought at an extremely high price point. There was contractual discussion.

By legal definition, a contract is a promise or set of promises that yields an agreement between two or more parties for which the law gives a remedy if it is breached (broken); it can also be an agreement that the law deems to have created a duty which is enforceable in a court of law.[9] In simpler terms, it is an agreement between two or more individuals or entities who promise to do or not do something, and their promises have legal force behind them. There should be four elements present to have an enforceable contract: an agreement, mutual assent, valuable consideration, and written terms. The redemptive work of the cross was born out of a contractual nature. I propose that there existed a legal contract between God the Father and God the Son regarding the "transaction" of the cross, and that all the contractual threshold elements were met. Firstly, there had been an agreement before the foundation of the earth for Jesus to "suit-up" in flesh to perform the atonement at the cross as the heavenly appointed high priest: *"Who is the Messiah…was appointed beforehand to this before the foundation of the world"* (1 Peter 1:19–20, ABPE). Secondly, there was mutual assent— or an element of the "meeting of the minds," which is the backbone of understanding that the agreement is built on. God and Jesus, with Holy Spirit present, often had a meeting of the minds. Consider that in the book of Genesis, they are recorded as saying, *"Let us make man,"* or, *"Let us go down and confuse their language"* (Genesis 1:26, Genesis 11:7, BSB; Emphasis supplied). In those passages, the plurality of the Godhead is seen in unified agreement. The same Elohimic collaborative of God's plural nature was seen at Jesus' baptism, which launched His sojourn of salvation (See Matthew 3:16). In short, God and Jesus got together and mutually set out to salvage humankind: *"God chose Him as your ransom long before the world began"* (1 Peter 1:20, NLT). This grand contract was just about complete. All that was needed were the elements of legal consideration and an accompanying writing for this heavenly contractual deal to be sealed.

Consideration must be an exchange of value. Let's look at the value of what was being exchanged between the Father and the Son. In this particular case, there was a leading inducement on both sides because, in exchange for Jesus' arduous journey to the cross, God would receive the most valuable benefit of being reunited with His creation. This reunion was of an inestimable value to God, who, after all, wrote His autobiographical story through the biblical portrayal of the prodigal son's return to his father. For Jesus' part, He would receive divine trophies of valuable honor. Jesus (the promisee) would receive a promise from the Father (the promisor) for four things: Firstly, He would get the honor of rescuing His glory-bride from the evil clutches of Satan and have his bridal body restored to Him. Secondly, since the crucifixion was the most honorless way to die known to man at that time, the second honor given to Jesus would be an honorable name; God was to extract Him from the grave with a crowned name that would exist above all names. Thirdly, God would grant Him a judgeship on the earth of a heavenly kingdom for one thousand years to be followed by honorable rulership over a kingdom that will have no end. Finally restored to Jesus will be the concomitant glory which He had shared with the Father before His emigration from heaven. *"But, we see Jesus, …crowned with glory and honour, that he by the grace of God should taste death for every man"* (Hebrews 2:9, KJV); *"He will reign over the house of Jacob forever, and His kingdom will have no end"* (Luke 1:33, HCSB).

Lastly, this contract was enforceable because it satisfied the legal writing requirement of the "Statute of Frauds," which is a law requiring contracts that cannot be performed within one year from the time that they are entered into to be in writing and signed. This contract could not be performed within one earthly year of Jesus' birth, and so was indeed in writing; in fact, in several places. Firstly, God had His earlier prophets write in detail about the fulfillment of this Messianic transaction for millennia to come, making sure it would serve as a public, enforceable document with His endorsement. For example, God, with His supernatural innovation, left the essential terms of the agreement on display for the whole world to see in Isaiah 53:4–12 with Isaiah's prophetic details of the crucifixion. Secondly, Jesus signed the contract in His blood. God emptied the legal repositories of heaven to get it done! It took gold, it took gumption, and it took blood! The gold was God's glory, the gumption was Jesus' passion, and the blood was the royal signatory proof. The signatory requirement was met there, for only the one signature of the party who pays the debt for another, and against whom the contract is enforceable, is legally required to sign under the Statute of Frauds.[10] Further, that law also provides that: "The signature may appear anywhere on the memorandum. Any writing, mark, initials, stamp, engraving or other symbol placed or printed on a memorandum will suffice as a signature."[11] Christ's blood, therefore, was the mark of scarlet ink; but one might ask, where was the memorandum which the statute requires the signature is to be written on? I submit that there were actually two memoranda that Jesus' signature comprehensively inked: One was a wooden memorandum that was initialed here and there by His gushing blood, and the second memorandum was His body itself which was covered in His signature blood. Importantly, the thirty-three-year-old Lamb of God was, in a veritable sense, "pure parchment" because parchment was made from a mature lamb! Looking at the productivity of the cross under this model of contract, I propose that humankind's soul would have been the commodity that was transacted for at the cross, for it was lost after Adam conceded to Satan in Eden's garden. In a contractual agreement with the Father, Jesus agreed to redeem-meaning to buy back—the soul of humankind by paying with the negotiable currency of heaven—His blood. Critical to the story of the cross is the fact that in the early church period of Jewish antiquity, a transaction involving a goods contract came with a "bill of lading" receipt once the contractual obligations of the contract had been fully and legally satisfied and it said, "Paid in full!"[12] Jesus emphatically nailed that receipt to the cross when he cried out, "*PAID IN FULL!*" (John 19:30).

I submit that God would see His promise to Abraham for one additional contractual observation: "Promissory Estoppel." God was legally obligated to keep His promise to give Abraham a big "star--seed" because God had represented to him that his seed would be as countless as the stars. God *had* to spare Isaac because Abraham kept his promise of faithful sacrifice and had relied on God to keep His. Those principles of reliance and enforceability are known legally as "Promissory Estoppel" and are based on the sequence where a judge may enforce one's promise in the interest of justice where another has reasonably relied upon it.[13]

In the legal, equitable sense, God was "estopped" from *not* keeping His promise to Abraham in order to prevent the loss of Isaac—and extensively the loss of humankind-since the representative of humankind was Abraham. Notably, Abraham had heavily relied on God's seed promise—and rightfully so—to the point that he was willing to imperil his son, so God had to "make good" on His representation. In the end, God, the Judge, enforced His own promise so that Abraham's innumerable seed through Isaac would not be detrimentally lost.

Crossology: The Legal Covenant of the Cross

"...and my grace shall not pass away from you, and the covenant of your peace shall not pass away, says LORD JEHOVAH, *the lover."*

ISAIAH 54:10 (ABPE)

God likes covenants. Jehovah actually began showing His passion to believers with stories of covenants and glimpses of His love under the old covenant, and He finished that same passion with a crescendo of storytelling that surrounded the cross and His New Covenant: *"The angel of the Lord went up from Gilgal to Bokim and said, 'I brought you up out of Egypt and led you into the land I swore to give"* (Judges 2:1, NIV). There is a covenantal law of God, and the redemptive work of the cross is a covenant because it rested on a *relationship* of promises. The crucifixion of Jesus Christ flowed out of a covenant between God and the covenantee, one which began with a patriarch of faith, Abraham. A covenant is different from a contract in its intention, scope, and execution. In a covenant, the emphasis is on the relationship rather than on the agreement singularly. In the covenant, two people promise to do something without a necessary emphasis on exchanging something of value. There need be no "consideration," just an agreement that is sealed with a vow or an oath by each party. As such, a covenant is relationship-oriented, with an emphatic connectedness and loyalty. Importantly, the relationship itself becomes the reward, which is different from a contract where the parties may not even know each other or otherwise have a relationship. The godly marriage covenant is an example of this type of strong relationship. In another example, a covenant existed between God and Abraham, the forefather of the Hebrew nation. God promised to bless Abraham and his seed, and Abraham promised to worship God as the one true living God. Abraham ("Abram" at the time) demonstrated his promise by building an altar of sacrifice to God, and God ratified His own promise by swearing by Himself because He couldn't swear by anything greater than Himself (See Hebrew 6:13).

Fast forward a few decades, and God tests the loyalty of the covenant—and the love of Abraham—by asking Abraham to sacrifice the seed that God had promised to bless him with, his son Isaac. Abraham set out for Mt. Moriah to sacrifice Isaac on an altar of fire. Intent to sacrifice Isaac at knifepoint before an angel stopped him, Abraham instead sacrificed a nearby ram that had been caught in a bush. Upon seeing Abraham's loyalty, God proved His own loyalty to the covenant as well; legally, God *had to* because a covenant is an agreement that is legally binding, meaning it has legal weight over the outcome between the parties because it is enforceable. God enforced it and blessed Abraham with innumerable offspring as promised. In the end, their inseparable relationship, above all else, prospered.

Although Abraham *intended* to sacrifice his only son, Isaac, on Mt. Moriah, later God *did* sacrifice His only Son on that very same mountain. It was there that Abraham saw the revelation of God as a provider and called Him *Jehovah Jireh*, which means The Revealing One Who Sees Beforehand. What I find exciting about this biblical account is the prophetic relational exchange: By saluting Him as *Jehovah Yireh*, there Abraham praised the prescient, all-seeing God because God *saw in advance* the sacrificial provision that Abraham would need; but, later, Jesus showed us that it was Abraham who actually *saw in advance* that Jesus would be the ultimate sacrificial provision that would free all mankind. Abraham was a "pre-type" of the archetype, Jesus Christ, and Abraham said, "In the mount of the Lord, it shall be seen;" in essence, he was prophesying the Lord's sacrifice on that mountain (Genesis 22:14, KJV). Jesus made it clear to His listeners that *"Abraham rejoiced to see My day,"* indicating that Abraham foresaw that there would be another provision taking place on that same spot where he attempted to sacrifice Isaac (See John 8:56, KJV). Abraham's vision of the crucifixion proved prophetic. What a covenantal relationship! Abraham had lifted up his eyes to see the ram that was caught in the bush, then lifted up his eyes and saw Jesus, who would be the superseding ram lifted up for all mankind to see. Abraham had lifted up his eyes to see the ram in the bush, but he also saw that Jesus was the ram, the male lamb, who, in that very spot, would be lifted up for all to see. Consider with me—Jesus, the Holy Temple, allowed His temple, which he raised back up in three days, to be razed on the very spot believed to be where Solomon built God's temple. God left no detail unrevealed—notice that both rams wore crowns! I observed that Abraham's sacrificed ram had a crown of thorns because his head's horns were caught in the thicket—which is a bush ornamented by thorns—and the sacrificed Lamb of God, whom God calls the *"horn* of our salvation," wore a crown of thorns pushed down on His head at the cross (See Luke 1:69, Genesis 22:13).

What does the legal covenant mean for the believer? The Bible refreshingly reminds us that even in our sinful state, God came toward us, giving of Himself. We were caught in a thicket of sinful mess, but He demonstrated a redemptive covenantal act towards humankind. Why? Because God "keeps covenant" with His people: *"They will come and bind themselves to the* LORD *in an everlasting covenant that will not be broken"* (Jeremiah 50:5). The covenants would not be broken by God, but these covenants were not absolute in that they could be broken if man did not abide by the terms of the covenant. God will always uphold His part of the covenant. God is so "pro-people" that Jesus shed His blood to disseminate a covenant that is superior to the Abrahamic one because it affords not only forgiveness but eternal life for the believer. *Breaking News!* This new bold covenant surpasses death and is intended to be irrevocable beyond the first light of eternity. Although a two-party covenant, it has the "in triplicate" effect that swivels between God and Jesus and between Jesus and humankind. It is blood clad. Jesus was the mediator between God and man, and this time, it was He who, in a sense, walked in blood between man and God as the high priest: *"This is my blood and with it, God makes his new agreement with you. Drink this and remember me"* (1 Corinthians 11:25, CEV) or *"This cup is God's new covenant sealed with my blood, Whenever you do it, do so in remembrance of me"* (1 Corinthians 11:25, GNT).

> *God is so "pro-people."*

The new covenant—or new agreement—is also superior to the old covenant because the old covenant was based on a covenant that God made with Abraham but was eventually broken by Abraham's posterity. The new covenant or New Testament, however, was based on a covenant that God made *with Jesus* who cannot break it for He is "the same today, yesterday, and forever," and is the everlasting promise keeper (Hebrews 13:8, BSB). The new covenant will always live in perpetuity because of the eternal attributes of its covenant makers; both God and Jesus are immortal, are sinless, are without error, and are incapable of reneging on a promise because "there is no variation or shadow of shifting" with them (James 1:17, ESV). The covenant with God is a holy covenant, and as we draw near to Him in holiness, He constantly ratifies His holy covenant: *"God has called us to live holy lives, not impure lives"* (1 Thessalonians 4:7, NLT).

Crossology: Covenantal Resurrection

There was a covenant involved in the resurrection. Jesus was raised from the dead because of the covenantal bond He had with God. The Bible expresses that one's bond is one's word, so God's Word was legally binding: *"All of our words are binding, because everything we say, we say before the living God"* (Matthew 5:33-37). Their relationship was built on a divine bond of trust, and God who had given Jesus His word would not abandon His soul in the belly of the earth; thus, on the strength of God's Word, Jesus trusted that God would uphold their bond. It's my unyielding opinion that the angelic courier who strengthened Jesus in the garden of Gethsemane before Jesus' trek to Calvary carried God's verbatim reminder of that promise: *"Because you will not abandon me to the realm of the dead, nor will you let your faithful one see decay"* (Psalm 16:10). I further propose that neatly tucked in that angelic reminder was also another message from God with a legal implication: *"So shall my word which shall go forth from my mouth; it shall not return unto me void, but it shall do whatever I please..."* (Isaiah 55:11, NIV).

"Void" is a legal term that means not having legal force. Jesus got the direct reminder that God was sending Him—the Holy Word—for the very purpose of having a legal effect at Calvary and beyond the grave! There was no turning back because to turn back means to void or to disable the legal effect of something. Jesus heeded the message and was strengthened for the work ahead of Him.

Jesus' work at Calvary did extend beyond death and the grave. The "why" of the resurrection, the purpose of having a legal effect at Calvary, was to efface the sting of death forever. Looking backward with a contemporary lens, #Thestingofdeath would be a relevant modern "hashtag" that Jesus could have used with the Apostle Paul. On the road to Damascus, Jesus emphatically sent Apostle Paul, known then as Saul, this communication, "Isn't it hard to kick against the pricks?" The meaning of pricks is sting. The precision and penetration of Jesus' message was so intentionally exact to a stunned Saul that later he would pen as Paul, *"Death where is your sting?"* (1 Corinthians 15:55, NET). So, Jesus, who had received His message before Calvary, sent His own underlying message after Calvary to Saul, which was two-fold: Stop opposing me or you will die a stinging death; embrace me, and you will truly live. Tellingly, Paul also went on to write, *"To live is Christ"* (Philippians 1:21, BSB). Paul had come to the realization that Jesus, in rising from the dead, took the prick out of death.

Crossology: The Legal Fluidity of the Cross

"Like a tree planted by the riverbank."

PSALMS 1:3 (NKJV)

The cross is not only the arc of the gospel, but it is a real legal picture of the work of the Father's heart. The work of the cross has a legal fluidity to it, and nothing can stop its seamless flow. With a panoramic of the cross in mind, below is my version of an acrostical construct of the cross, which will allow us to take a look at the dynamism of the cross from its humility all the way to its effrontery, and from its peacefulness to its weaponization:

C = Cross Examination of the Lamb of God

"Shall a faultfinder contend with the Almighty?"

JOB 40:2 (ESV)

The legal term cross-examination refers to the thorough examination of an individual witness by an opposing party's legal representative through in-depth questioning. I find it quite eye-opening that Jesus experienced an exhaustive cross-examination as both a person and as a typology of an animal. In ancient Israel, a thorough examination was traditionally carried out by high priests of a sacrificial lamb to see if a lamb were blemish-free before it could be used as an acceptable sacrifice for the atonement of sin; and in biblical recordation, a painstaking examination of Jesus as the Lamb of God was done through a type of cross-examination by the high priest Caiphas, and also by Pilate who proclaimed that He had examined an unblemished Christ. Pilate ostentatiously washed his hands and exclaimed, *"I find no fault in this man"* (Luke 23:4, KJV). Pilate's words are not lost on Jesus because a presumably unknowing Pilate had just strongly uttered the very words a high priest would say before selecting a lamb for its slaughter—"Behold the lamb, I find no fault in him." Both examinations of Christ, the person and symbolically as the Lamb-Christ can be categorized as "cross" examinations of Christ because they preceded His taking up His "cross," and because the questioners represented not the accused Christ but an opposing party. Caiaphas represented the opposition of ancient Israel, and Pilate represented the oppositional ancient Rome.

R = Resurrection Authority

Jesus had been given legal authority over His body, and He exercised it. Legal authority is often tied to legitimate power or legitimate governance from which the authority is issued. An example of this emanating authority is police authority which legally emanates from a legitimate governing body such as a city or town. In that city's name, an officer of peace can execute certain rightful acts. Similarly, Jesus, the Prince of Peace, was a peace officer of the highest degree and divulged that He had divine authority to save His life, to give His life and to also raise up His life (His temple) again (See John 10:18, John 2:19). This eminent authority came from God, the Father's power: *"Your right hand, LORD, was majestic in power"* (Exodus 15:6, NIV).

O = Obvious Demonstration of God's Love

The message of God's love splashes out from the cross. John 3:16 says that God loved His human world so much that He sent His Son to be the bearer of that love. Every drop of Jesus' blood on the cross strung together a vivid collage of God's love, which provided the backdrop for a picturesque intaglio of His affection; you could see the reflection of God's face in the cross. God's love was on exhibition for all to see as Jesus' blood oozed out from the temples of His forehead, from His wrists, from His ankles, from His back, and from His side. Jesus lost so much blood that He died while giving birth to save humankind. It was a bloody birth! He delivered into the world a healthy, newborn church!

S = Summons to Salvation

One type of court summons is a compulsory notice to appear in court as a witness; it is a command or a mandatory call to appear there on a specific day. God calls every believer to "show up" and fulfill the "Great Commission," for it, too, is a summons to be a witness and is compulsory: "…Compelling all men everywhere to be saved" (See Matthew 28:16). The Great Commission is intended to put the world on notice to appear before the cross. The message of the gospel is compulsory in that its content is compelling, for it is an urgent beckoning to salvation. As for the specificity of which day to show up—today! *"Now is the day of salvation"* (2 Corinthians 6:2, NIV).

S = Studies of Forensics Confirm Jesus' Death

Although the conventional labeling of Jesus' death is by crucifixion, I offer an alternate labeling. Notwithstanding the fact that Jesus technically died after being crucified, I submit that, more specifically, Jesus died of a broken heart over the humanity He loved. His heart hurt over the sinfulness of the human condition. His heart, I suggest, was disfigured on many levels; it was severed into chunks emotionally, squished anatomically, and sliced soulfully: *"A man of sorrows"* (Isaiah 53:3,

NLT). As a tandem observation, the study of modern forensics has had a positive bearing on confirming the veracity of Jesus' death due to a clinically altered heart. Forensic pathology is the scientific study of the injury and death of an individual and can be commonly used for the investigation of a crime, and further can be used in American court trials as exhibited evidence as to the cause of death.[14] Fortifying the reality and likelihood of Jesus' heart-induced death are reports of pathology doctors and scientists who discovered the probability of His death by heart failure. Let's tunnel through one such autopsy report. First, I will address the widely held assumption that Christ died *by* crucifixion. He did. The report verifies that Jesus' hands, actually His wrists, were likely impaled by nails, and He likely suffered excruciatingly and mercilessly from the wounds levied during His crucifixion: "This is a 5-foot, 11-inch male Caucasian weighing about 178 pounds. The legions are as follows: Beginning at the head, there are blood flows from numerous puncture wounds…The man has been beaten about the face, there is swelling on one cheek, and he undoubtedly has a black eye…there is a wound on the left wrist, the right one being covered by the left hand. This is the typical lesion of crucifixion… There is a stream of blood down both arms…On the back and front there are legions which appear to be scourge marks…The victim was whipped from both sides by two men, one of whom was taller than the other, as demonstrated by the angle of the thongs."[15] There, that forensic analysis portrayed a man who was crucified and was originally thought to possibly be the Jesus of the "Shroud of Turin," but later the portrayal was inconclusive as to the certainty of the Christ identity and has resulted in a disavowal of certainty of Christ's identity in some circles. What is certain, however, and has remained certain, is that the forensic analysis confirms that the above *type* of crucifixion is the same one that Jesus would have most certainly experienced, and the certainty of the death that would have followed it would have occurred in an extremely similar way. Jesus, therefore, did die by crucifixion.[16] Notwithstanding the exactness of Jesus' death—for it is true that He died on the cross and by the cross—I offer this finer thesis: It was the heart wound that Jesus felt for His church-bride that was the mortal blow which killed Him.

The cross was old, unattractive, and rugged, but it had gravitas because it was Jesus' platform of communication. We have heard the expression, "silence is golden," but those who were present at Calvary's crucifixion witnessed that silence is ruby. The rich, dark, ruby hue of Jesus' blood poured from His body in His silence. Jesus was silent, but He was not wordless! Although His mouth didn't verbalize anything most of the time while on the cross, that didn't matter because He is the Word of God, and it is impossible to muzzle the Word of God: *"The LORD roars from Zion and raises His voice from Jerusalem"* (Amos 1:2, BSB). Jesus, The Lion of Zion, delivered a great part of His oration with His cross-driven body; the Word of God spoke volumes, and the roar of the cross was heard in the Court of God. The outlet for speaking was His blood that spoke loudly, for the Bible makes it known how the blood speaks (See, Hebrews 12:24). On the cross, Jesus opined about the love of God; it was a divine, legal filibuster against death for six long hours as He atoned for the freedom of humankind's soul. There, the Word of God engaged in a *"fait accompli."* God sent the Word of God, His Son, to accomplish the cross: *"...My word...shall accomplish what I please"* (Isaiah 55:11, NKJV).

The expression, "wearing one's heart on one's sleeve," falls short of depicting the passion that Jesus displayed on the cross. It is more apt to say that Jesus wore His heart on His hands because when He died with His outstretched hands on the cross, He left *heartprints*. It was His heart that freed humankind on that cross, and it was His heart that would be medically and emotionally altered on that cross. Such is the mortal glance of the magnitude of Jesus' heart for humanity; Jesus died truly of a broken heart on the cross, and the donor-Christ donated a piece of it to every man, woman, and child who receives Him. There, God's love for humankind became inarguable. The immortal God dying on the cross for us, sheathed in mortal flesh, was more than a demonstration of mere sovereign hubris; it was love of the purest and highest order. In a very literal and spiritual sense, a heart transplant took place; there, He gave us His heart. Indeed, Jesus yielded His heart for His beloved church body and was willing to die to enkindle the spiritual rebirth of humankind's languished soul. Naturally, it must have severely saddened His heart that the inbred citizens of His own Israeli culture would plot His death. On a gut level, It may have severely frayed His heart to know that He was rejected as the Messiah by His Jewish-born compatriots. Combining that rejection with the emotionality of knowing that He also would be rejected by multiple Gentile countrymen as well, plausibly fractured His heart further: *"Jerusalem, Jerusalem, you who kill the prophets and stone those sent to you, how often I have longed to gather your children… and you were not willing"* (Matthew 23:37, NIV). One of the only three times that the Bible records the weeping of Jesus is over the incalcitrant heart of His native nation, Israel: *"And he looked upon Jerusalem and wept"* (Luke 19:41, NIV). There, His heart must have internally wept for the very heart of Israel. In retrospect, Jesus' dissonance with His fellow populus, and the enormity of the loss of communion with His Father during His station on that cross would surely have compounded, if not overwhelmed, His already sorrowing heart: *"Surely He has borne our griefs and carried our sorrows"* (Isaiah 53:4, ESV). A second time the tears fell from Jesus occurred just before He went to the cross: *"In the days of his flesh, Jesus offered up prayers and supplications, with loud cries and tears, to him who was able to save him from death"* (Hebrews 5:7, ESV). Jesus' sole purpose for leaving the heavenly cosmos and embracing carnal flesh was to save all humankind. The night before He died, the sorrow rolled in as Jesus was about to roll away the world's sins: *"I have deep sorrow and endless heartache"* (Romans 9:2, GW). Jesus martyred

> *Forensic pathology confirms that Jesus was heart-challenged.*

His heart! He did so because He wanted humankind to live forever, and He wanted to live forever with *them*.

Forensic pathology studies also scientifically confirm what I assert occurred viscerally—that Jesus was heart-challenged. Medically speaking, their studies shed light on the fact that Jesus, in all medical probability, died of cardiopulmonary heart failure. The expert finding of David Willis, an English physician and forensic scholar, points to Jesus' pericardium, the sac surrounding the heart, which would have expanded with fluid under the stress of His suffering and would have compressed the heart until His death.[17] In effect, Jesus' heart was flooded until it broke down. Pathologically, Willis concluded that the liquid compressed the heart of the Son of God, which produced His heart failure on the cross.[18] These modern forensics support scientifically what the Bible portrays spiritually—that Jesus did die of a broken heart. The Bible repeatedly chimes that there is a spiritual analog to every natural analog: *"What comes first is the natural body, then the spiritual body comes later"* (1 Corinthians 15:46, NLT). Bodily, both anatomically and physiologically, Jesus' heart was clinically overcome, but importantly, it was also shattered emotionally by a spiritual sensitivity. Jesus allowed it to be deconstructed for the whole world's sake. Having experienced this, it is no wonder that Jesus' first effusive order of business in His ministry was freeing the disfigured heart: *"…He has sent Me to heal the brokenhearted"* (Luke 4:18, NKJV).

Crossology: Treason & the Legal Progression of the Cross

In the case of *Garden v. Garden,* as I refer to it, treason visited the garden! Adam should have legally received the commensurate death sentence for committing high treason against the Most High God. To use the theological parlance of mercy and grace, Adam did not receive what He should have received, and Jesus received what He should not have received. Jesus graciously received a death sentence that He should not have received for a treason-less act in a garden that He had every right to be in. Mercifully, Adam did not receive a death sentence for a treason-filled act which he committed in a garden that he no longer had a right to be in. Adam forsook God's governance and preferred that of the enemy of God. He and his wife, Eve, capitulated to Satan by taking up arms, in a legal sense, against the counsel of God through reckless disobedience and adherence to God's enemy, which was legally tantamount to a charge of treason. Further, in a true sense, the Devil was a spiritual seditionist who toppled God's verdant order using his inciteful tongue. God had told Adam and Eve not to eat of the tree of good and evil. Roused by an enemy of God's State, the serpentine one, they ate of the tree of good and evil, and the Divine Crown had every right to charge them for their high crime. Notwithstanding American history and the well-accepted fact that the American Revolution led to liberty for numerous colonists who disbanded Great Britain, or the historically famous rebellions of Daniel Shays and Nat Turner, which sought certain shackled freedoms, sadly the garden dwellers misperceived the necessity of a revolt. In a dissatisfied moment of perversion, they wanted to declare their independence, but, regrettably, didn't recognize that there was never a need for their consternation because they already had abounding legal liberties and true freedom: *"Now the Lord is the Spirit, and where the Spirit of the Lord is, there is liberty"* (2 Corinthians 3:17, NASB1995). Regrettably, Adam acted in league with the enemy of God.

The cross was the conduit through which God legally fulfilled His grand plan to get heroic redemption to humankind. It was legally important for Jesus to die on a cross for a number of reasons. Firstly, the tree fits within God's apparent rule of law—within His symmetrical dictates and methodical axioms for redemption. There were symmetrical truths surrounding the tree that were essential factors and had to happen for legal redemption. For example, by bearing sin on a tree, Jesus put God in remembrance of the Adamic tree as He ate the wrathful consequence of Adam's consumed fruit—death, *Tree to Tree*:

death came in by a tree, and it would need to exit by a tree. Secondly, the tree was made of wood. The tree's composition was of significant magnitude because in the Old Testament, the sacrificial altar was oftentimes a structure of wood as set forth by the laws of God (Ezekiel 4:22). The word "altar" is from the Hebrew word, *mizbe'ah*, meaning slay; so wood from trees signaled the undergirding for a sacrifice that was to be slain and offered unto God. Symmetrically, Jesus was the sacrificial Lamb slain in accordance with God's law. This identity is so inseparable from Jesus that the Bible says to this day, Jesus appears in heaven like a slain Lamb in the middle of God's throne. Don't miss it—there is a lamb positioned dead center around the throne! (Revelation 5:6). Jesus was offered on an actual *slay-cross*, so He would be consumed unto death. Further, with respect to the wood, sometimes it was combined with stones. There is a crucial symmetry there also because stones were associated with Jesus' offering, too; in fact, Jesus provided the Stone—Himself.

Jesus said, *"Have you never read in the Scriptures the stone that the builders rejected has become the cornerstone. This is what the Lord has done"* (Matthew 21:42, NIV). Jesus had to die on a tree for a third reason. God's edict says, *"Cursed us everyone who is hung on a tree"* (Galatians 3:13, NIV). Because of that arboreal prerequisite, the only way to legally cancel the curse of the cursed Adam was to have the superior Adamic Christ lay in Adam's cursed place by Himself becoming accursed on a tree. I maintain there was a harmonization of those three elements that created a legal path to Jesus' redemption.

The exact location of the altar of sacrifice was located in the outer court of the portable tabernacle of Moses. The tabernacle's altar of incense, made of gilt wood, was positioned directly in front of the veil of the Holy of Holies, which concealed the presence of God. I find the location of the two in relation to each other of uppermost interest because I believe that the altar of sacrifice was located to the rear of that altar of incense so that the waft of sweet aroma would mingle with the stench of spilled, deathly blood. Symmetrically, on the cross, there was an outpour of Jesus' malodorous blood flowing forward and meeting the incense of His sweet sacrifice, which produced a double dulcet, honeyed effect in the Father's nostrils. There the intersection of the butchered dregs of Christ's fleshy surrender with the smoky embers of God's besieging fire was a legal discourse in the making. Keeping in line with the meticulousness of God and His fastidious emphasis on legal details, at traditional altar ceremonies, the Israeli handlers of the lamb sacrifice would call on the name of the LORD while sacrificing the lamb on the outskirts of town: *"From there he moved to the hill country… and there he built an altar to the LORD and called upon the name of the LORD"* (Genesis 12:8, ESV). Symmetrically, on a cross at the edge of a city's hilly slope called Golgotha, Jesus also called to the LORD God during His sacrifice: *"My God, My God, why have you abandoned me…When Jesus cried out again in a loud voice, He yielded up His spirit"* (Matthew 27:46, 50; NLT). All of the elements of God's law were present for the discourse. Jesus was the lamb of God: *"Behold the lamb of God who taketh away the sin of the world"* (John 1:29, KJV). The outcry of the servant, Jesus, was heard by His Lord. The wrath of God consumed Jesus's offertory of His lamb-breath. It is clear that the legal metric by which Jesus carried out His sacrifice was tactfully in accordance with God's law and was legalized on all squares.

"Run away…displaying your shameful nakedness" (Micah 1:11, ISV). There was a fourth reason for which Jesus' dying on the cross was a legal imperative—only a shamed Christ could legally reverse the shame of Adam. The cross was the defining pathos that evoked God's remedy for shame. After sinning, Adam was so ashamed of his sin and nakedness that he hid from God, so God engineered a methodology that would extract the dishonor of shame: *"Who told you that you were naked"* (Genesis 3:11, NKJV); *"Fear not, you will no longer live in shame"* (Isaiah 54:4, NLT). The style of Jesus' execution was key. Unwittingly, the Romans were being used by God. The Romans had perfected their heinous and extremely shameful style of crucifixion; it was not only the most gruesome method of killing an individual, but it

also involved the shocking ignominy of the victim appearing naked on the cross.[19] As a side note, while some historians plainly point to the nefarious Roman practice of completely stripping their victims, others hold to the notion that Jesus may have been only partially naked. I assert that there was ingrained shame in both scenarios, but due to the painstaking nature of symmetry and precision with which the Bible aligns itself, I believe Jesus was entirely naked as Adam was, and it is this harsher practice that would also be consistent with the widespread, conventional Roman custom of that day. By Christ's clothless profile of shame on a dead tree, He legally eradicated shame's muscle over humankind: *"I spread the corner of my garment over you and covered your naked body. I gave my solemn oath and entered into a covenant with you, declares the Sovereign* LORD, *and you became mine"* (Ezekiel 16:8, NIV); *"I am not ashamed of the gospel, for it is the power of God that brings salvation to everyone who believes: first to the Jew, then to the Gentile"* (Romans 1:16, ESV).

Crossology: Garden v. Garden

> *"Now Jesus himself was about thirty years old when he began his ministry. He was the son, so it was thought, of Joseph, the son of Heli…the son of Seth, the son of Adam, the son of God"* (Luke 3:23, 38; NIV). *"For your Maker is your husband, the* LORD *of Hosts is His name; …your Redeemer…The God of all the earth."*
>
> ISAIAH 54:5 (ESV)

What a beautiful, orchidaceous paradise God selected for the outdoor gallery of man. How was it that such beauty could unearth such ugliness? Man discarded his soul there! The garden ancestry goes like this: In the Garden of Eden, Adam lost his birthright as the eldest, created son of God because he ceded it away approximately four thousand years before God would place another Adam in the earth;[20] this one was begotten not made, and this one came bearing the birthright of God as the premiere Son of God: *"The first man was of dust; the second man is of heaven"* (1 Corinthians 15:47, NIV). Adam also ceded his birthplace, the earth, to the deceiver, Satan. From a legal standpoint, Satan, who the Bible correctly warns is a thief, in this instance did *not*, in fact, steal these birthright holdings from Adam. To clarify, yes, Satan did sneakily hoodwink Eve and baited Adam into handing over his botanical kingdom and his first-tier birthright title-deed; but Satan obtained it legally because, per fundamentals of analogous real estate law, Adam had legal ownership because God had given him the legal title to the earth, and with such, he could legally grant his property to whomever he pathetically chose—even to Satan. In short, if you own it, you can convey it—the whole thing.[21] *"For I am your God, listen…The whole world and everything in it belong to me"* (Psalm 50:12, NET). *"And the LORD GOD took the man and put him into the garden of Eden…to keep it"* (Genesis 2:15, NASB1995; Emphasis added). Adam, however, was supposed to *keep* the kingdom in the family of God, passing it down to believing, familial generations. Mercifully, God does all things legally, completely above board, for the Bible confirms that God is "Just in all His actions." God, of course, had a legal cure-all for the situation. What Adam legally gave away, Jesus legally retrieved. *"And I will restore to you the years that the swarming locust has eaten, the great locust, the grasshopper, and the caterpillar…"* (Joel 2:25, KJV). The first Adamic covenant was with God's created son, Adam, and he broke it in the Garden of Eden. The second Adamic covenant was with Jesus, the second Adam, and He upheld it in the Garden of Gethsemane, replacing what went wrong and making it right. In *Garden v. Garden,* the utopian would-be case, God's Court ruled that the second Adam could transact business in the first Adam's stead since they are both legal sons of God. Although the Garden of Eve's Adam was the archetypal Adam, Jesus was the perfected Adam, so Jesus, the last Adam, was the perfect solution to the first Adam who acted imperfectly. Regarding God's judgment, it was *"Res Judicata"*—in the legal field, meaning already judged and over with. God's gavel of grace seen in that matter gave humankind a second chance at freedom, if embraced. The cross was introduced as a legal intervening criterion for Adam's crime, and because Adam is the progenitor of humankind, God judicially took into account Jesus' act on the cross for every new Adam and Eve-to-come. Jesus' cross was exhibited both as a symbol of Adam's high sin, as well as a symbol of God's high mercy.

Crossology: Real Estate Law Meets Legal Redemption

How exactly did Jesus buy back Adam's property rights? Jesus redeemed or bought back Adam's soul, which was God's intangible property, with the proprietary currency of heaven—His death blood—which allowed it to remain within the family line. The book of Ruth was demonstrative of the "Redeeming Kinsman" right. That right illustrated that if a person owned some property but lost it, then a kinsman-redeemer would have the legal right to buy back this property in order to keep it under the family heading. In the biblical story of Ruth, Boaz acted as Ruth's kinsman-redeemer and was permitted to redeem her land. Jesus, in like fashion, acted as the kinsman-redeemer to Adam by legally redeeming His brother's ownership of the earth's land because Jesus and Adam were spiritual brothers. Adam had fed on a lie and discontinued His daily communion with God. Adam's new forbidden fruit diet contained an evil seed that was given to him to eat by that ancient reptilian cheerleader of revolt, Satan himself, who had revolted against God by committing treachery in heaven. When the Lord of Heaven yielded to the cross, He ate the heavenly fruit of loyalty which caused Adam's seedy consumption of disloyalty to be legally null and void (without effect): *"But whoever eats my body and drinks my blood has eternal life, and I shall raise him in the last day"* (John 6:54, NIV). When Jesus left glory, He took with Him the Father's command to be obedient to the cross by eating the fruit of sin, which is death. Why this command? Because in the garden, at ground zero, God had given Adam the command not to sinfully eat the fruit, but he broke it. Jesus obeyed the command to sinlessly eat the fruit and kept it. The holy seed from the bread of life yielded allegiance to God, so there on the cross, Jesus reversed the curse with fidelity instead of rebellion. The world would need a savior, a second Adam, who could restore law in the hearts of men: *"The first man is of the earth, earthy, the second man is the Lord from heaven"* (1 Corinthians 15:47, KJV). The second Adam was cross-bound. On His way to the cross, He would let no one and nothing stop Him from enacting the new covenant that God had forged for humankind. Adam had transgressed the law, and since Adam was the fleshly template of humankind, God's wrath was legally kindled against humankind. When Jesus died on the cross, He became the spiritual template of humankind to activate the new covenant that would re-instill the law of God in their gaping hearts: *"The spirit gives life. The flesh counts for nothing"* (John 6:63, NIV). Jesus' death toll canceled our death knell.

Crossology: A Lawful Revolution & an Illegal Revolt

> *"… He was counted among the rebels. He bore the sins of many and interceded for rebels."*
>
> ISAIAH 53:12 (NLT)

Rather than worldly revolution, Jesus had come to bring divine resolution for the oppressed soul.

Jesus' stance on earth was not so much a revolt as it was a refinement: *"You have heard it said by others, but I say…"* (Matthew 5:43–44, NIV). There were rebels on the cross the day of Jesus' death, and because

He was affixed on the cross between them, Jesus was numbered as one of them. In reality, not so! Jesus was not a lawbreaker of any of God's laws. The Bible, in an intriguing way, displays the difference between a revolt and a revolution. Jesus, not a rebel, came to bring a revolution; Adam, a rebel, revolted. A revolution is "a radical change in the established order," usually forcibly, suddenly, and resulting in a total change and direction in fundamental ideological thinking; it can be viewed as illegal because it disrupts the lawful, preserved government or religious order.[22] A revolt, however, is an illegal uprising with an armed refusal to obey ruling authority, and is usually associated with an ineffective rebellion.[23] The contrast is that Jesus' uprising led to everlasting change, but Adam's uprising changed his everlasting. Above, Adam rose up in rebellious defiance while *dismissing* the authority of God; Jesus, however, arose in furtherance of a new covenant that would *augment* authority with God. Jesus was more interested in revealing than revolting. Adam rose up in revolt and became an eternity-at-risk-statistic. Adam and Eve's attempt to hide, to self-reinstate themselves into the family of God with fig-relief, and to recapture God's glory was useless. They would need a Lord of glory, a Savior who could restore law in the revolting hearts of men. To a qualified extent, Jesus' revolution did involve violence; that is, not so much natural violence, but more of a macro-aggression of a spiritual nature, of a violent, force-producing faith. Jesus said, *"The kingdom of heaven suffers violence and the violent take it by force"* (Matthew 11:12, NKJV). Rather than a revolution against a natural government, Jesus had come to bring a violent resolution for the dissolution of humankind's condemned soul. *"What good is it for someone to gain the whole wide world and yet forfeit his soul"* (Mark 8:36, NIV). Jesus revolutionized His surroundings by coming to ground zero as the second Adam to reverse the revolt of the first Adam. Jesus, in a revolutionary twist, returned to the caution-taped scene of Adam's scene of the crime to redeem man from the fall out of that crime. Genesis is the storied scene of humankind's first encounter with lawlessness since Adam was history's first biblical lawbreaker;

he was the thief that stole from God's vineyard. God had given them permission to eat of every tree in the Garden of Eden except the one which they ate from, the tree of the knowledge of good and evil. The table was amply set, but Eve was tempted by the serpentine-looking, masked Devil who enticed her to break God's law. She gobbled the prohibited fruit and, in turn, tempted her husband to eat it as well; at that same point, they both became perpetrators of the crime of theft.

Adam and Eve were notoriously ambushed by that shiny-scaled, primitive con artist. Notably, under controlling real estate "Homestead" law in various states, a husband or wife cannot sell or transfer their real property that is owned by one of them without the consent of both spouses. I submit that a similar legal provision was in place in the garden. Assuming Adam had sole title and was the sole owner of the earth and its sphere, although the Devil had finagled Eve's assent, he needed Adam's, and he got it when Eve cajoled Adam to sell out by "eating out." Adam, thereby, sold earth proper, sold his birthright, and sold his soul. Adam and Eve did not know it, but they had just been involved in the worst "whole-sale" deal of a lifetime! I alternatively propose that Adam and Eve could have held joint ownership, or legal "Joint Title," to the Garden of Eden; alternatively, in some states, this same team ownership is known legally as "Tenants by the Entirety." God seems to have created a "level playing field" of ownership for husband and wife on the earth concerning their first enterprise together. I suspect theirs was one of co-ownership because of the continued emphasis that God placed on female ownership of property through the newly transformed Mosaic law in the Bible; that is, in conjunction with that of male ownership, God postulated the right of women to be landowners: *"So Moses brought their case before the Lord, and the Lord said to him, 'What Zelophehad's daughters are saying is right. You must certainly give them property as an inheritance...'"* (Numbers 27:5–7, NIV).

Crossology: God's Legal Strategy of Double Jeopardy

The legal concept of *Double Jeopardy* is relevant to every believer who wants to be condemnation-free in the kingdom of God. Double Jeopardy gets its teeth from the Fifth Amendment, which says: "Nor shall any person be subject for the same offence to be twice put in jeopardy of life or limb."[24] Straight and simple, two things are important to remember here as it relates to Double Jeopardy. Firstly, God decided the case of humankind's innocence when, through Christ, He exonerated (freed from blame) its ancestral representative, Adam. Secondly, because Adam was inextricably linked to us, God legally vindicated (cleared) humankind of its guilt, too; so humankind's free-flowing right to eternal life can no longer be jeopardized based on the sin Adam committed. In other words, our eternal life is no longer in jeopardy! God held court at Golgotha: *"No weapon formed against you will prevail, and you will refute every tongue that accuses you. This is the heritage of the* LORD, *and this is their vindication from me, declares the* LORD*"* (Isaiah 54:17-8, CSB. Emphasis mine). God's decision is final, and it is settled in heaven and on earth. Adam's verdict of "Not Guilty" is, therefore, the Court's verdict of all of humankind who are similarly situated in Salvation, and the decision stands which is legally referred to as *"stare decisis."* Under the principle of Double Jeopardy, humankind as the defendant does not have to defend itself against future litigation to avail itself of the eternal, finished work of Jesus. Jesus' sin offering was a once-in-a-lifetime occurrence that secured a post-lifetime of innocence. The antagonistic, satanic foe of humankind is barred from endlessly re-litigating his conjunctive claims of death and condemnation against an exonerated humankind. Double Jeopardy is our defense. The *cross and the gavel* are the legal reminders of the body of Christ's eternal triumph. When Jesus got up from the grave, He brought His heel down like a gavel on the head of Satan, and the cross was no longer the instrument by which the forces of evil could brag of His demise; instead, the cross became a legal torpedo in the war against Satan because Jesus' resurrection weaponized the cross and the enemy had no legal retort to it. The totality of Satan's defeat was the finality of Jesus' conquest; the totality of the redemption is in the finality of the resurrection. Jesus, Barrister of Heaven, won the case in favor of humanity so that never again could man be tried for the same damnable offense if he is in Christ Jesus. The Bible has its own version of Double Jeopardy that precludes relitigation, too: *"Therefore there is no condemnation [no guilty verdict, no punishment] for those who are in Christ Jesus…"* (Romans 8:1, AMP). *"He [Jesus] did not enter heaven to offer himself again and again… But our High Priest offered himself to God as a single sacrifice for sins, good for all time"* (Hebrews 9:25, Hebrews 10:12, NIV).

CHAPTER 4

Brilliant Attorney Jesus: A Legal Fight-Fest!

"This also comes from the Lord of Hosts, who is wonderful in counsel and excellent in wisdom."

ISAIAH 28:29 (BSB)

A Courtyard Becomes a Court: What Did Jesus Write and Why?

"For you...have neglected the weightier matters of the law: justice and mercy and faith. It is these you ought to have practiced..."

MATTHEW 23:23 (ESV)

It is no wonder that the practicing lawyers which Jesus encountered could not stump Him. Finite men were in contention with the Lord of infinity, the Counsel of heaven, and they constantly found themselves trapped by their own entrapments. *"The Counsel of the Lord stands forever"* (Psalm 33:11, BSB). Jesus' intellectual superiority was no secret even as a tween. At twelve, the discerning Jesus was in the Israeli temple, demonstrating His lawyerly prowess to the learned doctors of the law (See Luke 2:46). In Jewish tradition, a boy of thirteen would be turning into a man of accountability, and a hugely important *bar mitzvah* was to reflect that. As a practical matter, a boy at that age would have been under the tutelage of a rabbi, and the *bar mitzvah* showcased his attention to the teachings of the commandments and his ability to present an impressive speech about the first five books of the law—the *Torah*. The authoritative mastery of the Scripture which the divinely precocious Jesus had at the tender age of twelve was supernaturally remarkable and outshone any of this traditional instruction and recitation: *"After three days, they found him in the temple courts… Everyone who heard him was amazed at his understanding and his answers"* (Luke 2:46-47, HCSB). Interestingly, in Aramaic, *bar mitzvah* means "son of the commandment." I believe Jesus' commanding *tour de force* foretold that He was more than a son of the commandment; He was The *Son*, and the great enabler of the commandments: *"He existed in the beginning with God. God created everything through Him and nothing was created except through Him"* (John 1:2-3, NLT). Jesus formed the commandments and actuated them from Genesis to Revelation. Jesus is the personhood of the inscripturated gospel; He made the Word of God a reality, and the reality is—the lawyers had been reading about *Him*: *"You search the Scriptures because you think they give you eternal life. But the Scriptures point to me!"* (John 5:39, NLT).

Scripture records Jesus as the "wonderful counselor." He is indeed the wonderful "Counselor at Law" of the Godhead, for He was the very finger of God that wrote the commanding law which others received. Jesus' divine, digital ability to finger those ten hallowed tablets becomes pivotal in the biblical story of an adulterous woman. When a group of lawyers tried to ensnare Him with the woman whom they caught in the act of adultery, asking Him if they should stone her according to the law, Jesus extended the same finger that had penned the laws of the Ten Commandments and began to pen something that was filled with wonderment. I firmly believe that He was not only re-writing the Ten Commandments, but also that He "fired up" His writing as He demonstrated His divine, glyptic art. I am convinced that fire was present because the Ten Commandments were originally emblazoned by fire on its tablets. Also, when God appeared to Moses, to whom He gave the Ten Commandments, He first appeared as a burning bush. Christian scholarship refers to this burning wonder as a pre-incarnate appearance of Christ—a "Christophany." Fire emanating from Jesus' fingers as He wrote would line up with His pattern of fiery illustrations. Some theologians debate whether the ground that Jesus wrote on was made of dirt or was made of stone. Interjecting my thought, were it made of rigid stone, it would track with the miracle on Mount Sinai where the "finger of God" burned words into stone, the stone here representing the ultra stony hearts of the accusers. Comparatively, dirt could have rightly epitomized the accusers' dirty intentions or even their filthy hearts: *"I will give them an undivided heart and put a new spirit in them, I will remove from them the heart of stone and give them a heart of flesh"* (Ezekiel 11:19, NIV). I lean toward a stone supposition that is further supported by the illuminating scriptural passage where Jesus entered Jerusalem on Palm Sunday amidst rambunctious praise and said, *"I tell you that if these should hold their peace, the stones will immediately cry out"* (Luke 19:40, KJV). There, Jesus highlighted another one of His connections to stone; therefore, that courtyard's flooring begs further delving into regarding its probability of being covered in stone. I maintain that Jesus never wrote in the dirt as many have traditionally espoused, for I believe the finger of God-the-Son was at work in the stone that canvassed where He was standing. Further buttressing Jesus' finger illustration in stone is the biblical account of Belshazzar's feast. There, the wicked king desecrated the Israeli temple's holy libation vessels by drinking out of them as part of a debaucherous celebration. In judgment, a man's hand appeared and wrote on the wall:

> *As then they brought golden vessels that were taken out of the temple of the house of God…they drank wine, and praised the gods of gold…in the same our came forth fingers of a man's hand, and wrote over against the candlestick upon the plaister*

> *of the wall of the king's palace…the king's countenance was changed and his thoughts troubled him.*
>
> DANIEL 5:3-6 (ASV)

The text details that the hand wrote near a burning candlestick of fire which reinforces the concept of the finger of Jesus writing on stone with accompanying fire since stone was often under plastered walls back then. Jesus was indubitably teaching in the temple courtyard when the woman's accusers seemed to dash her to the ground. He was there because Scripture indicates that Jesus routinely taught in the temple courtyard (See John 8:2). This detail is important because of my assertion that the courtyard floor was made of stone; in fact, modern archaeologists have now uncovered pieces of stone belonging to the courtyard to Herod's Temple Mount, where Jesus was commonly found. A fairly recent Israeli discovery by the Temple Mount Sifting Project unearthed some compelling historiography that reinforces my supposition. The project recovered more than a hundred geometrically cut and polished *stone* tiles, *Opus Sectile*, meaning "cutwork" in Latin, with which the Temple Mount was paved under King Herod.[25] This Herodian temple's colored and regal-looking polished *stone* tile fit together so precisely, it was reported that one couldn't even "fit a knife blade between them."[26] First Century Jewish historian Flavius Josephus actually described the stones as indescribably rare, further said, "The open court loft of the Temple Mount was from end to end variegated with paving of all manner of stones."[27] This find is invaluable because it leads me to further theorize that when Jesus stooped down to write, it was highly likely that He was miraculously piercing stone. That fact is not lost given that the woman's means of death was supposed to be by infliction of stones; I think that Jesus had a concerted pause because of that, especially since He said: *"They will dash you to the ground, you and the children within your walls. They will not leave one stone on another, because you did not recognize the time of God's coming to you"* (Luke 19:44, NIV). Whatever the consistency, hard or malleable, the courtyard's surface hosted a definite miracle of a penetrating kind which made the male accusers walk away, every single one of them, without their stony, projectile missiles!

The Fire and the Finger

"Fire goes before Him and consumes His foes on every side."
PSALM 97:3 (NIV)

Fire flowing from Jesus' fingertips is credible. Significantly, in the first book of Revelation, Jesus appears to the apostle John on the island of Patmos with fire all around Him, flashing His prominent eyes and bronzed feet of fire. It is not uncommon for this repetition of fire to be connected with Jesus. Compounding my belief that fire met the stony floor of the courtyard is Gideon's encounter with the Angel of God, who was the Christophaneous, pre-incarnate Christ. There, when Gideon brought Him a meat offering, Jesus touched the rock that held the flesh offering, and with the staff in His hand, made fire come out of the rock. Gideon then called Him "Sovereign" (See Judges 6:19). Jesus also once appeared as the pre-incarnate Son of God, with three intrepid Hebrews teenagers by His side in a fiery furnace that was meant to host a human marshmallow toast (Daniel 3:13-30). It is significant that Jesus' presence was linked to fire; thus, it is totally fathomable that there was a fiery exchange between the rocky surface and Jesus' fingerprints. *"...The Lord my Rock, who trains ...my fingers for battle"* (Psalm 144:1, NIV). With a dramatic effect, it seems the stony courtyard venue was divinely orchestrated as the winning stroke of Jesus' case. Imagine the handiwork of Jesus' fingers acting like a rapier, with Him methodically dicing empty arguments by each letter! Further, Imagine seeing the living Scriptures spring to emblazoned life as the finger of God fingered the commandments which each man had broken, commandments which they had been admonished to bind to their very own fingers. At that moment, their Creator "put the finger" on their sin. Scripture encouraged them to use their own fingers to voluntarily tether the commandments to their own heart tablets: *"Keep my commandments and live…bind them on your fingers, write them on the tablet of your heart"* (Proverbs 7:2–3, NKJV). Arguably, they had not done it, so Jesus would have to use His own fingers to write those commandments on the courtyard's tiled tablets which doubled as mirrors to their hearts: *"Being manifested that you are a letter of Christ…written not with ink, but with the Spirit of the living God, not on tablets of stone but on tablets of human hearts"* (2 Corinthians 3:3, NASB). Jesus' "grounded" content evidently shook the doctors of the law so much that they were speechless and couldn't wait to disappear without so much as a murmur or any type of legal retort. In the American courts of law, when an attorney has so poignantly, definitively, and brilliantly presented His legal argumentation very often, the besieged, losing, and opposing attorney will state to the court that he has no further direct questions of his own witnesses, nor does he wish to cross-examine the counselor's witness either. The takeaway is that the attorney wants to move on—usually quickly. Similarly, the woman's opposition wanted to move on! As complimentary legal counsel for the adulteress, perhaps omniscient Jesus listed her accusers' names, their co-sinners' names, and maybe He even added the dates and times of their transgressions as exhibits. A bunch of men with nefarious motives did not shut up easily nor entirely, and they certainly did not walk away without the least bit of resistance unless something utterly revealing and overwhelming had assailed them. Although they fled the court, they could not outrun the truth. Surely, the forcefulness of Jesus' legal abilities had rushed to the forefront. None of us knows for certain what Jesus wrote on the *terra firma*, for the Bible does not record His written argument. What is not in doubt is that Jesus' writings contained content that brimmed with such a high degree of evidentiary value and were so ripe with anointed, rhetorical efficacy that it staggered the very legal faculties of these men. They became consummately speech-challenged. In a word, Jesus' lawyer's skills were… brilliant.

Gender Representation and Legal Loopholes

"For you…have neglected the weightier matters of the law: justice and mercy and faith. It is these you ought to have practiced…"

MATTHEW 23:23 (ESV)

In Ancient Judaism, a broad swath of society demonstrated misogynist tendencies. How did Jesus navigate through His society's negative vilification of women? He evaded the normative, cultural traps of His day by utilizing "legal loopholes," which I will expound upon in chapter 6. Strictly speaking, a legal loophole is a legal calculation or technicality that is used to steer clear of a restriction of law without directly violating it.[28] More directly, they are strategic devices, which an attorney can legally use to secure a desired outcome if he is skillful enough to identify and properly utilize the defect in the law. Jesus did just that, but He did it faithfully with mercy and justice and without any illegality or dirty hands. Importantly, Jesus did not engage in any ill-intentions to evade well-intentioned law. Again, Jesus always worked within God's intended legal purview. Consider, for instance, that the prevailing law said the adulteress had to be stoned. Jesus did not thwart that prevalent Mosaic law directly in that He did not impugn the law itself—He did not oppose the restriction of the law itself—but cleverly and dexterously held court right there on the spot where He tried the fitness of the vilification of her handlers instead. Jesus had heard the eyewitness testimony, which was supplied by her enthusiastic would-be executioners who were totally on board with her having been "curiously" caught in the act. The astuteness of Jesus' observation of the three-step syllogism of their case and the reception of His opposers is telling: 1. Their presentation of the law (Thou Shalt Not Commit Adultery—an act that carries a sentence of stoning). 2. Their presentation of the facts (The woman was caught in adultery). 3. Their presentation of the conclusion (The adulteresses should, therefore, be stoned according to the law). Jesus did not obfuscate the law, but He retorted with the mirror of God's law: Let the sinless man, therefore, go ahead and stone the adulteress. Jesus had presented His written testimony which He wrote on the ground, and then waited for her accusers to carry out the lawful sentence of death by stoning. They did not. They *could* not. They vanished one by one: *"They dig a hole to trap others, but they will fall into it themselves"* (Psalm 7:15, NLT). Jesus had not trounced the law on its face but seized upon a legal strategy to indirectly allow the men's own sins to *"surely find them out,"* as the Bible puts it in Numbers 32:23. Jesus was successful in allowing the device to take its natural course, resulting in His outwitting the opposition and steering clear of the death penalty. Jesus' legal adroitness cut through the substrata of the men's motives like a scalpel and was masterful at drawing out forethoughts, mid thoughts, and afterthoughts of their faith to effect His meaning. Judicious Jesus was both a brilliant legal practitioner and a faith practitioner.

> *Jesus was both a legal and a faith practitioner.*

The Trial Venue: The Chosen Courtyard

"… and having set her in the center of the court."

JOHN 8:3 (NASB)

A trial's venue—the proper location where the court case takes place—is very important to the case that is being tried. Attorneys expend considerable effort to make sure that the trial takes place in the location that is most favorable to their client because a trial's venue can greatly influence the outcome of a case. The courtyard was the destined venue of choice in the above story of the adulteress and proved to be influential in Jesus' counsel presentation, as noted above.

Jesus was literally holding two types of court in the courtyard; in one of them, He introduced Scripture and doctrine as instruction, but also He introduced trial testimony in another:

> *At dawn he appeared again in the temple courts, where all the people gathered around him, and he sat down to teach them. The teachers of the law and the Pharisees brought in a woman caught in adultery. "Teacher this woman was caught in the act of adultery…the law of Moses commanded us to stone such a woman. Now what do you say?"*
>
> JOHN 8:2-5 (NIV)

As a matter of routine, Pharisees, teachers of the law, and doctors of the law did not always take part in legal court procedures; they did, however, at times. Contextually, there seems to have been a full-blown trial in progress here with them spearheading the charge. The facts seem clear. She was roused from her illegal, adulterous activity by her handlers unfairly—without her male partner who had been an accomplice and who contributed to the pandemonium. An uproarious confrontation ensued as she was conceivably flung at Jesus' feet. Notice that Jesus' words in this story were poignantly legal; it is as though the listener is hearing audio from a legal lexicon or watching a legal film. He said to the woman: *"Where are your accusers?"* and "neither do I condemn you." Later, the text records, and "they went away *convicted* one by one." Continuing, the words of the Pharisees were also strikingly legal and were meant to stab at the core of both Jesus and the woman: "She has broken our law and that of Moses" (See John 8:5). The conspicuously legal avalanche of terms point to only one thing—a trial was going on. Their question to Jesus was loaded. What they were really doing was introducing evidence against the woman known as *"In flagrante delicto,"* a legal term meaning in the act of a blazing misdeed, interpreted as caught "red-handed." They actually said, *"Teacher, this woman was caught in the very act"* (John 8:4, NIV). In lawyers' parlance, it was their "smoking gun"—known in court circles as the inarguable, undeniable piece of incriminating evidence that is said to "win the case." Since the woman's accusers were, in essence, her prosecutors, Jesus would have assumed the adversarial role of defense counsel, whose role it was to introduce testimony that would prove advantageous to her defense. It appears that was exactly His methodology. Legally speaking, if the covenant law—the commandments of God—is testimony, then when Jesus wrote the Ten Commandments in the stone of the court's yard, as I assert, He would have been, in effect, introducing testimony: *"And thou shalt put into the ark the testimony which I shall give thee"* (Exodus 25:16, KJV. *See* also Exodus 40:3).

Bristling with opprobrium, the men proceeded to smugly present what could be legally called *Prima Facie* evidence, or evidence which on its face, or at first look, appears to be enough to get a ruling in their favor on the facts. The problem, however, which the men had with their *Prima Facie* evidence was that no matter how convincingly true the evidence looked, it was still subject to a rebuttal. Not only did Jesus introduce God's testimony, but He also offered what is called "rebuttal evidence;" in other words, through a written statement, Jesus offered a repelling contradiction that was meant to erode the adverse party's evidence. Their sole evidence was offered by them only, and *Jesus introduced evidence that called into question their own trustworthiness, and by doing so, pitted their uprightness against her wrongness.* By striking at their hypocritical hearts, he struck at the heart of their offense.

At first blush, it looked like the Pharisees and company had this case all tied up, with a bow, too! I do not want to up-play the sinfulness of the high elitism of the Sadducees or the vaunted ritualism of the Pharisees more than any other sinner because Jesus hated all sin equally and loved all sinners equally, but these groups consistently made themselves available to be the vehicles of white-washed evil. Legally, if the character of those eyewitnesses could be discredited in some way by their own actions, then it could render their eyewitness accounts so ineffective as to turn it on its head. This seems to be the effectual route that Jesus took. With a legal wince, Jesus impeached their character because each witness, indeed the whole prosecution who appeared to be one and the same, left the court's yard apparently invalidated, taking their crippled prosecutory evidence with them. Given their acquiescence, in simple terms of legal procedure, where there is no longer any evidence of culpability, coupled with no prosecutorial pursuit, there is no viable case to be pursued. The defendant is usually free to go. This case could have been regarded as a dismissal in the legal world. Jesus shut down her marauders of death! Five words from Jesus freed this woman from the trauma and the drama of her past: *"Go now, and leave your life of sin"* (John 8:11, NIV).

Leaning in closer, Jesus wore many legal hats that day. He was defense attorney, and a zoomed-in look at the text supports that He was also the judge that day. Judicially speaking, although there was no pronouncement of a condemned sentence by Jesus as Judge, it was verified that He had the judicial capacity to condemn her, for Jesus clearly stated to her: "Neither do I *condemn* you." Legally, to condemn means to pass sentence upon; in an ironic manner, there was no sentence given out, but the trial *did* result in two sets of convictions; both the woman defendant and the accusatory men of the prosecution experienced inner, spiritual convictions in the place that mattered most—in their deepest cores. One of them left seemingly terrified, and the other left happy and relieved: *"When justice is done, it brings joy to the righteous but terror to evildoers"* (Proverbs 21:15, NIV).

How was justice accomplished? In our American society, the accuser or at least his representative must be present at a legal proceeding for it to go forward—and should remain there for its duration—or a judge has the authority to dismiss the case. Case in point, when the woman's accusers, who were the self-same legal representatives, vanished, and indeed, failed to appear any longer at the trial, the case against the woman defendant could not legally proceed. Because her accusers, nor their representatives, were no longer present, I submit that Jesus, outfitted in an invisible judicial robe, adopted His judicial authority and dismissed the case. Throughout her case, Jesus had stepped into the role of a defense attorney, victim's advocate, and ultimately judge. Jesus adjudged her free with the caveat not to repeat her offense. Importantly, Jesus was not ratifying her sin; she had with certainty broken the law of adultery, but having her accusers go to lengths to stratify the law by gender and splinter justice by remaining silent about their own "crimes" was not acceptable. Jesus butt heads with a cultural staple that wrongly discriminated against women, and He righted it; Jesus went "counter-cultural" on them. He had stepped in as her attorney in fact, articulated a winning legal defense, and saved her from the grave in stunning advocacy when He introduced evidence that countered the credibility of their witness testimony. He had directed His hulled argument toward her accusers who were also her self-appointed prosecutors and unmasked her cloaked executioners: *"There is no longer male nor female... for you are all one in Christ Jesus"* (Galatians 3:28, NIV). Finally, judicially speaking, there was no need to condemn the woman because Jesus was able to, in effect, dismiss the case.

The related text says Jesus stooped down, not once but twice, and I've often wondered why did He posture Himself in this downward motion (John 8:6-8). I view it as *gender humility*, with two goals in mind; not only to meet the woman where she found herself—at the bottom of her lamented class—but also to raise her afloat with genteel correction and newfound dignity. It was an intended foray by Jesus, for He meant to destabilize the old normal and rectify the gender divide.

At that moment, her victimhood was surpassed by her victory. She was transformed. Stooping, He lifted her. The buoyancy of His love had elevated her! *"The goodness of God is gently drawing you to repentance"* (Romans 2:4, WNT).

Jesus, Champion of Women

"He who vindicates me is near."

ISAIAH 50:8 (NIV)

Come see a man, she proclaimed! The irony is that Jesus had come to see a woman, this woman.

Contrary to first glance, the Samaritan woman at the well is one of the most heroic and intelligent women in the Bible. Although long seen by traditional thinkers as only polytheistic, unattractively amoral, one-noted, and unpleasantly one-dimensional, conversely, this beheld female could have been an apt attorney if the emergence of the women's movements had been salient in her time. Even though such was not the case thousands of years ago, or even hundreds of years ago because of the unapologetic dearth of gender equality, Jesus apparently recognized her impressive, timely, and logical acumen. This woman showed a cerebral mix of fortitude and truthfulness. She didn't speak in speculative terms; in contrast, she spoke of a definitive and formative liturgical worship: "Our ancestors worshipped on this mountain, but you Jews claim that the place where we must worship is in Jerusalem."[29] She, moreover, engaged Jesus in a linear fashion with questions of geography and history. Neither did she simply blurt things out, but was contemplative and volleyed facts to Jesus: "You are a Jew and I am a Samaritan woman. How can you ask me for a drink?"[30] The Bible records their discourse, and as it turns out, it is notably the longest colloquy ever to take place between Jesus and a woman. She further engaged Jesus with questions about physics and commentary about theology: "…You have nothing to draw with and the well is deep."[31] "I know that Messiah is coming. When he comes, he will explain everything to us."[32] She unabashedly fired off questions about His identity: "Are you greater than our father, Jacob, who gave us this well?"[33] She refuted presumptions about her identity: "I have no husband."[34] She was not afraid to go toe to toe with a man, even the man, Jesus, whom she deemed was different: "I perceive you are a prophet."[35] She was bold with untrammeled courage and yet sagacious enough to know she needed a Savior: "Sir, give me this water so that I won't get thirsty."[36] How did Jesus react? He was intent on guiding her to her breakthrough. He knew that there was a victory in the offing, a sure miracle in the making. He knew that He was about to see an unsuspecting woman transformed into a missionary-evangelist before her very own eyes. He knew that what she was about to do would inject her into the popular discourse for centuries to come. With laser precision, He thrust His words: "I, the one speaking to you—I am he."[37] She ran to spread the good news, and her weighty impact proved to be the beginning of a mass harvest of believers in Jesus throughout Samaria (See John 4:39).

While we know the name of her city, we don't know this woman's name. She may have been nameless, but Jesus wanted her to know that she wasn't faceless. There can be no doubt He wanted to see her face, planting Himself near her because her vindication was near. Directly in front of her on the well, He sat *tete-a-tete*, purposely wanting to see her face because she resided in Samaria, known to the Jews for having nothing good coming out of it; this stereotype would have belonged to Him, too. Jesus had lived through that stigma that was oh so familiar to Him regarding His own hometown of Nazareth (See, John 1:46). Yes, I believe Jesus sat down as a practical matter because He was tired after His journey, but even more, I believe Jesus was tired of the other half of His creation being reduced to inferiority. For example, at that time, a father could sell his minor daughter into slavery but could not sell his son into slavery.[38] I am convinced that Jesus intentionally wanted to stare precisely into the face that represented the miniature face of countless women whose cause He would legally champion by stressing His Father's pertinent laws: *"For there is neither... male nor female, for you are all one in Christ, Jesus"* (Galatians 3:28, NIV). *"...God is not one who shows partiality, but in every nation the one fearing Him and working righteousness is acceptable to Him"* (Acts 10:34, BSB). Jesus wanted to break down systemic barriers to women in evangelism on that prodigious day at the well, which was marked on God's calendar, too. Jesus radically dented gender bias by upholding the practicality of the woman's role in His kingdom. Her nondescript face was the distinctive face of innumerable women whom Jesus would inclusively pray for in the garden the night before He would give His life for all humankind; some of whom would become unsuspecting female, city-changing, missionaries, evangelists, and preachers upon a new, dotted landscape of history and... her-story. There, Jesus shattered bigoted, sexist conventions and not only interfaced with this woman but made a missionary out of her; for after receiving His warm attention and emotional healing, she canvassed her town with the good news of Jesus. Before He left her, He made sure she had enough "water" to drink: *"The LORD ...will strengthen your frame. You will be like a well-watered garden, like a spring whose waters never fail"* (Isaiah 58:11, NIV). Jesus single-handedly democratized female ministry!

> *Jesus democratized female ministry!*

CHAPTER 5

Jesus: Enfranchisement, the Sixth Amendment, and Women

Jesus brought Himself proximate to the feminine condition repeatedly. In His travels, Jesus approached a village and saw a very distraught mom who had lost her only son. Widowed and overcome by the funeral procession, the Bible caught hold of Jesus' tender reaction: *"When the Lord saw her, his heart went out to her"* (Luke 7:13, NIV). Instantly, Jesus touched the coffin and gave this grieving mom her living son back. I submit that the predictive Christ who knew the end from the beginning, also knew there would come a time when His own mother would be similarly grieving at a cross after the death of her first born son, too: *"Jesus …said to his mother, 'this man is now your son'"* (John 19:26, CEV). Jesus literally had the whole world on His mind—like saving them—in addition to the fact that His earthly sonship was about to come to an end and John would be His mother's replacement. He, nevertheless, paused in a carefully crafted moment of stilled time to passionately assist that widow and to entrust His widowed mother to His friend.

In a different scenario, Jesus reached out to a woman with a disability: *"Jesus turned and saw her. 'Take heart, daughter,' he said, 'your faith has healed you'"* (Matthew 9:22, NIV). I read that account as saying, "Daughter, take my heart" because Jesus wore His heart more than on His sleeve; He wore it as a crest on our hearts. The plight of every woman mattered to Jesus, for He would say things like *"Wherever the Good News is preached…this woman's deed will be…discussed"* (Matthew

26:13, NLT). A third time, the practical application of gender and the law can be seen in the earthly life of Jesus. Mary, whether debatedly known as Lazarus' sister of Bethany or that Mary Magdalene out of which Jesus cast seven demons, this woman was toting a very expensive alabaster box of perfume when she crashed a party where Jesus sat reclining just two days before His death (See Luke 7:36–50). The first debatable Mary was a beloved ruleress; the second Mary was scorned and lacking in Proverbs 31 virtuousness; nonetheless, it was a Mary whose worship of Jesus was ornamented with her tears. Her story is punctuated by her "stand-out" name and by Christ's praise of her anointing of Him, and so, she became the quintessential, posterized woman of worship for future millennia. Her story is a preserved snapshot of her disheveled hair and pricey perfume, featuring cantankerous men against a backdrop akin to a closed gentlemen's club, with her presence so hotly contested by the chauvinism in the room. A cacophony of pitched disgust could be heard regarding her ill repute despite her fierce temerity. Although her audacious presence was regarded with a certain amount of vitriol, Jesus wanted her importance recorded, and God wanted it told for posterity. Since Jesus immediately muted their male protestations, it begs the question of her relevant presence through His eyes. Jesus actually included women on His itinerant kingdom team, like Joanna, Susanna, and Mary Magdalene, which reflected not only His respectability for femininity; it revealed pivotal, fearless, and focal striations of real feminine upgrade and female resourcefulness. Both the long and the short of it is, Jesus loved to liberate women, all women. Historically in America, women have had struggles of liberation. Suffragettes marched for women's voting rights under Susan B Anthony's leadership that ushered in the 19th amendment to the US Constitution, which established voting rights for women. Also, civil rights groups under Reverend Dr. Martin Luther King Jr. demonstrated for equal enfranchisement and integration of races which had a bearing on the upward trajectory of women's rights. Federal law, Title VII of the Civil Rights Act of 1964, gave legal protection from discrimination and sexual harassment of women in the workplace. All of the above efforts were monumental milestones. In a similar fashion, Jesus' posterization of that abysmally marginalized woman was His historical contribution to the spiritual enfranchisement and societal elevation of women as a whole. Regardless of the fact that the prideful prayer of a Jewish man of that era would commonly include His soiled gratitude for having not been born a woman, Jesus was making the statement that He came to bring and enforce something greater, something infinitely genderless—a universal, unreserved, and "equal opportunity" love. There, Jesus stepped in to intentionally invade a module of cultural disparity and gender inequity towards those women. Jesus was the great equalizer long before it was politically correct or socially savvy, and He rectified the gender divide long before our federal laws were enacted, like the Lilly Ledbetter Act, which amended the Civil rights of 1964.[39] Women mattered to Jesus. Little thought has been given to the fact that Jesus took the role of a first-century civil rights lawyer on behalf of women, but He did.

> *Jesus was a civil rights lawyer.*

Sixth Amendment & The Bible

"In His justice and great righteousness, he does not oppress."

JOB 37:23 (NIV)

The adulteress suffered mercilessly on the wheels of systematic gender insobriety in Ancient Israel. Jesus, however, sought to equalize and empower women. It is unimaginable in this country not to be able to face your accuser at trial. To ensure that this travesty of justice could never happen in this country, James Madison, along with our leading forefathers, built in the constitutional protection called the Sixth

Amendment, which guarantees a citizen's right to face her accuser at trial. It looks like God feels equally strong about this legal protection—even stronger—because God's sense of virtuousness is always greater than man's greatest level of virtue and intensity: *"…Who then will bring charges against me? Let us face each other! Who is my accuser? Let him confront me!"* (Isaiah 50:8, NIV). That amendment to the Constitution includes witnesses. Since the male co-adulterer who could become a primary witness for the prosecution against the adulteress in that patriarchal society, turning "stateside" to corroborate the offense against her, suspiciously disappeared as he did, a faceless accuser is exactly what we read about in John's recorded passage.

Before he was a teenager, Jesus knew His place in the world at twelve. God-the-Son knew that over a thousand years later, Israel would have one of the most architecturally complex and stunning Supreme Courts in the world.[40] He also knew there would be etched in the grandiose marble of the aesthetically exquisite United States Supreme Court, America's highest court in its land, these lofty words, "Equal Justice Under Law." He surely knew it is where systematic gender and deprivation of rights would be ruled upon one day. On His watch, Jesus ameliorated the gender polarity of His day and intentionally battled for the embattled female. The Sixth Amendment is the shoulder that a US citizen can lean on to protect their right to face their accusers. Jesus, too, established a right to face one's accuser, whom the Bible defines as Satan. On the night when Jesus was about to be arrested by a detail of temple guards which was led by the Satan-possessed disciple, He told the remaining disciples: "Let's go and look at Judas, in other words, face him!" (See Matthew 26:46). In actively approaching Judas, Jesus forever epitomized the Sixth Amendment provision—that we have the right to face our adversary. This legal concept has its roots in the English notion that no one is to be accused anonymously in a court of law, thereby ensuring the best defense. God also demonstrated this concept in Ephesians 6, where the apostle Paul lays out the weapons of our spiritual warfare against our spiritual adversary. Paul emphasizes a body armor for the front, which is dismissive of anything to be worn on the back; therefore, indicating a frontal assault only and the need to face one's enemy to launch the best assault. It's worth re-noting that the adulteress's complicitous male offender was never produced during her trial. Although the text supports that there were other accusatory witnesses present, strangely enough, the probable co-defendant and potential "state-turned witness"—the male party to the whole "his and hers" illicit affair—was nowhere to be seen. Culturally, the adulteress was not allowed to speak in legal proceedings because of her womanhood, which may explain why she had no opportunity to implicate her male half of the "crime team." His absence was a glaring omission, and this type of unilateral bias against legal freedoms for women was the notable norm of that ancient period.

The biggest legal "face-off" involved Jesus when He faced our enemy at Golgotha's hill. There, He defeated the devil, and it is so interesting that the shape of Golgotha's hill is that of an image of a huge skulled face. At Calvary, Jesus would have set His face toward the skull as He approached it to be hung on it—talk about facing your accuser! Because Jesus faced down the enemy for every believer, He grants us the right to face Him in victory, too.

The Esther Effect: Dare to Touch Me

"Bring joy to your servant's life because I appeal to you."
PSALM 86:4 (CSB)

What is "the Esther Effect?" In short, it is " the Favor Effect." Jesus had it. Esther had it. It is God's touch: *"Jesus grew…gaining favor with God and people"* (Luke 2:52, GNT). The people of God have it, too: *"Surely, LORD, you bless the righteous; you surround them with your favor as with a shield"* (Psalm 5:12, NIV). Recognizing the flow of judicial procedure and judicial review in American federal courts is helpful in understanding God's favor-full order of divine review. In order to have one's federal case reviewed by the United States Supreme Court, this nation's highest court of appeal, permission from the court must be obtained. This permission is granted as a *Writ of Certiorari* which is a formal order to appear before the court to argue the case, and it is only granted to approximate one hundred favored recipients per year. Similarly, the authoritative Word of God is the Holy Writ that grants permission for the believer to appear before God's high Court to argue her case, which is founded on the Word of God. There is no automatic right of review before the United States' distinguished high court of justice; in fact, to receive an invitation to appear before this audience of elevated Supreme Court jurists is exceptional. Only certain qualified and distinct cases which meet the federal requisites of review and which are desirable for appellate review by this Court are actually granted permission for review. This notion is reproduced in the Bible's story of Esther (circa 357 BC), where we can glean an understanding of how humankind's permission for review before God became automatic. In the book of Esther, royal permission is required before an appearance and review of a matter before the King in his court. Queen Esther desired to present her case before King Darius of Persia regarding an injustice posed as a genocidal threat to her people by his corrupt, top government official, Haman. Haman considered the Jewish people an enemy of the Persian State, and Esther, who had hidden her Jewish race, desired to appear before the king to ask that she and her people's lives be spared. There was only one problem. No one could have an audience regarding royal business with this powerful king without his expressed permission—without his unambiguously holding out his scepter to the petitioner. Without this gesture, it would amount to a breach of court protocol, and decisive death would be in the air for the one approaching him. This sequence replicates God's procedure of review before His regal and highest Court. To explain, there were three courts in the tabernacle. The first two courts were the outer courts and would be the equivalent of the lower trial and appellate courts in an American model of courts. The third and innermost court would be the counterpart to the American highest court of review, the Supreme Court, for it represented God's divine Supreme Court where He convened His presence. In order to appear in this highest court which was situated in the preeminent *HaDvir*—the "Holy of Holies" in Hebrew—one had to have permission from the King of Eternity, and to enter into it without permission was to do so upon pain of death. It was similar to *not* receiving "heavenly Certiorari," for in the Old Testament, to come before God's Ark of Covenantal presence without permission was to be improperly credentialed or uninvited before His high Court. To expound, to stand before The Exalted Jurist of all the earth in His highest Court without being of the Levitical high priestly lineage, and without proper cleansing and extensive sanctification, was to, in effect, have no invitation at all. As with Esther's king, It meant certain death by The King. To look at this set up more deeply in terms of our American Supreme judiciary, I classify the priestly, Levitical representative of the nation of Israel as a legal representative because He had a legal right by virtue of His ancestral Aaronic order to advocate merciful atonement for Israel's behalf. There were no other legal avenues of appeal; it was in the Holy of Holies where God's Law was actually contained, and by it, He judged all of Israel. There was no higher divine judiciary, no greater earthly forum, and no more prime venue where God held Court on earth. To violate His protocol by coming before Him without obtaining the mandatory procedural permission would lead to a deathly outcome, so in the divine parallel, no Certiorari had been granted. In parity, the appearance was, hence, violative.

Reflecting, it causes pause that the book of Esther is the only book of the sixty-six books in the Bible that does *not* contain the name of God. Nevertheless, it is unmistakable that God's providential hand was very much present in Esther's life, and perhaps it is a reminder: If God is not so obviously visible in our everyday lives, then we should expect Him in the unexpected and in the unobvious. To end the story,

Esther's king held out the royal scepter, and she was safe. To end the believer's story, when Jesus died, God extended the divine Royal scepter so that we could dare come near to His Holy of Holies. We would not die...

> *God put man on legal notice: Don't touch Me!*

only His Son. Unbounded by His consuming love for us, the scepter would fall on His Son, but we would be safe. The outstretched arms of Jesus seen delineated against the mid-evening sky configured His own far-reaching hug upon the world. He came for us. #World Hug. Jesus to the rescue! The Bible points out that Jesus satisfied all the just wrath of God and, therefore, successfully averted the deserved judgment of guilt and punishment of imminent death away from humankind. Jesus opened up the holy Court of heaven to us, and we now have safe passage; heavenly certiorari is ours! Jesus accomplished in fireworks fashion the presentation of the scepter between God and man. Looking back, it first had to be handed from God to God: *"But about the Son He says, 'Your throne, O God, endures forever and ever, and justice is the sceptre of your kingdom'"* (Hebrews 1:8, NIV). This Scripture elucidates for me that God handed the scepter over to Jesus once it was held out to us. When Jesus stretched out His hands on His death cross, I submit it was equal to His extending the scepter to humankind and coaxing it closer to God like never before. It was a handwritten invitation of beckoning to His throne. It was a bloody instrument of welcome—the ultimate welcoming party to the family of God! It was grandstanding permission to have a safe audience with the Almighty—to touch Him. Before this watershed moment, God legally untouchable by humankind. Man was put on spiritual notice: Don't touch Me! One man tried and died. The Bible mentions that Uzzah stretched out his hand to steady the Ark of the Covenant, which contained the presence of God, and lost his life as a result. His intentions were pure, but the way to touch God had not been purely perfected yet. Jesus did that with

His completed work of the cross. That prohibition was clear from the book of Genesis, where God admonished Adam by lit angelic swords that his days of touching Him in the Spirit was over, to John's book where Jesus warned Mary, "Don't touch Me!" God had even left strict and detailed instructions with Moses that no one was to dare touch His presence in the Ark, or he would die (See John 20:17, Genesis 3:24, numbers 4:15, 2 Samuel 2:6). It was Jesus who reopened the way for tactile expression between God and humankind…"Touch me and see," Jesus said upon being resurrected (See Luke 24:39). So, let the touching begin!

It is exciting to realize that God had freedom for His creation on His mind dating back to the Garden of Eden, and all the time, He had planned to secure it with the hand of Christ and a touch. Jesus was crucified under the Roman legal system. In an ironic divine twist, God would use principles from their own Roman system to redeem humankind. Under ancient Roman law, there was a legal ceremony before the judicial authority of a praetor or magistrate where *"vindicta"* took place where one extended a rod from his hand to the enslaved as a sign of intervention into their slavery and as an activation of their new lawful freedom.[41] *Vindicta* comes from the Latin root verb to set free or avenge—*"vindicare"*—and is where we get our English word vindication. Notably, the Bible calls Jesus the "Rod of Jesse," and Jesus extended Himself on the cross before the Judge of heaven to intervene and legally free us from sin's enslavement with the touch of His outstretched hand: *"But it was the LORD's good plan to crush him and cause him grief…and the LORD's good plan will prosper in his hand"* (Isaiah 53:10, NLT).

God's Heart Coloration: A Lesson in Diversity

Why would God not promote diversity? After all, He demonstrated the multi-diversity of the union of the Holy Trinity. Each member of the unified Godhead has unique and singular personhood as well as corresponding diverse roles. The Holy Trinity is a harmonious mutuality, a divine comity, a triangulation of blessedness. Building on the theme of godly diversity, the last book of the Bible distinctly alludes to heterogeneity in heaven. It points out that there will be multitudinous worship in every language and native composition. The apostle John saw an innumerable heavenly population from every tongue and tribe: *"…and they cried out in a loud voice: Salvation belongs to our God' I, John, saw an innumerable heavenly population from every tongue and tribe"* (Revelation 7:9-10, NIV). Further sobering is the thought that the saints of God are to be "caught up together"—a unification by aggregation, without segregation: *"Then we which are alive and remain shall be caught up together with them in the clouds, to meet the lord in the air: and so shall we ever be with the Lord"* (1 Thessalonians 4:17, KJV; Emphasis supplied).

We can learn a lot about diversity from God's heart. What color is the heart of God? To answer this question, I will take my cue from the colors that God has chosen to surround Himself with. The range of colors which God opts for are extremely important because, indeed, He is the God whom a person would be hard-pressed to find that perfect, novel, and colorful gift for; there is no surprising Him as He actually created all the hues of the palette. Ponder the thought, what color gift would you bring to a party that God has thrown? A clue may be in God's habitat—inside His personal, third-heaven throne room at the Holy City, where its dimensions are perfectly square and about 600,000 stories tall.[42] A closer look at John's panorama reveals that God's throne is situated in this third heaven, is arrayed with a bevy of assorted colors, and is flanked with an encircling rainbow that acts like a crystalline halo. Even more, God's regal city is bordered by pearl gates, making it the ultimate "gated community." For the optical reader, the Bible also paints a colorful mural of perfectly appointed gold-carpeted streets with jasper walls that would be characterized by today's gemological tables as the finest colorless, sparkly diamonds.

Additionally depicted in John's vision are sardius stones that are embedded in the walls of heaven. These primeval carnelian gemstones are dazzling in stark red.

There is an expression that an individual has a "heart of gold," but this is more than an expression as it pertains to God. Based on the colors that God intimately surrounds Himself with, I deduce that God's heart is golden, inlaid with red, overlaid with pearlescent accents, and sparkles heavily like a transparent diamond that bears all the colors of the rainbow in its inclusive prism. Admittedly ultra-analytical, my rationale for God's heart coloration is confirmed by two main thoughts. Firstly, God's self-styled heavenly mansion is subjectively outfitted and prepared by Him, and since God can choose anything He wants and has chosen to "gilt-gold" heaven and to saturate its surroundings in high definition precious gems, it appears these choices are precisely reflective of Him. Secondly, Jesus said He would go to heaven and "prepare" a mansion for every believer. From the time Jesus first heard man's heartbeat, He wanted to prepare the best for Him. The verb "prepare" indicates a preparation that will be perfect. In the self-same preparatory fashion as His Son, God, too, has prepared for Himself a heaven that is also particularly fitting for Him. Such specificity, such colorful and imposing surroundings, therefore, must have preferential meaning to God. Lastly, Jesus Christ identified Himself as the *Alpha* and *Omega*—the first and the last (Revelation 22:13). Pursuant to this, the Bible records that the first stone which God commanded to be near the heart in the breastplate of His chosen, Levitical priest was to be the smooth, bright jasper (white diamond), and the last stone to be set in the breastplate was to be the rich, deep sardius (red carnelian, which is a modern day ruby). I believe these essential colors were meant to correspond with the heart of God and also with the first and last act of Christ in redeeming mankind. Christ's first act toward the legal redemption of humankind was to leave the jasper, or diamond-studded walls of heaven, and His last act toward legal redemption of humankind was to bear the red-stained, carnelian, bloody cross at Calvary. To sum it all up, there would be no salvation without the shedding of the sardius blood or without Jesus' departure from the diamond divide. There is no doubt that this colorful majesty reflects the heart of God.

At Calvary, God stroked watercolors of His heart and of His plan of salvation for the whole world to see. The display shone in vivid 3-D as diamond-colored piercing glory amidst a red fountain of blood, replete with the pearlescent splendor of the dawn's resurrection. It calcifies the aforementioned, mainly that God's heart radiates a profusion of multi-colored golden, rouge, diamondized, and pearl-dipped hues. Finally, I propose that God's heart prism emits a rainbowish color of diverse light which represents the innumerable and diverse people groups He died for. The heartful God sent Jesus to heal the heart that was cracked. In relevance, this question struck me—what color is the intolerant heart? I surmise it is pale and monochromatic, for a heart such as that had to have lost its diverse coloration. One should never lose heart since God is divinely good and the healer of the contrite heart and the restorer of its vivaciousness. The following are God's preferred heart-scapes: *"God, create a clean heart for me…"* (Psalm 51:10, CSB). *"Do not look at his appearance or at the height of his stature… for God sees not as man sees, for man looks at the outward appearance, but the lord looks at the heart"* (1 Samuel 16:7, NASB1995).

Have you had a heart-to-heart talk with God lately? May our hearts burn!

CHAPTER 6

The Legal Instrument by Which God Gets Things Done

Religiosity Collides with the Legal Supernatural: Lightholes

"You've heard it said…but I say unto you…"
MATTHEW 5:38

In Jesus' time, Jewish religious law had become very ritualistic and cumbersome to its adherents. Jesus invaded the scene to minister relief. To do this, it meant that Jesus would sometimes have to rebuff a religious system that strayed from its origin and divine purpose and whose enforcement now had become legalistic. It was illegal for Jesus to administer healing to the Syrophoenician woman's daughter. He did. It was quasi illegal at the most and unethically prohibited at the least, for Jesus to talk to the Samaritan woman in public, at the well. He did. It was illegal for Jesus to heal a man with a shriveled hand on the Sabbath. He did. It was illegal for Jesus to touch an "unclean" woman who had a fountain of blood flowing from her. He did. In all of these unlawful scenarios, there existed a supernatural that legally superseded the natural encumbrances of that law—a divine response to a legal quandary. The closest thing to it in the legal vernacular is a legal "loophole," which is an exception, ambiguity, or inadequacy in the law that furnishes a route to avoid it without violating its literal requirements.[43] I like to express it like this—technical maneuvering within legal nuances. Going further, with the acts of Jesus specifically, I prefer to call the process of finding loopholes as "finding supernatural navigation" because I view the newly found courses as *lightholes* rather than loopholes in that a sliver of light breaks through in every situation where Jesus injects justice. To be clear, every lighthole or supernatural navigation of Jesus was legal. Jesus circumvented the man-made laws of His day because He denounced them as being inadequate, fraudulent counterfeits of His Father's real law. Much of the Pharisaic law had disintegrated into white-coated deception. They tried to use methodical legalism to stop Jesus, but Jesus used a spiritual lasso to stop them. Jesus noted, *"Their worship is a farce, for they teach man-made ideas as commandments of God"* (Matthew 15:9, NLT). As a result of that denigration, the radical and unprecedented acts of Jesus were to cure the defects in the doctored man-laws. In the example above of the woman with the abnormal flow of blood, it is worth taking a deeper look to see how the loophole component legally worked there. It was illegal for Jesus and the woman to actually touch physically, but the woman never technically physically touched Jesus; she touched His promises. She did so by touching the bottom of Jesus' priestly, rabbinic garment called *a "tsit tsit."* It was really the hemmed fringe of Jesus' traditional prayer shawl that contained the 600 plus promises of God wrapped up in them. The Bible says, *"For all of God's promises have been fulfilled in Christ with a resounding Yes!"* (2 Corinthians 1:20, NLT). Notice the preposition "in" that precedes Christ. The woman's faith reached *inside* of Jesus to get her miracle; that is why Jesus could feel *inside* that someone had touched Him *inwardly*. Not only that, but the woman, too, felt her healing *inwardly*. It was actually an *inward* touching for both, but not physical, so therein lay the lighthole; it was not illegal. According to God's law, it was perfectly legal for the woman to draw virtue and power out of Jesus by touching Him with her faith: *"… If two of you shall agree on earth as touching anything that they ask, it shall be done"* (Matthew 18:19, ASV). The tall of it is that Jesus navigated these miracles by a redirection of the origin of the miracle; that is, although Jesus always remained the source of the miracle, it was the believer's declarative faith that brought the miracle into being. It was the woman who kept declaring, *"If I only touch him I will be healed"* (Matthew 9:21). Faith germinates miracles!

By the way, I am convinced that this woman had one more revelation on her mind as she crept toward Jesus. I believe that she discovered, as I have, that wings that can be found on the traditional prayer shawl. To clarify, I noticed that when the prayer shawl is worn across the shoulders and both arms are extended, the material forms shapes of spreading wings. Why is this important? It makes a great difference because I believe the woman grasped the Old Testament promise of Psalm 84:11 (NIV) that says, *"For the LORD God is a sun…"* and with it, she could have ruminated on Malachi 4:2, too, which says the Messiah, or the Sun of righteousness, would rise with healing in His wings! To use some appropriate idioms, "She got her faith on!" "She went for it!" She headed straight for the wings! (See Mark 5:25–34). Another revelation that I received fortifies this promise of healing. While it is widely held that Jesus received the legal limit of thirty-nine lashes—or stripes—on His back, the Latin language supports the miracle of Jesus rising with healing in His wings. Biblical text describes how Jesus received these stripes on His back; the whip would have lacerated certain muscles on His back known in Latin as *Latissimus Dorsi*—meaning, widest of the back. What is most interesting is the fact that this muscle, the widest of all the back muscles, wraps around the whole back, extending to each side, behind, and beneath the arms, and anatomically looks like a set of wings; in fact, is known in athletic circles as the "wing muscle" or "developed wings!"[44] It, therefore, is quite revelatory that when the Bible notes, "by His stripes you are healed," an extrapolation of that truth could read, by His wings you are healed, which is a direct reference to Jesus having healing in the wings of His striped back! (1 Peter 2:24). In conclusion, the legal principle of the lighthole was actually a type of legal supersension because, in a legal sense, the miracle was attributed to the adamant faith of the believer. In every example above, God had left a way for the believer to navigate through the waters of legalism with oars of faith: *"I tell everyone… God has distributed a measure of faith to each one"* (Romans 12:3, CSB).

The Human Rights Legacy of God

"Again I saw all the oppressions that are done under the sun. And behold, the tears of the oppressed, and they had no one to comfort them! On the side of their oppressors there was power, and there was no one to comfort them."

ECCLESIASTES 4:1 (ESV)

Human rights are the recognized "equal and inalienable rights of all members of the human family," and as such, they are universally claimable rights for every individual without question and without distinction, including basic rights, freedoms, and benefits.[45] Human rights sparked Jesus' attention especially since human rights include basic, internationally recognized benefits. Jesus illustrated that healing should be an undeniable benefit, so He left His imprint on the human condition. He made it clear that faith was the great counterweight that insured one's basic right to kingdom dividends, one of which was healing. The Syrophoenician woman's story shines because Jesus trumpeted the fact that she was no less of a woman or mother just because she was of a different racial, ethnic, and regional persuasion. The Syrophoenician woman wanted Jesus to heal her daughter but was Greek and, therefore, was considered a gentile or an "ethnic outsider." As such, she was not an Israeli or a "daughter of Abraham," and it was unlawful for Jesus to minister to her needs above the needs of the sons and daughters of Abraham. Jesus, however, supernaturally navigated the law by demonstrating that the active pedigree that God ordains outranks the sedentary lineage of man. It is the faith of sons and daughters of God's spiritual lineage that was designed to accommodate the Syrophoenician mother, although she was not a part of the Jewish house of the covenant to which Jesus was sent. Because of one word—faith—the woman was ahead of her time spiritually, which caused her to be right on time. The Father and Jesus had already made provision for the gentiles to be grafted into God's redemptive plan at the cross. There, the human rights passage of *whosoever* would believe in Him would not perish, but have everlasting life was solemnized. Later, God gave Peter an "anti-racist" vision in which He similarly communicated to him that in God's eyes, all races of the human race were equally precious to Him: *"But God has shown me that I should not call any person common or unclean"* (Acts 10:28, ESV). Only the colorless, cultural-less creed of faith was needed to activate the legal lighthole here. That mother would qualify for a miracle, to the right of healing, because she legally met the race-blind threshold of faith. In a technical legal sense, it was the mother's faith that drew forth the miracle and allowed the course of the lighthole, for Jesus never laid a hand on the child.

Because I love atmosphere-changing faith, let's take a closer look at the Syrophenician woman's impenetrable faith-reasoning. Jesus said, *"I was sent only to the lost sheep of Israel…It is not fair to take the children's food and throw it to the dogs"* (Matthew 15:24–27, NIV). The Bible typically uses animal motifs like sheep, goats, dogs, etc., to signify categories of association, and there, the term dogs indicate a foreigner or one who is impure spiritually. Unflappable, the woman, in a demonstration of lucidity, lobs a dogged counterpunch thought that is as much faith-filled as it is humility-filled. The force of her riposte and the tenacity of her faith-words got her the miracle she longed for: "Yes, Lord, yet even the dogs eat the crumbs that fall from their master's table." Jesus then exclaimed, *"Woman, great is your faith! Let it be done for you as you wish"* (Matthew 15:28, ESV). Again, the woman's tenacious faith was the determinant factor that allowed Jesus to legally sidestep the rigid course of the historicity of law and adhere to God's overarching course of justice within His laws of faith; He used a lighthole. It is crucial to know that Jesus would die on the cross not long after seeing this woman, and it was part of His crucial mission to die for

Jesus experienced prejudice.

all humankind, and by doing so, graft the gentiles—different human beings like her—into the family of God. Weighing in, prejudice is an unreasonable, ignorant or odious presumption or prejudgment against an individual, all of which is enabled spiritually by an underlying, evil spirit of fear or strife. Further chiming in, prejudice is uninformed, unpleasant, and subjective guesswork about someone that is motivated spiritually by concealed fear or strife. In my opinion, racism is similar to prejudice in that it is unfairly judgmental, but it is driven by an evil spirit of hatred, as well as fear and strife. Both prejudice and racism are antagonists of human rights, but the good news is that Jesus destroyed the root of these intercontinental and intracontinental antagonists to abundant human life and is still setting the world free from it with His love!

A little-observed fact is that Jesus, Himself, was no stranger to the vestiges of prejudice while sojourning on this earth. He experienced regional prejudice because He came from the town of Nazareth; it was said of Him: *"Can anything good come out of Nazareth?"* (John 1:46, ESV). He also clashed with scathing prejudice because of His birth status. Consider that after finally divulging that He was the Son of God, malcontents plotted to assassinate Him day and night. While this targeted prejudicial unrest did not unnerve Jesus, it was apparently impactful to at least the point of His telling a biographical story that reflected the unpleasant pangs of persecution. In Matthew 21:33, Jesus told how the master of a vineyard went on a trip to a faraway land and sent his son to do business in his stead with the tenants on his land, but the heartless, contrition-less men hated the son because of his birthright, prejudged him because he was an heir, and murdered him.

Unbeknownst to many, but refreshingly clear, is my proposal that Jesus was actually the first New Testament human rights advocate who set the groundwork for an enduring civil rights footing with His overturning of the infamous notion of "Separate but Equal" in His day. Jesus made it clear by the miraculous action and His interaction with the Syrophoenician woman that the ethnocentric wall that separated the races and bred prejudice and racism between Jews and non-Jews needed to come down, there and now, in order for there to be equality in the kingdom of God: *"God is no respecter of faces"* (Acts 10:34). Approximately 1900 years later, the United States would have its own notorious law of "Separate but Equal" that was violative of civil and human rights overturned in the landmark case, *Brown v. Board of Education* (1954). There, the United States Supreme Court ruled that segregated education did not produce equal and fair education, and therefore, was not fair and equal. That Court officially overturned *Plessy v. Ferguson* (1896), which was the outdated, iconic-standing "Separate but Equal" case, and decisively ended officially-imposed segregation in public education. With a unanimous decision, the Earl Warren Court held that "separate but equal" facilities are inherently unequal and violate the protection of the Equal Protection Clause of the Constitution's Fourteenth Amendment.[46]

Extending the metaphor from the Syrophonecian story, one could say that the Court signaled that everyone should be able to have an equal portion at the table of benefits. A long, sobering look back in time shows that Jesus had already established the timeless, fair virtues of human rights and civil rights. The Brown case demonstrated that a long-established precedent can be legally overturned when the application of the law no longer represents a constitutionally protected right and an interpreted pure intent. Put simply, such a displacement occurs when the "rule of law" no longer reflects the "spirit of the law." This recognition seems to be what Jesus was alluding to with His conclusory remarks to the Syrophoenician woman. There, the Spirit of God's heart superseded the *status quo ante* law or the rule that stood before Christ. Thereafter, faith in Jesus would prove to be the catalyst of equal conversion of all nationalities, ethnicities, and races and their claimable rights and benefits. Jesus' conclusion was perfectly legal and legally perfect, but how did He arrive at it legally? The framers of the Constitution set forth a standard of interpretation by which judges are to interpret the law. Under American jurisprudence, the judiciary can use " rules of construction" to ferret out the true meaning of a law through, among other things, an examination of a framer's purpose of the law under the light of words, the contemporaneous climate at the time of the words, the intent of the speaker words, all coupled with searching out the true spirit of the law, and the evolving time intersecting those spoken words. It is an exercise of extreme balance in the application of the letter of the law and the interpretation of the spirit of the law. Above, Jesus "hit a home run!" The timeless spirit of God's heart was clear, and the Light of the World enforced His Framer's intent and purpose of equality-based love. "…*We understand that by God's word all the world was framed*" (Hebrews 11:3, NKJV).

On balance, in the best of configurations, the Constitution should have the teeth of the intention of the law without losing its bite of the spirit of the law. I suspect that Jesus used a similar calculus. Given the vastitude of Jesus' divine skill set, His examination of the Father's intent of law would have been infinitely greater than any earthly advocate; however, the rudiments of the American judicial thinking seems to have had its roots in Jesus' construction. Consider the exchange between Jesus and the Syrophoenician woman. Jesus spoke legal words of applicable law, the woman responded with a legal rejoinder. Jesus considered her words in light of the interpretation of the Spirit of His greater mission and rendered a decision. What is quite interesting in the text is the Greek translation of Jesus' response to the woman's words during their word-fest: "Because you have said this, the demon has gone out of your daughter." The Greek reads, *"For this word (logos) the demon has gone out of your daughter"* (Mark 7:29, NASB1995). There Jesus, The actual *Logos-The WORD*, examined the exact *logos -words* from the woman. He combined it with the interpretation of the Spirit of His true mission and the true and greater intent of the Father's lit up words which say, *"God sent His* WORD *[the Logos] and healed them"* (Psalm 107:20, NIV). After inspection, Jesus acted on the intent and purpose of the Father's literal words, along with the Spirit of the Father, to legally overturn the previous exclusionary legal practice that was religiously applied unequally to this woman. It had deprived her of her faith-ignited freedoms. Our current American Jurisprudence model reflects God's forward-thinking of this full picture of the word-based Law *and* the Spirit which Jesus employed way back then: *"But we know God accepts only those who have faith in Jesus Christ. No one can please God by simply obeying the Law. So we put our faith in Christ Jesus, and God accepted us because of our faith"* (Galatians 2:16, CEV).

Weighing the Bible with a Legal Scale

"Thou art weighed in the balances, and art found wanting."
DANIEL 5:27 (KJV)

Above, we saw how unjust treatment was repudiated by a just God; the legal scale of justice is supposed to be balanced: *"Let justice roll on like a River, righteousness like a never failing stream!"* (Amos 5:24, NIV). Apparently, God wants the same measured standard of justice, which He dispenses to be the same calculus that we dispense to each other. There should be a tipping of the scales towards justice. He also demands we come before Him justly, and this Scripture helps us to understand what that shaping looks like. God wants a full-fledged, frontal explosion of heart-telling worship, not a fleeting "camera appearance" in His presence: *"Even though you bring me burnt offerings and grain offerings. I will not accept them…"* (Amos 5:22, NIV).

Ministers, especially, have to be found not wanting in their worship and in their ways of justice, for judgment begins at the house of God. *"My sons, do not be negligent now, for the Lord has chosen you to stand before Him, to minister to Him..."* (2 Chronicles 29:11, NIV).

> *Jesus left no one behind who needed deliverance.*

This, then, is how you ought to regard us: as servants of Christ and those entrusted with the mysteries God has revealed (1 Corinthians 4:1-2). The scales of authentic worship and godly ethical integrity were out of balance at the temple where religious leaders used tactics of illegal extortion in forcing worshippers to pay exorbitant prices for animal sacrifices and charged usurious money-changing fees—literally *pigeon-holing* them—through profiteering schemes when selling pigeons and more. Jesus weighed in with a hand-made whip! (See John 2:17). It is very interesting that Jesus says, *"The zeal for your house consumes me..."* (Psalm 69:9, NIV) because one of the American attorney's foremost ethical rules of professional conduct and responsibility is to *zealously* represent your client to the fullest of your zeal within the boundaries of lawfulness.[47] Jesus exemplified just that when He zealously broke up the shady ring of thieves, representing the Father with all His zeal. He came to earth from the Commonwealth of heaven with a legal mandate to destroy the works of Satan, two of which were sickness and oppression, and He did that also with zeal: *"...God anointed Jesus of Nazareth with the Holy Spirit and power, who went about doing good, and healing all that were oppressed of the devil, for God was with Him"* (Acts 10:38, NIV; See John 5:15-19). Jesus replicated exactly what the Father did by putting the Father's commonwealth law into practice; He pursued salvation for everyone, healing for all, and left no one behind who needed deliverance. Neither did He and tolerate materialistic abuse in His Father's house. *"The zeal of my house has eaten me up"* (John 2:17), *"I am consumed with passion for Jerusalem!"* (Zechariah 8:2).

Weighed in the Balance

Our salvation was completely predicated on the grace of God and on the purity of heaven securing justice for us as He balanced His cross between heaven and earth. Our souls hung in the balance, teetering between death and hell as His skewered body weighed down one side of God's scale of mercy, while on the other side of the tottering scale hung our unappeased damnation. In this post-cross era, may we weigh the scales of eternal life against the scale's pre-cross eternal chastisement that could have weighed us down forever.

God's Power of Attorney, Angelic Agents & Celestial Legalities

> *"Bless the Lord, ye his angels that excel in strength, that do his commandments, hearkening unto the voice of his word."*
>
> PSALM 103:20 (KJV)

I am certain that angels are endowed with a type of "Power of Attorney" (POA).

A POA is a written instrument that gives someone that you have chosen the legal authority to act as your designated legal agent with all the general abilities and authority that you, yourself, and have spelled out unless you specifically limit her.[48] The limited authority instrument is called a limited POA, and the more expansive general authority instrument is called a general POA. In Exodus 23:20–21 (NHEB), God sent an angel of provision to the Israelites with what I categorize as a type of general POA, for God was careful to instruct the Israelites to be aware that God's name was in

Angels have Power of Attorney authority.

the angel and that he surely represented the very name and expansive agency of God: *"Look, I send an angel before you… Do not provoke him, for he will not pardon your disobedience, for my name is in him."* A varying version reads: *"I am sending an angel to protect you…Carefully obey everything the angel says, because I am giving him complete authority and he won't tolerate rebellion"* (CEV). A second example in which this POA is seen is in the *exordium* to the Christmas story where the angel, Gabriel, appears to Zechariah to announce the birth of Jesus. In the middle of the discourse, Zecharaiah did not embrace the supernatural agency of God, and as a result, did the forbidden and provoked the angel with his unbelief, to which the angel responded by striking him with muteness. Gabriel emphasized his representative authority to Zechariah by telling him that he had just come from the presence of the Almighty. I find it interesting that Gabriel means the "might of God," so the Almighty purposely sent His might, which is a reflection of His name and authority, to bear that all-important message. Gabriel genuinely bore the POA of God, and it is happy news that believers, too, are endowed with a type of POA through which Jesus allows His believers to enjoy when they walk in the authority of His name. For example, we have the authority to condemn or forcibly mute any rebellious tongue that arises against God's plans for our lives: *"…No weapon turned against you will succeed. You will silence every voice raised up to accuse you"* (Isaiah 54:17, NLT).

CHAPTER 7

Nine Fascinating Trials: God's Legal Response to Sin

Four Trials of Christ Jesus

"Therefore this says the Lord God: 'Behold, I lay in Zion a stone for a foundation, a tried stone, a precious cornerstone, a sure foundation.'"

ISAIAH 28:16 (NKJV; EMPHASIS ADDED)

Jesus was the stone that was tried four times, undergoing several trials. When a person is tried in a United States court of law, it means he must withstand the intensive scrutiny of a trier of evidentiary and admissible facts, as well as a trier of questions of law. In a jury trial, a jury panel—or alternatively a tribunal panel—determines questions of fact, and a judge will determine questions of law; but in a bench trial, there is no jury, and a judge must determine both the questions of fact and law. Jesus faced both of these types of trials relentlessly within a matter of only hours. Put simply, in a "trial," someone can be "tried" by a "trier" of fact and a "trier" of law in an adversarial setting to determine guilt or innocence based on legal claims. Jesus was tried as Scripture predicted, being immersed into four interesting trials that bear mentioning. All of these hostile trials resulted in a decision of guilt.

God's Word is His law. When He spoke it, it became absolute and could be tried for its evident certitude. God laws, which are His formulaic factual words, have been rigorously tried through the ages, in the lives of men and women, and even in His own Court, and through it all, have been determined valid and good—without any stains of guilt: *"As for God, his way is perfect; the word of the Lord is tried…"* (Psalm 18:30, BSB). Jesus was tried. A different result was yielded.

1. A Trial by the Jewish Council of Elders

There, the trial was before a judicial body of instructors of law, Elders, and chief priests, also known as the Sanhedrin Court, which was ancient Israel's analogous Supreme Court.[49] Jesus' trial was centered on a false, unsubstantiated claim of blasphemy and was a farce (See Luke 22:66). Under the High Priest, Joseph Caiphas, this tribunal reached its verdict of guilt of blasphemy for Jesus "claiming" to be the Son of God and unanimously sanctioned His death sentence (See Mark 14:64). It should be noted that prior to this trial, immediately after Jesus' arrest, He was first brought before the High Priest Annas, who was the father-in-law of Caiphas and the first High Priest of the Romanized Judea, for a lesser, formal session of preliminary questioning; but I do not regard that session as having the makings of a trial. It is, therefore, excluded.

2. A Trial by Prefect Pontius Pilate

There, the inquisitor Pilate initially dodged the issue of punishment for the charge of blasphemy, as he was more intrigued by questions of divine personification and was more preoccupied with questions of divinity, kingship, and existentialist "truth." Pilate made a point of asking Jesus if He were really a king because he was curious if Jesus were one of the kingly deities that existed according to his own Roman polytheistic culture. I find it very telling that even in the midst of Pilate's elephantine question of divinity, Jesus exercised the American constitutional Fifth Amendment right not to legally incriminate Himself on Pilate's witness stand: "Nor [shall any person] be compelled in any criminal case to be a witness against himself."[50] Jesus knowingly never admitted the claim that He was King of the Jews before Pilate; instead, He wisely somersaulted the question by attributing the answer to the words coming out of Pilate's mouth as follows: *"Are you king of the Jews?' 'Is that your own idea,' Jesus asked, 'or did others talk to you about me?'"* (John 18:33–34, NIV). In a roundabout way, Jesus affirmed the answer without giving a head-on admission. Jesus knew exactly what He was doing because earlier He had intentionally admitted His divinity before Caiphas in no uncertain terms in order to advance Himself to Pilate, but before Pilate whom He would spar sandal to sandal with, He chose not to. Not only was the tactic legally savvy, but it was also in tandem with prophecy. Jesus' legal approach was extremely effective because it allowed the prophetic cause of Jesus' death to remain Jesus' decision without earthly provocation. To clarify, without Jesus being ultimately convicted by something He had admitted and which was used as evidence against Him. I describe it this way, Jesus was prophetically compliant. Without a direct admission from Jesus, there was no real evidence of blasphemy because Pilate, as the sole trier of both fact and law here, saw through the disingenuous, dishonest testimony of Jesus' jealous accusers.

3. A Trial by Herod Antipas

There, Jesus appeared before the Tetrarch Herod only because of the legal technicality of jurisdiction known as "proper venue" which controlled where a case could be appropriately tried based on one's connected residency or the connected incident before the court. Jesus was recognized as a Galilean since His base of operation was in the Galilean city of Nazareth, and as such, Herod could try him in his court since Herod's authorized jurisdiction pertained to Galilea (See Luke 23:7–15). For that legal procedural reason, Pilate sent Jesus' case to Herod.

4. A Second Trial by Governor Pilate

There, Jesus was put on trial before Pilate a second time—it also could be seen as a continuation of the first trial. In actuality, Jesus made three appearances in total before Pilate. He initially ended up before Pilate by default since the ruling Jewish body of judges, known alternatively as the Sanhedrin "Council," were not vested with the judicial power to lawfully execute His death. Legally, there needed to be a state-sanctioned execution since it was a capital punishment case. This time, Pilate reluctantly presided over the bench trial inside his grand praetorium and had to focus on the alleged offense that Jesus claimed to be the King of the Jews. Since Pilate had this type of judicial authority to issue a legal death sentence, he knew exactly how to carry it out because he had not been shy about spilling Galilean blood before according to apostle Luke's text (Luke 13:1); but this time, he hesitantly pronounced the gubernatorial-judicial sentence, reluctantly condemning Jesus to death by crucifixion. What had occurred with Pilate's and Jesus' encounter with each other on a sublevel was deeper than what meets the eye. The Bible points out: *"Where the Word of a king is, there is power"* (Ecclesiastes 8:4, KJV). During the trial, Jesus wanted to be emphatic that it was not Pilate who took His life. In reality, He lay it down as a kingly ransom: *"…You have no power, except that given to you from above"* (John 19:11, ASV). For Pilate, the trial became a legal conundrum. There, in Pilate's praetorium, two kings were pitted against one another, each with their back against the pavement. In Pilate's hall, also called "The Pavement" in Hebrew, one Roman king was an enemy of the cross, the other a Jewish King who was declared an enemy of Rome. Pilate represented the Roman titan, the king Caesar, and Jesus represented Himself by appearing *Pro Se*—legally meaning for oneself. They were both reputed as kings. One, an emperor playing dress-up in God's universe, and *One* supreme God who dressed the universe. One who impersonated a god, and *One* who was God. One who pretended to be a heavenly ruler, and *One* who ruled all of heaven.

One who thought he was powerful, and *One* who had all magisterial power. One who thought he controlled the fate of another, and *One* who actually controlled the other. It appeared, at first, that Jesus had lost this trial when the throng yelled: *"We have no king but Caesar"* (John 19:15). Pilate finally caved into the skewed wishes of the potentially riotous leaders because not succumbing would threaten the increasing empirical rule of Rome's first emperor, Augustus Caesar. Caesar Augustus—as he is alternately called—was an imperator who was very preoccupied with increase. Fittingly, Augustus means "increaser" in Latin. Jesus, however, had not lost, for He increased a great veritable empire with His death. There was an empiric clash: Pilate thought he was part of the best empire, but time has been the judge and has revealed that it is Jesus' Holy Empire, not the Roman Empire, that has stood impregnably against the barrage of time. A band of motley twelve, armed with the laws of God, carried a message that withstood and outlasted the empire of Rome. *"These who have turned the world upside down"* (Acts 17:6, NKJV). Jesus inevitably won this trial in the long haul because Pilate ended up doing God's bidding by sentencing Jesus to death. God's masterful, providential hand used Pilate to land Jesus exactly where He wanted Him—in front of a crucifixion squad. Pilate ejected himself out of the true deliberative process, refusing to render his final judgment of innocence, and instead handing Jesus over to handlers of the cross by pressure. It did not matter because the divine stage had already been set. On to Calvary! *"But let the Scriptures be fulfilled"* (Mark 14:49, ESV).

I submit that God allowed these four trials because they lined up perfectly with the legalities of atonement. Consider that in order for there to be a legally acceptable atonement by God, it had to have all the staples of God's law and instruction, one of which mandated that its sacrificial lamb had to be inspected for four days to assure it had no blemish. Since Jesus was the beheld lamb of God, and since He said that He came to fulfill the law, He would have had to be inspected four different times before He was sacrificed. Four trials produced four inspections. I think it is also very significant that at the culmination of these four examinations, Jesus was pronounced faultless by the highest-ranking examiner, Prefect Pontious Pilate, who had done the most thorough examination of all. In Psalm 19:7, the Hebrew word describing God's perfect law is *"tamim,"* which means without blemish or blameless, so God's law is just like Him and the blemishless lamb. Of note is the fact that Pilate's great hall where Jesus was tried was called the Hall of Hewn Stones. A hewn stone means a split or cut stone; how divinely ironic it is that Jesus was being tried there, especially since the Bible calls Him "the Stone which the builder rejected" and since His back was split and cut.

Above, I discussed why God allowed Jesus' trials which were emblematic of His will.

It seems appropriate to ask why does God allow believers to go through trials also? The answer is because trials are expositional; they uncover the core of the believer. I believe that when a believer undergoes a trial, it brings to light what has been entered into evidence about them by the trier of their faith. Sometimes it is an adversarial proceeding, and the examination can be initiated by a hostile enemy. Other times, God the Judge could be looking for an admission from you as to your true identity in Him. Remember, what you exhibit is actually evidence which can be examined to determine a final verdict about your faith, your identification, and your loyalties*: "Beloved, think it not strange concerning the fiery trial which is to try you…"* (1 Peter 4:12–13, KJV).

I am convinced that the believer's trials test three things: our faith, our identity, and our will.

As Job said, *"when I am tried I shall come forth as pure gold"* (Job 23:10). So once the trial is over, and the evidence is in, and we have presumably shown our lasting faith, then we are acquitted in that acquittal is tantamount to gold. Obviously, if there is lack of evidence of our faith, or if there's mounting evidence which convicts our wills and identities, then we've got some work to do. The Bible says that

God has given to every believer a measure of faith, so trials reveal how we are using that faith as well as provide a vehicle for that faith. God has a law of faith: *"The just shall live by faith."* God reserves the right to test our observance of that law:

> *"I may test them, whether they will walk in my law or not."*
> EXODUS 16:4 (ESV)

One really important find that Jesus' trials showed was not about Him, but about the heart of God. Jesus on trial showed God's heart, how God was willing to put His Son through gruesome, agonizing, shameful, and pitiful treatment in order to redeem us. I think the trial was necessary to show God's redemptive nature, that He was willing to go to any length to redeem us. It is a great mystery that God allowed Himself to be on trial and allowed Himself in the form of His Son to be beaten without a cause, to be dealt deathblows without any wrongdoing. *Who does that?* Only a God who so fully and so rapturously loves His creation! What more did the trial reveal about Jesus? It revealed that He truly loved us and demonstrated before our very eyes that no greater love does a man have than to lay down his life for his friend (John 15:13). Jesus, thus, was revealing His vast love for us as the second person of the Godhead; Jesus is the friendship arm of the Trinity. God is obviously the sovereign arm, and Jesus is that great friend that you bring home, and because your parents like your friend, they may even gather another opinion of you. In other words, He's that faithful friend you always want around.

5. The Inner Trial of Jesus' Faith

The Garden of Gethsemane was the trial of Jesus' faith. There, Jesus' faith was tried when His will came head to head with the Father's will. In this joust of wills, to drink of the cup of suffering would separate *Himself from Him.* The Father and He would no longer be shoulder to shoulder—or throne to throne—although still in close collaboration. Jesus prevailed in His trial of faith, for He put His faith in the Father's plan. Because the Father's face would be hidden from the fit Savior, the unfit Adam who had chosen his will over God's and who had given God the "cold shoulder" in the Genesis garden, could now be legally exculpated. The Blameless One had cleared him of blame; it was a legal exchange fit for all eternity.

6. The Temptation of a Baker's Delight

The three wilderness temptations were a trial of Jesus' heart. Jesus made this key remark, *"For where your treasure is, there your heart will be also"* (Matthew 6:21, NIV). There, in the arid desert, the desires of Jesus' heart were tried triply. Jesus was tempted in three distinct areas, all dealing with misplaced aspirations of treasure. It seems the triple temptation shone light on the triple threat of those three leaden weights that can injure a Christ-follower's spiritual walk: The lust of the flesh; The lust of the eyes; The pride of life (1 John 2:16).

During the first wilderness temptation, Jesus was asked by the tempter to turn stones into bread for sustenance. This request tried Jesus' ability to overcome the lust of the flesh. The underlying test was whether Jesus could dodge the pleasure of feeding His physical hunger in order to embrace the spiritual hunger that hungers after the things of God. Jesus prevailed. This request strikes me as one which Jesus would have despised on several levels, one being that the *Stone* was being tempted with a stone, and the *Bread of Heaven* tempted with bread. In any case, Jesus showed that doing the will of His father was His satiety. After all, He would later tell His disciples that He had "food to eat that you know nothing about" when they tried to coax Him to eat while He was ministering (John 4:32). I might add that in a "fast forward" to a "rewind moment" of temptation, the tempter appealed to Jesus' dining faculties when He offered Jesus a drink on the cross just like he had "baited" Him before in the wild desert, but Jesus refused. Only after Jesus' six-hour ordeal in the emotional wilderness of the cross did He take the vinegar drink at the appropriate time. Do you see it? Jesus "rocked it" because it was also written: "Indeed, I will make a way in the wilderness and streams in the desert" (Isaiah 43:19, BSB). Eventually, and just before Jesus gave up His Spirit, He would drink at the permitted time. Doing the will of His Father filled Jesus up; it was the obedience, itself, that was a great trove. In my view, that wicked, engineered temptation was really a double goblet of sorts; that is, not only was Jesus being tempted to eat prematurely before His fast was over, but there was temptation within the temptation. He was also being tempted to prematurely demonstrate His miraculous powers. Keeping in line with that fact, soon after Jesus performed His first miracle of wine at the Canaan wedding, He would indicate to His mother that He had a predetermined interval for performing His miracles (John 2:1–12). It is clear, therefore, that Jesus had been tempted by the Devil to haughtily flaunt His power by transforming the stones into bread, which is another type of lustful pursuit of the flesh. Jesus prevailed there, too. Because Jesus treasured being satiated by spiritual food more than physical food, which Adam did not, humankind could now be pardoned. It was a culinary legal exchange.

7. The Temptation of a Quenching Drink

"They gave Him sour wine mingled with gall to drink. But when He had tasted it, He would not drink."

MATTHEW 27:34 (NKJV)

As a corollary thought, I find it interesting that Jesus refused the drink for two reasons. Firstly, I believe Jesus refused the sedating vinegar-gall made of wine and myrrh because if He drank it, it would have amounted to a repudiation of His avowed obedience in the Gethsemane garden. There, He had proclaimed within earshot of the Father that He would drink from a different cup, the cup of God's spiritual wrath at full strength, and would not let it pass from Him. Therefore to have drunk from another cup containing a vinegar-based sedative, or even the Roman soldier's sour vinegar wine, "*Posca*," at the onset of His suffering would not have allowed Him to spiritually taste the full wrath of God, which was the full magnitude of the separation. Had He drunk it, Jesus would have suffered a watered-down castigation spiritually because He would have bowed to fleshly accommodation. Secondly, in the natural as well, it would have been technically a watered-down pain also because if He prematurely consumed the myrrh, which was an ancient pain reliever, Jesus would not have felt the full weight of the physical suffering on the cross, which was necessary for a full physical redemption for humankind. This was a deficit that tempting "Old Slewfoot" would have liked.

I find it meaningful that there were a lot of *firsts* at this *last* event. Jesus' first days on earth included a gift of this analgesic from a wise man, and Jesus' last day on earth, before He died, included myrrh also. Additionally, Jesus' first miracle featured wine, and His last miracle before He died also featured wine—the miracle being the miracle of salvation which we will "drink to" during heaven's welcome home feast: *"Mark my words—I will not drink wine again until the day I drink it new with you in my Father's kingdom"* (Matthew 26:29, NLT). I propose there was another often overlooked miracle at the cross. Jesus' death WAS a miracle—because it would have taken a miracle for Him to die!

8. Temptation of Self-Regard

The second wilderness temptation by the tempter involved egoism, or the pride of life, combined with the lust of the eyes, which includes a focus on materialism. There, the tempter requested that Jesus worship him in exchange for a whopping world of wealth and treasure. Jesus schooled this former celestial worship leader with a refresher's course on the tenets of worship by reminding him that it was He, his Lord and God, whom the X-leader must worship. Jesus' heart was in the right place and could not be beguiled by this tempter who bet on the fact that Jesus would miss His inestimable, glorious wealth after stepping through heaven's ante-room to earth. The tempter also knew it would take Jesus' lifetime to get it back and hoped he could influence Him to detour ahead of schedule by appealing to egoistic pride. What the tempter obviously did not count on was that although the splendid treasure was inestimable, it was not invaluable to Jesus. The value that Jesus put on it appraised at a lower value than the soul of humankind. Adam, however, had done the opposite and underpriced the value of his soul while overpricing the value of the knowledge of good and evil. Jesus prevailed over the temptation. Humankind could now be pardoned. It was a valuable legal exchange.

9. The Temptation of Enticement

In the third wilderness temptation, the tempter enticed Jesus to hurl Himself from the pinnacle of Jerusalem's Herodian temple to show off His angels' catching abilities. There, Jesus was tempted by the pride of life, which I view as the pride of power. I further view this temptation as the "Climax of Two Temples." Fathom this: Jesus, who was the Temple of God not structured with hands, was standing upon Jerusalem's structural temple. In freeze-frame—the Temple was standing upon a temple—the very Ancient of Days transported to an ancient daily temple. I am further struck by the fact that Jesus was positioned at the pinnacle of the temple because it was there at the pinnacle that a priest would customarily blow the shofar for the people at a spot known as the "The Place of Trumpeting."[51] Jesus' standing there is significant especially because the Bible instructs that a shofar is to be blown just before Jesus' second coming.[52]

Consider that Jesus was reminded right there that His second coming as King could not occur until His first coming as High Priest of the atonement was completed, that servancy must precede power. With the tempter, there is always a motive behind the malevolence, so why was his angel there? It was tied to the fact that Jesus would later prophecy that the dazzling, Herodian temple would not have one stone left unturned, but that He, the chief cornerstone of the temple of God, would raise Himself up in three days after the destruction of His own temple. I deduce that the tempter chose the location of the temple as a distraction during this temptation, hoping to appeal to Jesus' obvious love for the temple since His boyhood, and trying to persuade Him that hurling Himself downward would righteously activate His power to command an angelic safety net at His favorite place. The ruse was a sentimental power trap. The stratagem didn't work. Jesus answered, "Do not put the Lord your God to the test" (Luke 4:12, NIV). Jesus recognized the trick for what it was, one involving the resident companions of pride, power, and ego. In essence, the tempter attempted to attack and taunt Jesus with His divine identity. In a psycho-analytical twist, He tried to make Jesus question His identity by actually asserting His identity. That is, by questioning if He were the Son of God, while at the same time positively asserting that the same Sonship would protect Him from harm if He would come downward. Jesus prevailed in His servanthood.

Now for the second "fast forward-rewind," looking back, the tempter introduced the same ploy at Jerusalem's high point of Calvary where Jesus was heckled: *"He saved others, but he can't save himself! Let this Messiah, the king of Israel, come down now from the cross… If you're the son of God why not save yourself"* (Mark 15:31–32, CSB). Jesus did not come down. Adam doubted his identity as the son of God, which caused him to doubt the very words of God when he was tempted. Jesus, on the other hand, knew His identity was inexorably linked to His Father and did not doubt His identity nor the Father when He was tempted. The great difference, Adam toppled a tree to get enough fig leaf coverings to clothe his shame, but Jesus propped up a tree on His way to Calvary to remove Adam's shame. Jesus prevailed. Adam could be subsequently pardoned. It was a legal exchange.

The Trial of Humankind

Jesus did something very interesting as the defense attorney in humankind's trial. Usually, in a case when there are no other character witnesses for the defendant or there are no witnesses that are up to par, or maybe no witnesses that are really prime good witnesses, the defense rethinks strategy. Perhaps the mounting, incriminating evidence against the client seems so insurmountable that it can't be overcome, and the client could lose the case. In a desperate juncture like that, the defense may choose to call the accused to the stand as a witness. This is customarily an absolute last-ditch and an undesirable option where a vulnerable witness is called upon to tell his story and risk a poor showing under cross-examination by opposing counsel. Such a strategy might be deployed to evoke mercy from the court. Another way that a defendant might evoke mercy is to "throw himself on the mercy of the court," hoping to sway the court for a lighter sentence. What is so astronomically interesting about this mercy maneuver is that it is usually the defendant who throws himself on the mercy of the court, obviously with the direction and or advice of his attorney, by admitting his guilt in hopes of a mitigated sentence. In the trial of mankind, however, Jesus throws *Himself* on the mercy seat of God for *our* sentencing. Jesus absorbed the guilty stain of our sin, which canceled our sentence. Story over!

The Trial of Satan:
The Condemnation of Satan

Under our American judicial infrastructure, it is possible to find a defendant guilty of a crime and to have that defendant appear at a later court date for sentencing. In similar fashion, Satan is awaiting sentencing similar to that of our judicial sentencing under which sentencing can be imposed at a later date; that delayed sentencing of Satan and his angels will be meted out later by the Court of God: *"God chained* them with everlasting chains and is now keeping them in dark pits until the great day of judgment" (Jude 1:6, CEV). I believe that the saints of God will be present

> Satan is now a death row angel.

as a jury when God does sentence Satan and his angels because the Bible states that we, saints, shall judge angels (See 1 Corinthians 6:3). Satan is a condemned angel, and in a true sense, he is a death row angel, in that he and death will be sitting on the same row in hell: *"For God did not spare even the angels who sinned. He threw them into hell...where they are being held until the day of judgment"* (2 Peter 2:4, NLT). Satan has his irrevocable ticket to hell, and He already has been adjudged guilty by God as an unfit angel, as is evidenced by his being stripped of his former stripes of rank. In God's hierarchical pecking order of throne angels, Satan was once one of the celestial top brass with the glorious title of "son of the morning," but he was stripped of that holy insignia. No longer allowed to hold his position of raising the dawn because of his wicked downfall, the angelic agitator started the clock for his demise. The law he broke—"Thou shall serve the Lord your God." Satan acted fractiously, for he wanted to break away from God and be served instead of serve, and he attempted to raise his throne higher than God's. The short-term penalty for his infraction was his being exiled from heaven with only limited future access. The long-term penalty for Satan will be immersion by chain into an infernal pit for a thousand years—a type of infernal pit arrest—followed by serving a life sentence without the possibility of parole.

One of the most important trials of all time has already taken place with Lucifer, known by his criminal alias as Satan, having been found guilty of treason. For now, Satan is a condemned prowler, for The Bible paints that he stalk-walks to and fro, seeking whom he can devour. Since the Bible says that by one's words, one is condemned or acquitted, Satan is surely condemned because he was ensnared by his own words: *"thou art caught by thy own words"* (Proverbs 6:2, KJV). Consider his condemnatory speech of the highest rung of treason: *"I will ascend… I will raise my throne above the stars of God… I will make myself like the Most High"* (Isaiah 14:13–14, BSB). Not only did Satan, himself, commit this treason against "The Throne," he also illegally incited "high" treason against the Most "High" God—by "aiding and abetting" the insurrection of one-third of God's angels to join him in his attempted crime to overthrow The Divine Crown. In retrospect, Satan's first direct attempt to overthrow "The Throne" was lost upon himself, but he attempted another *coup d'etat* indirectly to seize God's exalted throne also. Although his physical pawn was different, his mental motive was the same; instead of inciting angelic beings this time, he incited human beings to rebel. With malicious animus, Satan communicated the same evil, psychological refrain that condemned him—"I will be like God"—except he contorted and uncoiled the words when he whispered them to Eve. He said to her, *"God said that because he knows that when you eat it, you will be like God and know what is good and what is bad"* (Genesis 3:5, GNT; Emphasis added). Satan, that old serpent, wisely disguised his baked-in immorality as appetizing morality, and he served it to Eve and Adam.

Under our American constitutional laws, which mirror God's laws in large part, I've observed that Satan also broke the law of unlawful assembly that is related to the First Amendment to our Constitution, which protects lawful assembly. God is very much in favor of lawful assembly, for the Bible promotes this in His Word: *"Forsake not the assembly of the saints"* (Hebrews 10:25, KJV). God, however, is judgemental of unlawful assembly, and Satan assembled his wicked angelic consortium for evil-spirited, prohibited, and unlawful means. Following the world's end, he will be forever confined to a lake of fire, along with his accomplices to his depraved crimes. Satan premeditatively conspired with a third of the angelic guard for the intended, attempted, and violent overthrow of God's kingdom, as exhibited by his military engagement in using his tail as a weapon of force to violently drag a contingent of heaven's angelic assembly with him: *"For their power is … in their tails, for their tails are like serpents"* (Revelation 9:19, ESV; See Revelation 12:4).

There was treason in the Garden of Eden, and blood had to be spilled! Satan introduced treason, but Jesus introduced the cross. The cross was the progressive avenue through which God fulfilled His epic plan to get redemption to humankind. It was legally important for Jesus to die on that tree-cross for a number of reasons. Firstly, the tree fits within God's legal axioms for redemption. There were symmetrical truths surrounding the tree that were legal factors and had to happen for legal redemption. For example, by bearing sin on a *tree*, Jesus put God in legal remembrance of the Adamic *tree* as He ate the wrathful consequence of Adam's consumed fruit—death. Secondly, the tree was made of wood. The tree's composition is of legal magnitude because, in the Old Testament, the sacrificial altar was oftentimes a structure of wood as set forth by the laws of God (See Ezekiel 4:22). The word "altar" is from the Hebrew word, *mizbe'ah*, meaning to slay; so wood from trees provided the undergirding for the sacrifice that was to be slain and offered unto God. Symmetrically, Jesus was the sacrificial lamb slain in accordance with God's law. This identity is so indivisible from Jesus that the Bible says to this day, Jesus appears in heaven like a slain lamb in the middle of God's throne. Don't miss it—there is a slaughtered lamb positioned dead center around the throne (Revelation 5:6). Jesus was offered upon an actual wooden altar—the cross—so that He could be consumed unto death. With respect to the wood, sometimes the wood was combined with stones. There is also a crucial symmetry here because there were stones associated with Jesus' offering. Jesus, in fact, provided the Stone—Himself: *"Jesus said to them, 'have you never read in the Scriptures: the stone that the builders rejected has become the cornerstone. This is what the Lord has done…'"* (Matthew 21:42, CSB). From a legal view, Satan was adjudged guilty but has a deferred sentence:

> *But the court will sit, and then the sovereignty, power and greatness of his power will be taken away and completely destroyed forever. Then the sovereignty, power and greatness of all the kingdoms under heaven will be handed over to the holy people of the Most High. His kingdom will be an everlasting kingdom, and all rulers will worship and obey him.*
>
> DANIEL 7:26-27 (NKJV)

Eventually Satan's power will be taken away; this provocateur of wickedness will serve a sentence of life imprisonment according to Scripture, and he will be confined to hell's lake of fire forever (Revelation 20:10, See Matthew 25:41).

Trial by Fire: Jesus' and Peter's Friendship

> *"A man with friends is to show himself friendly."*
>
> PROVERBS 18:24 (YLT)

Jesus and Peter's friendship was tested by fire—literally. Their relationship would twice endure a burning fire. Their rapport was one of torrid loyalty on both sides. A tempestuous Peter determined to commit mayhem the night of Jesus' arrest to "save" Him. Without hesitation, he took on a mob, wielding a daunting sword against one of Jesus' captors. Only after Jesus admonished him did he eventually sheath his angry sword. For Peter, shrinking in the face of the danger surrounding his friend was not an option. Theirs was a "do or die" relationship. In his steadily raging mind, Peter stayed ready to cross blades for his giant friend; nevertheless, the mettle of their relationship was to be tested on a cold night in front of hot coals fire. With only a rough-shod trial, or more accurately a cloak-and-spear inquisition taking place inside of the high priest's home, Peter denied knowing the man for whom only a short time earlier he had been willing to wage an all-out personal assault. He made his denial while reluctantly warming himself with the comfort of a cozy fire. At the time, it made no sense to Peter why Jesus had warned him that he would deny their friendship, but the rooster's annunciation of the morning would be the wake-up call to his sleepy memory. Although Jesus had been absent when Peter tendered his shocking false claim against his Savior-friend, the very next glimpse of Jesus' presence would make it bitterly clear to Peter that he had uttered a double denial—one of himself and one of Christ. By denying the truth of who his best friend was, he also denied the truth of who he was. The two identities were so intertwined that to belie one was to belie himself; after all, it was he who Jesus had commended for knowing the truth about His messianic identity. Peter probably flashed back to the day he had demonstrated that unrelenting courage to speak up with the truth when Christ questioned, *"Who do men say that I am"* (Mark 8:27, ASV). Peter had spoken forth with such a clarion, oh so spirit-filled, bold truth that Jesus exclaimed that He would build His church upon that very rock bed of truth. It was a momentous day for Peter; Jesus gave him a new identity, a new name. No longer Simon Bar Jonah, but Peter, the two of them now linked with Peter as a stony *Petros*—side by side with Jesus—The great *Petra* rock. Regrettably that night, however, Peter toggled between Jesus' identities, the man he knew and the man he claimed he didn't know. What Peter uttered near the fire was a devastating falsity since the apex of Jesus and his friendship had been truth, dating even back to that morning of infancy when Peter first met Jesus. There, Peter realized that it was none other than the Messiah who had miraculously bid the fish to overtake his net. That kinetic overflow evoked such a rushing truth within Peter that he admitted he was a "sinful man!" and way back then, called Jesus by His true identity, *"Lord"* (Luke 5:8, ESV). It was an inner truth so comprehensively tender and self-owned by Peter that Jesus initiated him into his circle of kingdom fishermen: *"Come, follow me… and I'll make you fishers of men"* (Matthew 4:19, BSB).

It was that welcoming ability of Peter to court the truth with all abandon that made him express to Jesus, *"if it's truly you, call me and I will walk on water"* (Matthew 14:28, NIV). It was patently clear that Peter and Jesus had a reign of truth going in their relationship until Peter lost the reins. It all came to a halt when Peter lied and falsely denied knowing Jesus; then truth became a distant object in a rearview mirror for Peter. There was a trial indoors, but Peter underwent his own trial outdoors. He brooded over his sin and regretted his misstep. He knew very well the law that he had broken and the law around which his trial revolved: *"You are truly my disciples if you remain faithful to my teachings. And you will know the truth ,and the truth shall set you free"* (John 8:31–32, NLT; Emphasis Mine). What was left of their relationship if the very foundation of truth had been eroded by Peter's denial? What came next gave new meaning to the expression, "trial and error." Peter had erred maximally, and there would be a trying of his faith. The comforting news about this duo is that Jesus did what all good friends do for one another—He prayed for him: *"Satan has asked to sift each of you...But I pleaded in prayer for you that your faith, Simon, should not fail. So when you have repented...strengthen your brothers "* (Luke 22:31, BSB). In truth, Peter's faith faltered, but it never ultimately failed. In symmetry, Peter's greatest trial would take place next to a second cozy fire, but this time it would be a beach fire that his friend, the resurrected Christ, had built. I submit that Jesus started a fire to symbolize the trial of Peter's faith by fire. Peter seems to have agreed because later he penned: *"Beloved, don't be astonished at the fiery trial which has come upon you, to test you..."* (1 Peter 4:12, WEB). In essence, Jesus lit a fire under Peter at the breaking of day in pursuit of him in the same way a good shepherd goes after his stray sheep. Realistically, the burning passion of the shepherd for his sheep makes him track them down indefatigably. There flowed out of the trial of their friendship, a trial of Peter's faith which would later prove to be unwavering. After three successive calls of vocation from Jesus to Peter, the trial ends with Jesus presenting His conciliatory offer of forgiveness and His grace-laced love to Peter. Peter is free, having been converted and falling headlong into the lap of Jesus' love while accepting His call to apostolic ministry. There the relationship of two friends surely had been rekindled by fire.

God on Trial: The Trial of God's Heart

When Jesus stood trial before the Jewish tribunals and before Caesar's Roman ambassador, He was never on trial by Himself. It was the heart of the Father that was on trial beside Him, all along! I submit that "God on trial" was the most important trial of all time, even more important than the very important trial of humankind's soul because the outcome of the soul would depend upon the heart of God. In this trial, we see a great mystery: It was God who was both the real trier of fact here, and simultaneously the one being tried; it was God's justice on one side, and His heart on the other, that made up the scales upon which all evidence would be laid.

As I view it, this trial can be summed up as the case I've dubbed *Heart of God v. Heart of the Matter*. The heavenlies produced a trial of the composite of God's heart, and it is that composite which would answer these essential earthly inquiries: Did Jesus' death *really* satisfy the Father's wrath? Would a Holy God *really* allow an unholy people to come in His presence? Would the blood of Jesus *really* cause God to forget our past? Would God really never forsake us? Would relational reconciliation *really* be accessible to us? The answer to all of these questions is a resounding yes! Conclusively, in the long run, it mattered not what type of earthly trial Jesus received, nor did it matter if that mode of trying Him was unfit because it was actually God's heart—not man's actions—that would ultimately be judged. In other words, God made the potential converts to

> *Potential converts serve as jury members.*

be the all-important jury. He actually gave the would-be believers the gift of deciding the credibility of His heart. Regardless of the excellence of Jesus' sacrifice at Calvary, and irrespective of the nobleness of God's shepherdly heart, God arranged it so that the lost sheep whom His heart went after would render the crucial vote for His loving heart. Would the believer choose the heart of God because He chose to give up His Son's heart for her. Choiceless love is not real love; it's robotic. When it gets right down to the matter of it, to accept Jesus as Savior is to cast a vote ratifying the credibility of God's heart. To believe in the name of Jesus is to embrace the reliability of God's heart to both slay Him for *you* and raise Him from the dead for *you*. Firstly, humankind would have to vote if God was a Father who loved it enough to do that. Secondly, humankind would have to vote if God's self-sacrifice through "The Way," which created a full-proof avenue to Him, was enough. Thirdly, humankind would have to vote if eternal life that is to be celebrated on streets paved with gold, which was preceded by the *true* gold rush of His fountainous blood, was enough. In American court trials, jury members are usually given a set of instructions from the Judge by which to arrive at their vote. In this case, God the eternal Judge might instruct the jury thusly: If the jury believes that God's heart handily passed and unequivocally met the three above tests, that it was indeed enough, you may cast a vote of acceptance. You are further instructed that a vote of acceptance is to also accept Jesus as Savior, and such will instantaneously seal your vote in favor of God's heart.

The Mistrials of Jesus

"Keep far from a false charge, and do not kill the innocent and righteous, for I will not acquit the wicked."

EXODUS 23:7 (ESV)

Within our American criminal system, a defendant on trial is presumed innocent until "proved" guilty, but conversely, in Jesus' unfair trial by the Jewish leadership, He was presumed guilty until "proved" innocent. It was clear from the procession of circus trials that Jesus endured that even the most robust defenses would not have made a difference in the staged presumption of guilt that was waiting for Him. That guilty presumption flies in the face of true justice. From the outset of the legal mazes, it was clear that Jesus had been targeted. Notice that Caiphas should have never adjudged Jesus' guilt because he was politically motivated to have Jesus dead; in fact, he said regarding Jesus: *"And you do not consider that it is profitable for us that one man die instead of the nation…"* (John 11:50, ABPE). Jesus should have never been tried as a criminal offender because He should have never even been arrested. According to His accusers, His only purported crime was that He called Himself the Son of God. In other words, He told the truth. Blasphemy? I think not. The fabricated basis of His arrest was unfounded under Israeli law because it had no basis in fact, and unwarranted under America's criminal branch of law, too, because it would not have withstood a legal probable cause test for a warrant to be issued; such an issuance required more than a mere suspicion of a crime. The bogus criminal charge of blasphemy was suspect since most criminals don't senselessly and blatantly commit crimes in broad daylight with an abundance of witnesses looking on! Jesus even balked at their soiled attempts and stood solidly by the same things which He had said openly and during daylight: *"I always taught in the synagogues and at the temple, where all the Jews come together. I said nothing in secret"*

(John 18:20). Jesus' arrest was obviously an illegal railroaded, or reflective of the time chariot-roaded, attempt to politically silence Him, and that is why the temple "police" sneakily arrested Him under the cover of darkness which prompted a violative night trial under Israeli law.[53] Jesus even chided the temple guards on the night of his suspicious, illegal arrest; *"Have you come out with swords and clubs to arrest me as you would an outlaw? Every day I sat teaching in the temple courts..."* (Mark 14:48, BSB). Jesus, of course, knew what Leviticus 4:16 (CSB) said: *"Whoever blasphemes the name of the Lord shall surely be put to death."* Jesus, however, made an adept comment to the police, "For which of these things do you arrest me," in other words, Jesus was asserting His right to know what was the charge against Him. This right is mirrored under our constitutional Sixth Amendment.[54]

What followed was the first of sham trials. The lethargy of justice displayed itself in bureaucratic trappings aimed at destroying whom Jewish leaders deemed a political opponent. Jesus' trial was conveniently convened in the covert and peril of night, and He was swooped up in treacherous fashion and carted off to detention. The mock trial that took place did not permit any witness testimony from any of Jesus' supporters, sympathizers, or even His disciples. Scripture reveals that there was at least one of Jesus' followers present at the night owl trials, the young apostle John, and although John apparently enjoyed some influence that gained him access, it obviously was not enough to have him included on the witness list. Despite the biblical mention of at least two witnesses who testified falsely and uncorroboratedly of each other, there were no recorded congenial witnesses for Jesus who were permitted to challenge that testimony. Importantly, under Ancient Jewish law, it was illegal to use the witnesses' dissimilar testimony to convict Jesus because an accused could not be convicted in a death penalty trial unless at least two eyewitnesses observed the act and testified to the same observation without dissimilarity. According to the Jewish *Mitzvah* commandments, the trying body must reject any non-conforming testimony.[55] The Jewish Torah states, "You shall not give false testimony against your neighbor"[56] (*See* Exodus 20:16). By the way, unscrupulous witness testimony that matched was difficult to find, but the religious leaders tried the tactic anyway under Caiphas, and it resulted in a fiasco of inconsistent, non-credible testimony (*See* Matthew 26:60–61).

Jesus' trials were unfairly mined with antagonistic pitfalls. If a trial falls to the level of unfairness, one remedy is the motion for a mistrial by the defense or the related declaration of a mistrial by the judge. A mistrial is a trial that ends prematurely without a determination on the merits due to misconduct or procedural error during its proceedings; it can also be declared by the successor judge if the presiding judge recuses—legally disqualified—himself.[57] Jesus' trials should have ended in mistrials because Judge Caiphas, Judge Herod, and Judge Pilate should never have presided over Jesus' trials, and all of them should have recused themselves from conducting those trials. Caiphas should have recused himself because he was so openly and politically amped about Jesus dying; recall he said regarding Jesus: *"Nor do you understand that it is expedient and politically advantageous for you that one man die for the people, and that the whole nation not perish"* (John 11:50, AMP). He was, therefore, devoted to preserving his political platform above preserving justice. He enjoyed a high position in the Israeli nation for sure but had never drawn crowds of five thousand as Jesus did. Next, Herod should have recused himself based on the fact that he had earlier sentenced Jesus' cousin to death, John the Baptist, because of a personal vendetta he had against him and his holy beliefs, which also typified Jesus' belief system. Also, he was the same *King* Herod, tetrarch ruler of Galilee, who was very leery of anyone the people of his domain hailed as king. It was a family trait undoubtedly picked up from his father, Herod the Great, who sought to slaughter Jesus as an infant. He, therefore, could not conduct a trial without an offensive, prejudicial bias against Jesus. Previously, Jesus had even called him a cunning and unclean "fox" and disdained his behavior so much that at the trial, He refused to respond to any of his trial questioning. Finally, Pilate should have recused himself because he had a conflict of interest with Jesus' case in that he perceived Jesus as his territorial, political rival. Jerusalem was a hotbed of insurrection against the Roman rule at that time; therefore, Pilate had been sent there as a washed-up military representative, and this was his last chance to salvage his own political career by keeping the peace and stifling any Jewish uprising. During his interrogation of Jesus, Pilate finally realized he was dealing with one he gauged as an "equal," a man of power and destiny in the earthly realm. It was quite the juxtaposition, Jesus standing robe to toga with Pilate, but He made it clear to Pilate that although he seemed to be in a position to determine His mortality, Pilate was of the lesser kingdom and possessed only borrowed authority from the Father: *"No one can take my life from me. I sacrifice it voluntarily. For I have the authority to lay it down when I want to and also to take it up again. For this is what my Father commanded"* (John 10:18, NLT). In a real sense, Pilate should have recused himself because he was not in a position to be just-minded.

Prosecutorial Misconduct & Grounds for Mistrial

Fully knowing this, Jesus said, *"For truly I say unto you, until heaven and earth pass away, not an iota, not a dot, will pass from the Law until all is accomplished…for I tell you, unless your righteousness exceeds that of the scribes and pharisees you will never enter the kingdom of God"* (Matthew 5:18-20, ESV).

The Jewish prosecutorial leaders demonstrated prosecutorial vindictiveness by intentionally convicting Jesus of blasphemy and by intentionally assessing His unjustifiable death under the guise of the severest of crimes. Under the professional conduct rules of the American Bar Association, such capricious conduct could fall under "crime misrepresentation;" for a prosecutorial representative to misrepresent the commission of a crime in order to engage in plotting a murder for political gain is, indeed, unethical misconduct. Given that the hostile leaders who were also cultural icons of Jesus' day held judicial sway over His trials, it is not inconceivable that there was an undisguised exhibition of errant trial noncompliance, lack of judicial fitness, judicial impropriety, and prosecutorial trial misconduct, which should have resulted in a mistrial. From a legal point of view, I identify the following rampant abuses which were contained in Jesus' trials:

1. Tampering with witness testimony: tainted hand-selection of false witnesses (See Mark 14:55; Mark 26:59).
2. A faulty closed-door, night capital punishment trial: inaccessible to the public, and in direct contravention of Sanhedrin law, which regulated trials by day and in public forums: "Therefore, since capital cases might continue for two days, the court does not judge cases of capital law on certain days, neither on the eve of Shabbat nor the eve of a Festival"[58] (See also Mark 14:53).
3. Pre-planned Judicial bias which is impermissible in a capital punishment trial (See Matthew 27:1).
4. Guard brutality by all three judges' guards which exceeded dictated corporal punishment: It involved, but was not limited to, pressing down lacerating thorns on top of Jesus' head, punching, slapping, and spitting on Him while in custody: "I gave… My cheeks to those who pulled out My beard" (See Mark 14:65; Matthew; Isaiah 50:6; Mark 14:65; Luke 22:64; John 19:2).
5. Bribery by a judge: By implication, Judge Caiphas is associated with the cadre of Jewish leaders who paid money to Judas—who was an operative for them—to entrap Jesus (See Matthew 27:4-7).
6. Intimidation of a jurist: Jewish leaders inciting a crowd in order to directly influence the trial's outcome (See Matthew 27:20; John 19:6; John 19:12).

7. Hostile venues: The trial should have been moved to a neutral venue. Herod's trial was held in lower Galilee in which Nazareth was located and which was hostile toward Jesus. Jesus identified Nazareth as hostile home territory when He stressed that, "No prophets are liked by the people of their hometown" (Luke 4:24). Regarding the Pilate trial, it was held in Jerusalem—in Pilate's Great Hall—which categorically was hostile to the cause of Jesus also because Pilate was a surrogate of Caesar who opposed the monotheistic truth of Jesus. The fact cannot be overlooked that Pilate had been sent to Jerusalem to stomp out all Judean opposition which Jesus, Himself, personified. In essence, the people who Jesus appeared before were His nemeses and held power within the surrounding communities at large and at small, and as such, had the ability to inflame injustice and suppress justice.

8. Biased members of the Sanhedrin Council: Council-member Gamaniel demonstrated the need to remind the other members of the council of their role to be objective and of the presumption of Jesus' innocence (See Acts 5:38). Nicodemus felt the same inquietude: *"Does our law convict a man without first hearing from him to determine what he has done"* (John 7:51, BSB). The council who was empowered to convict or acquit Jesus on the charge of blasphemy would have functioned much like American jurors in that they were to present their vote after hearig the testimony. That council, however, was not made up of Jesus' peers as American juries are. Importantly, Ancient Israel had no official "jury" system.[59] Constitutional forefather John Adams warned that trial by jury, as is protected by our Sixth Amendment, was the *heart* and *lungs* of one of the greatest underpinnings of our judicial system, signifying that it was meant to

ward off bias because its absence could leave the accused in the hands of a capricious body who performed less than deliberately fairly.[60] Jesus' trial was booby-trapped with unfavorable bias and ambushes and with a subplot of jealousy atop political pride. It's especially interesting that Adams expressed this concept in terms of anatomy since Jesus' death involved the piercing of His heart and the disabling of His lung capacity on the cross, so the picture Adams anatomically referenced was also related to His trial.

9. Festival violation: The trial was held in violation of three Jewish Festivals (Feasts) that occurred that weekend, so it was illegally carried out, as mentioned above. The three festivals were: The Passover Feast (Friday); The Feast of Unleavened Bread (Saturday); The Feasts of First Fruits (Sunday).[61]

The trials were nests of above misconduct and impropriety which comprised fundamental error that was prejudicial (harmful) to the defendant, Jesus, and should have rendered Jesus' trials as mistrials both two-thousand years ago as well as today: *"He has told you, O man, what is good; and what does the* LORD *require of you but to do justice, and to love kindness and to walk humbly with your God?"* (Micah 6:8, ESV). The Jewish *Talmud*—the deeply revered encasement of the ancient Jewish law of Israel—expresses a similar, legal intolerance in its laws for dishonesty and misconduct:

> *Do not spread false reports. Do not follow the crowd in doing wrong. When you give testimony in a lawsuit, do not pervert justice by siding with the crowd. Do not deny justice to your poor people in their lawsuits. Have nothing to do with a false charge and do not put an innocent or honest person to death, for I will not acquit the guilty. Do not accept a bribe, for a*

bribe blinds those who see and twists the words of the innocent.[62]

Despite the horrific instrumentality of the crucifixion process itself, the mean Roman guards, or the egregious behavior of envious Jewish leaders, they were all unwittingly part of God's delegation of preordination. They were all delegates of God's plan to rescue the world; in fact, Jesus' planned ruination was cloaked in a powerful journey to the cross that would become an out-of-this-world transformative moment in the life of every future believer: *"My kingdom is not of this world. If it were, my servants would fight to keep me from being handed over…"* (John 18:36, NIV).

CHAPTER 8

The Shalom Breach and Its Legal Repair

> *"...Pray for the peace of Jerusalem: 'May those who love you be secure. May there be peace within your walls and security within your citadels.'"*
>
> PSALM 122:6 (NIV)

In ancient Jewish history, the wall has always been of paramount importance. Consider that Joshua led a putatively noisy Israeli brigade that launched a conquering praise against its enemy's walls at Jericho. Consider also that Nehemiah showed unflappable courage in the face of opposition as he toggled back and forth with a weapon in one hand and construction materials in the other—cautiously militaristic—all for the sake of rebuilding a city's wall after enemy occupation. Both of these men, and their contingent, risked life and limb because of a wall. Fast forward to the first advent of *Yeshua HaMashiach*—Jesus, The Messiah, to see another type of wall that was imperiled and another enemy's fortification. The internal, superstructural wall of the spiritual tower in which Adam had comfortably made his abode, ensconced by the love of God on all of its sides, had collapsed under the weight of sin. Not only was the inner wall of the tower broken down, but also there had arisen an outer wall of hostility between God and Adam's descendants due to that same sin, and it further ripped apart the original peaceful rapport between God and His creation; these bleak barriers of antagonism separated the Potter from His clay. The absence of the retaining wall of obedience gave way to a double breach—the crumbling of a wall within a wall. The decaying interior wall of humankind's heart reflected the ill status of the dilapidated exterior wall of humankind's will.

In steps, Jesus, the Prince of Peace, the authorized divine mediator and curer of the breach. The Bible casts Jesus in the role of the great Mediator between sinners and a sinless God, *Jehovah Shalom:* "*For there is only one God and one Mediator who can reconcile God and humanity…the man Christ Jesus*" (1 Timothy 2:5, NLT). Critical to this schematic is the fact that the *Yeshua* spoken about here, in a very organic and real sense, is "Judeo-Christian." He is fully Jewish and fully the Anointed Christ, and I underscore here that Jesus is God the Son, and His oneness with God is regardful and not intended to belittle the divine exclusivity of the holy oneness of Jehovah, for He alone is God; but ultimately God is not alone. In other words, He alone is God, but He is not a lone God, and Jesus' sameness with Him is not meant to be, nor is it a violation or a supersession of the sacrosanct "One God" Jewish orthodoxy. "*When you've seen Me, you've seen the Father,*" Jesus said, for He is fully God and fully man (John 14:9, CEV). God and Jesus, the mystery of a binary unison, two persons of the triune assemblage, two parts of the sacred threesome, all separate but wholly one. In sum, a unity of individualism. Monotheism is not lost in the Trinity. Jesus is both the Son of God and God the Son; He is God of God. It is the very nature and essence of God to confound the finiteness of earthly understanding. Out of love, God undrapes the vastness of His immortality and enables us to get a serial look at His eternality using the technologies of spiritual bifocals—His lucrative endowment of understanding to actually partake of Him. Indeed, the present One God showed a multi-constituency of His loneself—both plenary and single: *"For God was in Christ, reconciling the world to himself"* (2 Corinthians 5:19, NLT). The Hebrew word, *Adonai,* is in its plural

> *Monotheism is not lost in the Trinity.*

form, which literally means "Lords;" in Jewish tradition; however, it is expressed singularly as "The Lord" and commonly refers to God. This word study of Adonai crystalizes for me the strong notion of the Father and Son converging as two Lords in One—as the "Lord God." Thomas received a similar revelation when he saw the freshly risen Yeshua: *"'My Lord and my God!' Thomas exclaimed"* (John 20:28, NLT). By extension, Thomas was saying, My Lord and my *Lord*—or "Jesus is LORD God." In reflecting on the meaning of Jehovah Eloheenu, which means "The LORD our God," it is, therefore, rational to denote "Jesus is Lord" as "Jesus is LORD God." That day Thomas heard the voice of Christ and the voice of God as one: *"And the LORD said to me what they have spoken is good. I will raise up for them a Prophet like you from among their brethren, and will put my words in His mouth and He shall speak to them all that I command Him"* (Deuteronomy 18:17-18, NKJV). Moreover, in Judaism, a most prominent declaration from the Torah is known as the Shema: Hear O Israel! The Lord is our God, the Lord is one. Interestingly, the Hebrew word for one there is "echad" which is the same word used in Genesis 2:24 where the Bible paints a husband and wife as one flesh—another type of ordained unison found in a pairing.

At work on the cross—which was the instrumentality of the chosen mediation—Jesus properly drafted a new covenantal agreement with the stylus of His red, diamond blood, for only a diamond can cut into another diamond: *"The sin of Judah is engraved with a pen of iron, with the point of a diamond"* (Jeremiah 17:1, ESV). The diamond of Salvation cut into the diamond of sin. Jesus' blood cut away humankind's sin, so there, in that mediation, God-the-Father agreed to deliver man from his broken places—to repair his walls—in anticipation that one day man would agree to adore The Son of the broken tree. *"For my Father's will is that everyone who looks to the Son and believes in him shall have eternal life"* (John 6:40, NIV). Even as Nehemiah completed his work amidst adversity, Jesus similarly withstood the virulent attempts from religious leaders to derail Him from His spiritual itinerary. Like

Joshua, who endured an alliance of hostile spectators, Jesus endured a hostile cadre of legal minds, including lawyers, chief priests, and scribes who watched His every move, conspiring to overtake Him with their machinations. Jesus succeeded in His earthly mission as the mediatorial conductor of repair of the breach in the walls of separation between estranged man and God. Yeshua Hamashiach was the gift within a gift, for God gave the gift of His Son, and the Son gave the gift of Himself: *"See, I have engraved you on the palms of my hands; your walls are ever before me"* (Isaiah 49:16, NIV). *"...But my Father who lives in me does His work through me"* (John 14:10, NLT). *"Shalom"* in Jewish thought is defined—among its many other meanings- as the peace that results after a breach is repaired. This association with its meaning would explain Jesus' relentless exuberance as He effused, *"Shalom"* or "Peace be with you!" to His disciples after His resurrection: *"But when it was evening of the first day of the week... Yeshua came and stood in their midst and He said to them, 'Peace be with you.' He said this and He showed them His hands and His side"* (John 20:19-20, ABPE).

According to Jeremiah 10:24 (NIV), the Bible gives some insight as to how chasmic man's estrangement with God was. It was not only strained but wreaked of acrimony: *"Discipline me LORD, but only in due measure- not in your anger, or you will reduce me to nothing."* In Jewish teaching, *shalom* can actually be broken, as in a broken relationship between a father and his children. The pointed hostility, then, would need to be legally excised from the relationship in order for it to flourish or even to continue. *Yeshua*, which literally means "Salvation" in Hebrew, would ultimately finish His singular expedition of salvation and rehabilitated two collapsing spiritual walls: *"No longer will violence be heard in your land, nor ruin or destruction within your borders. But you will name your walls Salvation..."* (Isaiah 60:18, NIV). More than a rabbinic sage, Jesus of God, Yeshua Hamashiach, was the Jesus Christ of the long-awaited *rapprochement* between the Father and His children. In Mark 14:36, Jesus notably refers to *Yahweh* as *Abba Pater*—meaning "Daddy Father"—a transliteration of Jesus' daily Aramaic speech into the Greek.[63] Remarkably, Jesus' reference is the New Testament's first mention of the warm, affable "daddy-hood" of The LORD God Almighty, and most likely would have been a very unfamiliar reintroduction of The Holy One to adherents of Old Testament Judaism. To this point, they had primarily, almost entirely, focused on the familiar distant rigidity and aloof mightiness of the majestic Creator, *Elohim* (See Deuteronomy 32:6; Psalm 80:19; Isaiah 64:8). Pursuant to this newly revealed, divine proximity to God, Jesus taught His disciples to pray by invoking this cozier and inclusively godly presence with "Our Father." Jesus legalized affectionately calling God, "Father:" *"I am ascending to my Father and your Father, to my God and your God"* (John 20:17, NIV). That novel, primary mention of divine parenthood signaled a coming hallmark of warm reconciliation and divine intimacy as God's *mishpochah*—family in Hebrew. Jesus overarchingly came to be a bridge over the chasm of separation, which was the fallout of sin: *"For there is one God and one mediator between God and mankind, the man Christ Jesus"* (1 Timothy 2:5, NIV). Jesus took on a multi-detailed repair: The road to Salvation was broken; The will of man was broken; The fellowship between Jehovah Shlomi—The one who reveals my *shalom*—and humankind was broken; The door to man's blessing was broken.

How was Jesus legally able to conduct these repairs? Firstly, Jesus declared He was *"The Way, The Truth, and The Life," and further that "No one comes to the Father except through me"* (John 14:6, NIV). Therein, lay the legal roadmap to having a lawfully obtained relationship with Father God; so legally, Jesus repaired the broken way to the Father and to eternal life by *becoming* both the way of repair and by *showing* others the true way to get back to the Father of life spiritually: "Philippus said to him, 'Our Lord, show us the Father, and it is sufficient for us." Yeshua said to him, '…whoever has seen me has seen the Father…" (John 14:8-9, ABPE). Jesus sharpened the image of the Father for humankind by showing them God's Fatherly essence in walking "3D." Secondly, by the surrender of His own will in praying His Gethsemane prayer, "Father not my will, but your will be done," Jesus lawfully restored the power of free will to the relationship on humankind's behalf. Thirdly, Jesus lawfully restored obtainable fellowship with the Father by fusing that all-important will of man with God's will. Typically, God-The-Father waits for that moment of intense volition in which His child willfully chooses Him by choosing Jesus. It is a moment of the highest, categorical order of the wills: *"I will be a Father to you, and you will be my sons and daughters…Says the Lord Almighty"* (2 Corinthians 6:18, BSB). The desire to have Almighty God be a part of one's life, indeed to quench the Adamic thirst, is a marriageable moment; saying "Yes" to Christ, the bridegroom of the Church of God, is the ultimate-intimate moment of divine fellowship. Lastly, Jesus lawfully restored "The Blessing" by incorporating the Abrahamic blessing into His Messianic blessing:

> *The Messiah redeemed us from the curse of the law by becoming a curse for us. For it is written: "A curse on everyone who is hung on a tree!" This happened in order that the blessing promised to Abraham would come to the gentiles through the Messiah, Jesus, so that we might receive the promised Spirit through faith.*
>
> GALATIANS 3:13-14 (ISV)

As mentioned, Yeshua in Hebrew means Salvation, and Yeshua fixed the spiritual wall; so by logical reasoning, the spiritual wall, therefore, was repaired by Salvation: *"… You will call your walls Salvation"* (Isaiah 60:18, NASB). It struck me that there is an assortment of "walled" solutions occurring between Yeshua's first and second coming. His objective during His first earthly and "lackluster" appearance was to rebuild the "retaining wall" pertaining to *Elohim a*nd His creation, that is, to bring Salvation. Contrastingly, Jesus' second earthly, luster-rich return will take place specifically after the demolition of the man-made erected wall between Jews and Gentiles is completed. In His name, Jesus has begun the crumbling of that divisive wall spiritually and has opened the way for the emergence of the biblical, future "one new man:" *"For He is our peace—He who has made Jews and Gentiles one, and in His own human nature has broken down the hostile dividing wall, by setting aside the Law with its commandments, expresses, as they were, in definite decrees"* (Ephesians 2:14–15, WNT). Yeshua's design was to unite the two sections of humanity in Himself so as to form one new man. I find it intriguing that the apostle Peter, who was a devout Jewish separatist and purist, received a vision from God in which Jews and Gentiles were united in a commonality of the Christian faith: *"What God has cleansed, no longer consider unholy"* (Acts 10:15, NASB). Crucially the vision showed that Jesus, by fulfilling all the laws of God, had set aside the wall of separateness as it pertained to those laws because He, Himself, became the fulfillment of the Law and would enable united humanity to walk out God's kingdom laws. *"Until we all shall be one entity in the faith and in the knowledge of The Son of God, unto a perfect man, unto the measure of the stature of the fullness of Christ"* (Ephesians 4:13, ABPE). It is both ironic and amazing that *Hashem*'s will was ushered in during the past by one wall being repaired and re-erected, but in the future, *Hashem*'s will is to come into being when another wall is obliterated: *"But the crowds which were going before him and coming after him were crying out and they were saying, 'Hosanna to The Son of David! Blessed is he who comes in the name of the LORD JEHOVAH! Hosanna in The Highest!'"* (Matthew 21:9, ABPE). *"For I say to you that you will not see me from now on, until you will say, 'Blessed is he who has come in the name of the LORD JEHOVAH'"* (Matthew 23:39, ABPE). When the wall of blindness is overcome by God's precious and chosen Jewish people, the one who is to come will come. The most devout and highly learned Apostle Paul wrote: *"Satan, who is the god of this world, has blinded the minds of those who don't believe. They are unable to see the glorious light of the Good News. They don't understand the message about the glory of Christ, who is the exact likeness of God"* (2 Corinthians 4:4, NLT).

Unspooling the divine thread of the gospel, one can see a thread of continuity between the Jewish and Gentile narrative that is further illustrated by biblical design. On his deathbed, the biblical patriarch, Jacob, blessed his twelve sons, who were heads of the official twelve tribes of Israel. In particular, Jacob pronounced upon his son, Judah, a blessing above all the other sons when He announced the symbol of Judah's tribe as the lion, referring to Judah as a lion's cub (Genesis 49:9). Jesus bears the appellation of the "Lion of Judah" in the Book of Revelation by divine ordination. Judah means law, and Jesus is titled the Lion of Judah, and thus, by logical extension, I refer to Jesus as the "Lion of the Law." This labeling is important because of the association of Judah with the law; Judah not only means law, but also Judah is known as the lawgiver, for it is his tribe from which the law originated: *"Judah is my Lawgiver"* (Psalm 60:7, KJV). Connectively, Judah is also the tribal lineage from which Jesus genealogically descended, passing through forty-two generations posteriorly, including King David's. I find it a forceful symmetry that in Jewish tradition, a symbol of Judah's venerable lion decorates the *Torah*—the Law of God of the first five books of the Bible, the *Pentateuch* in traditional Christianity. Similarly, in the last book of the Gentile Bible, the book of Revelation, which details the eschatological second coming of Jesus, Yeshua is depicted as the Lion of Judah. In both traditions, thus, the lawgiver is celebrated. Importantly, in Revelation, just before His return, but after Yeshua is directly referenced as the Lion of Judah, He opens the sealed heavenly citizenry from every nation… and tribe! Isaiah 32:22 (OJB) says, "HaShem is our Lawgiver… He will save us."

In the sheerest of theological reveals, it is apparent from above that *Yeshua* came to perfect repair and maintenance between Adonai and humankind, but He also came for a third and fourth reason. The third reason is exemplified in what He was doing on the un-coveted cross. To sort it out in a different context, *Yeshua* was "shalom-ing" man as

His third goal. As pointed out, *Shalom* in the Jewish vernacular is a multitudinous word, and in one of its most fundamental applications, it is also a verb meaning to repair by putting a lost stone back in the wall. Excitedly, this definition gives a new visual dimension to the work of the cross. Jesus is the cornerstone of humankind's salvation, and it is His lively stones that embody His built church; so, in essence, the Savior was putting lost man—or His lost stones—back together again. Jesus undertook the cross for a fourth reason—to bring justice. *Shalom* also means the justice of God. Within the American legal system, an outside party who has a significant interest in a case may intervene in the case of another to influentially offer relevant information to the court regarding an action, and that party is legally recognized as *"Amicus Curiae,"* meaning friend of the court in Latin. Jesus was the friend who sought our justice and legally intervened with relevant salvific information on behalf of humankind; the model of significant interventionism for a friend was He, for Jesus self-proclaimed that friendship: *"No one shows greater love than when he lays down his life for his friends"* (John 15:13, ISV). God's Court took full note of Jesus' intervention! Yeshua's words were fitting because not only did he self-confer best friend status on Himself by dying for the entire world, making Himself "our" best friend. He also dubs humankind "His" best friend. Jesus' legal status of *Amicus Curiae* in God's Court on our behalf gave new meaning to the #"BFF!" *"No longer do I call you servant but here on out a friend."*[64] Having shown Himself to be *our* friend, should we do no less? Let's show that we are *His* friends: *"You are my friends if you do what I command…"* (John 15:14, NIV).

Joshua Goes to Court

"And the Ancient of Days took His seat; His Vesture was white like snow."

DANIEL 7:9 (NASB1995)

Many biblical scenes, when conflated, conjure up a succession of courtroom interactions like in the story of Job and in the story of Joshua. Looking closely, the unusual story of Joshua

> *God's redemption is told by the blood-dipped gavel!*

opens where Satan, the accuser, takes pleasure in accusing Joshua before the high bar of heaven. There, Joshua's is fitted in an unholy array, that of filthy and bloody clothes, which is a motif of sin. I propose that Jesus, shown here as the pre-incarnate Christ or Angel of the LORD, actually takes up Joshua's case before the High Court. This story knits together electrifying imagery of the future Christ who would disrobe Himself of His royalty so that He could re-clothe redeemed humanity in the finest of pure white robes. In the storyline, Joshua literally goes from "rags to riches" via an exchange of his bloody clothes. I envision the very compassionate move by Jesus as he nullifies Joshua's culpability of sin by literally giving him the clothes off His back; remember, it was Jesus' expensive robe that the Calvary Roman soldiers cast dice for. I believe Jesus gave up His robe that day as a prophetic reference to the fact that He would willingly disrobe again if it meant being able to re-clothe humankind with the holy raiment of righteousness, which symbolizes its salvific acquittal: *"You have a few names even in the church Sardis who have not defiled their garments; and they will walk with Me in white, for they are worthy. He who overcomes shall be clothed in white garments, and I will not blot out his name from the Book of Life"* (Revelation 3:4–5, NKJV). Jesus, or "Yahweh is salvation" in Hebrew, shares a root meaning with Joshua in Hebrew—"The LORD is salvation." At Calvary, Jesus exchanged His robe for the bloody array of sin which Joshua symbolized and, in doing so, God's salvation came to humankind. This biblical allegory is a moving scene that foretells God's angular plan of redemption, which is the judicial relief a believer receives unto salvation in the courtroom of God when God brings His *blood-dipped gavel down!*

The Joshua narrative is one of many narratives that represent the high point of the Gospel, and it does it by invoking the bare bones of the Gospel in a colorful way and by wrapping its head around this fact: *"Because when we are clothed, we will not be found naked"* (2 Corinthians 5:3, NIV). To be found naked is to be found without the glory of the living God inside of you, which clothes you from the inside out.

The Bodywork of the Gospel: A Legal Mechanic

"… After you have done everything to stand. Stand firm then…"

EPHESIANS 6:13-14 (NIV)

There are essential parts to the Gospel that make it legally "run." Let's look at an essential part under the "hood of the gospel." One such part is "legal standing." Litigants are not allowed to come before a court unless they have proper standing, and to have such, an individual must show that there has been a sufficient injury to his legal or constitutionally protected interest. The court uses this prerequisite of standing to determine if someone has enough cause to "stand" before the court to petition it because not just anyone gets to bring a lawsuit before a United States court for any conjured up reasons.[65] Similarly, God has prerequisites for standing in His Court, too. Spiritual, legal standing is the equivalent of having sufficient right standing with God, and that is what allows a believer to stand flat-footed, with shoulders back, before God's courtly throne. It is by God's politeness and grace—mixed with faith in Jesus' atoning blood—that the believer can walk and stand uprightly before Him. This doctrinal mix is known as "justification," and that person is "justified" in courageously coming before the court of God to inquire of God via his advocate, Jesus. In a real sense, no sinful man could have stood firm against God's Holy anger, so he could never have achieved legal standing on his own. To make it doubly plain, he could have never had any spiritual legs of legitimacy to stand on, but for the substitutionary work of Christ Jesus. God is a judicial God and within His judiciary, and just like in that of the United States, there must be lawful justification before receiving anything: *"And having called them, he gave them right standing with himself"* (Roman 8:30, NLT). What exactly is upright standing with God? Spying closer, I deem it as the redemptive status that one acquires after Jesus *stood* in the believer's place on Calvary's "skull hill." Because the damnable believer would not have been able to with*stand* the damning vengeance of God, Jesus took a *stand* for him on the slopes of Golgotha. His uprightness made us upright! *"…A God of faithfulness and without iniquity, just and upright is he"* (Deuteronomy 32:4, ESV). Receive this. To have standing as a believer is to be the blessed recipient of the ability to rightly stand before God's throne not once but twice, and not be consumed by his Holiness—once while a living earthly, petitioning resident, and a second time occurring after the believer's death at "The Judgment." God's plan of redemption *stood* before the foundations of the earth and will *stand* for all time.

Jesus' Posture, Shame, or Shameless Victory?

> *"I am not ashamed of the gospel of Jesus Christ, for it is the power of God unto salvation… Anyone who believes in him will never be put to shame."*
>
> ROMANS 1:6; ROMANS 10:11 (NIV)

An act of disgrace and infamy is what Satan wanted the headlines to read for successive millennia concerning Jesus' death on Mt. Calvary. Instead, Jesus' death on the slopes of Calvary came to be broadcasted as a lasting act of inarguable nobility and reputable love. Subjugated to die inhumanely, akin to "human trash," next to the town's dump with stagnant heaps of refuse, the un-robed Savior took His pitiable position. *"I hid not my face from shame and spitting"* (Isaiah 50:6, KJV). Consider this: A naked Adam hid himself from God, but on the cross, the naked second Adam hid Adam's sin in Himself. Where Adam couldn't, Jesus could: *"I heard the sound of you in the garden, and I was afraid because I was naked, so I hid myself"* (Genesis 3:10, ESV). That day, Jesus re-clothed humankind with attire that is invisible to the naked eye: *"So I advise you to buy gold from me, gold that has been purified by fire… Also buy white garments from me so you will not be ashamed by your nakedness, and ointment for your eyes so you will be able to see"* (Revelation 3:18, NLT). Adding to Satan's glee was the prospect that all eyes would be fixated on the humiliated Christ, but Satan and his horde of darkness failed to comprehend the nature of God's humility-based laws. While humiliation usually debilitates, it functions differently under the profundity of God's rule of law; there, humility exalts: *"Humble yourself before the Lord, and he will exalt you"* (James 4:10, KJV). It sounds oxymoronic to say that shamelessly Jesus assumed a posture of abject shame on the cross, but that is exactly what He did. The posture of His greater reward contradicted the posture of the penalty; it was shameless shame. The unthinkable had really been thought of by our visionary God. Within God's great scheme of salvation, this shameful degradation was really Christ's joyful, poised posture by which He would be lifted up, in His own words, "for all men to see" so that He could draw them all to Himself (John 12:32). Jesus was not only deliberately lifted up from the earth on the loathsome steeps of Calvary for perceived loss to the untrained eye, but God intentionally used it in such a gainful manner to draw the eye and the emotion toward Jesus unforgettably. *"I let them beat my back and pull out my beard. I didn't turn aside when they insulted me and spit in my face. But the Lord God keeps me from being disgraced. So I refuse to give up, because I know God will never let me down"* (Isaiah 50:6–7, CEV). I find it totally revealing that Jesus has a titular description as *"Jehovah Nissi,"* which means The Lord, my banner, or The Lord my flag of victory (See Exodus 17:15). Locked up within these two titles are two key details that pointed to Jesus' significant posture on the cross. In biblical times, a rod or a *shebet* in Hebrew was depicted as a wooden club-like pole. The Bible foretold this Messianic scene through the prophet Isaiah who prophesied that Jesus would be the "Root (or Rod) of Jesse" and would be a *"Banner for the peoples"* (Isaiah 11:10, NIV). Notice with me that Jesus died on two wooden poles that formed a cross which was perpendicular to the earth—or lifted up (*See* Galatians 3:13, NIV). What further intrigued me was that a banner of victory was usually a flag or cloth that had a degree of identifiable, vivid coloration. Notice that the Lamb of God wore a vivid, identifiable red crimson flag of blood about Him when He died that flagged His slain posture for eternity. The "Light of the World" postured Himself as a bright rod, dying on a pole, and wrapped in a luminous flag of blood for us!

More about Jesus' very specific, shameful posture on the cross. From a positional perspective, Jesus' hands were functionally handcuffed since to handcuff means to restrain or manacle a person's hands, usually with metal, in such a way as to render them ineffective, powerless, or defenseless.[66] Jesus's hands were confined to the cross by Roman-era, metal nails, leaving Him helplessly without the use of both His hands and arms and producing the same type of subservient and vulnerable position which handcuffs do. The Romans chose this posture-driven torture both for its gruesome nature as well as for its shameful configuration. It is beneficial to mull over that although Jesus is the Son of God, His dying on the cross was no "walk in the park." Importantly, Jesus didn't die just "reclining" in an upright position; He endured real suffering. The crucifixion was the vilest and vicious way of taking a life at that time. At first glance, one might think that all the negativity of the cross counterpoised its positivity, but not so! *Au Contraire*, God, in His magnificence, did not waste one minuscule aspect of the cruel posturing in the crucifixion. When Jesus held out His blood-ripped hand, God saw it not as hand-cuffed but hand-stuffed with our salvation. The two extended their hands toward one another when Jesus said, *"Into your hands do I commit my Spirit"* (Luke 23:46). It was a lordly communion, a hand-held ceremony of two Kings touching: *"For a brief moment I abandoned you, but with deep compassion I will bring you back. In a surge of anger I hid my face from you for a moment, but with everlasting kindness I will have compassion on you, says the* LORD *your redeemer"* (Isaiah 54:7–9, NIV).

The Shame Exchange: The Weight of Justice Meets the Nails of the Cross

"I turned my face to shame."

ISAIAH 50:6

A divine exchange took place on the cross. The shaft of shamefulness met the spike of mercy on the cross. There was nothing "soft serve" about the unprincipled vulnerability and nail-scarring castigation Jesus received; in fact, He redeemed us from every possible shameful shadow and shameful calculability of every kind, all because He endured the unjust shame of the worst kind: *"Fear not, for you will not be put to shame; And do not feel humiliated, for you will not be disgraced; but you will forget the shame of your youth…"* (Isaiah 54:4, NASB).

The Five Postures of Christ: Standing, Standing Ovation, Stooping, Sitting, Sleeping

Standing Still

A beggar who needed healing cried out to Jesus twice. The Bible gives us insight that it was his second cry which surmounted the opposition of the crowd, as it was louder and apparently more forceful than the first. At this cry, Jesus suddenly stood still. What was the motivation for Jesus' still posture there? The catalyst to stilling Jesus was the rush of the beggar's faith which contained a bullish force. The Greek translation of that section connotes aggression and turbulence with the word "faith," as does this verse: *"The kingdom of God suffers violence and the violent men take it by force"* (Matthew 11:12, AMP). Jesus perceived the rambunctiousness of the beggar's force of faith, and that level of faith caused Jesus to instantly stand still.

Standing Ovation

There are three distinct places in the Bible where the post-resurrected Jesus is standing in heaven, and one takes place during the death of the Apostle Stephen. In Acts 7:54-56 (NIV), Stephen is being stoned for his faith in Jesus. Just prior to his death, he gives a literally glowing testimony, for the text says his face shone like that of an angel as he spoke. The text continues, indicating the words of Stephen: "Look, he said, I see heaven open and the Son of Man standing at the right hand of God." I submit that Jesus was cheering for the virtuous martyrdom of Stephen by giving him a standing ovation; simply put, because Stephen stood up for Jesus, Jesus stood up for him! The other two dramatic sightings where the post-resurrected Christ is seen standing occur in the book of Revelation where Christ stands in the midst of seven candelabra, which represent the seven churches of Asia Minor, and where He stands to knock on the door of humankind's heart (See

Revelation 1:12; 3:20). Both observations conjure up the image of Christ Jesus' intense desire for involvement with His churches and with humanity's heart, but only upon invitation.

Stooping

As discussed earlier, I believe Jesus stooped down to be at eye level with the accused adulteress in order to show His compassion and to lend His support. To sum up His compassion, it was as if Jesus were saying, "I am only a stoop away."

Sitting

Jesus sat at the table with sinners often. This sedentary posture was head-scratching to the Pharisees, for they viewed Jesus negatively for inviting tax collectors and others whom they considered the dregs of society into His midst this way. Even Jesus' dinner host who invited Him to his home said to himself, *"if this man were really the Christ, he would know what type of woman it is who is sitting [with Him] at his feet"* (Luke 7:39). There, the text referred to a reputedly "loose" *woman*. Jesus sat with sinners and every type of man, woman, and menace to society for one simple reason—He loved them: *"I came to those who are lost and in need of a physician"* (Luke 5:31). I find it telling that Jesus sat with the same type of people who sat with Him at His birth—outcasts. Shepherds were considered veritable outsiders, the lowest of the societal lot, but were known to invest a lot of sitting with their sheep. Jesus, the *Veritas* of God, called Himself the "Good Shepherd" and was also called the "Son of David." Putting it all together, that translates to: The Good Shepherd, who was seen as the Son of a kingly shepherd (David), and who sat with His house of lost sheep. That sounds like a rightful posture to me.

Consider that when Jesus sent His Spirit back, Holy Spirit, He sat again on the Day of Pentecost, for the Bible records Jesus' fiery spirit *sat* on each of the disciples (See Acts 2:3).

Sleeping

It seems Jesus did not get very much sleep while on the earth. The Bible characterizes Him as very industrious. He was always working ministerially and traveling from one town to another. Jesus, Himself, said man must work intentionally because an hour was coming when that would no longer be possible (See John 9:4). The gospels report that He would get up early and then teach not only for hours but for days!—#logging man hours! Therein lay the message that Jesus was fully man and fully divine, and he was always conscious of His approaching divine hour to intersect with the cross. One day, however, He did sleep; it was on a boat, in the middle of a tempest. The tempestuous storm was so bad that some modern-day scientists categorize it as a probable hurricane. Jesus slept through it until He was awakened by a ruffled Peter who went into a tirade about Jesus not caring for Peter's imperiled life. Jesus' relaxed actions were not those of an apathetic master who casually ignored His disciples; rather, Jesus' posture reflected a master who was spiritually at rest and a man who was perhaps fatigued, given His hearty schedule. The coexistence of the nature of the lofty Messiah with the lowly man's nature was constantly elusive to the comprehension of the twelve who studied Him. The disciples would finally learn that Jesus' posture was not one of cavalier evasion but was evocative of a mysterious combination of both powerful readiness and divine repose. Put another way, Jesus knew how to rest in His might.

The Gatekeeper

Jesus' seated posture found Him seated in some interesting circles, but none more interesting than at the right hand of God's throne; it is a visual mainstay of triumphant authority. The Bible attests to the fact that the believer has assumed a similar posture as one seated with Jesus in His heavenly quarters (See Ephesians 2:6). God intended the believer to do something with this posture, to walk in audacity because she is an authoritative victor and, therefore, is not to be stymied by victimization. Scripture says that the gates of hell are not able to prevail against God's believers (Matthew 16:18). Why not? Significantly, because there is a greater gate than the gates of hell, and that ancient gate is Jesus, Himself! *"I am the gate. If anyone enters through me, he will be saved"* (John 10:9, BSB). Jesus' believers who are strongly situated as He is, are spiritually brawny, "lifted" mini gates, and are gates which should also "lift up" praise. Scripture further says, *"Lift up your heads, oh Gates! Be lifted up, oh gates of eternity, that the King of glory may enter!"* (Psalm 24:9, ABPE). That Scripture is notedly written in the imperative mood—as a command—and projects the following, gratifying image. Envision Jesus with me: The great exemplar of victory is returning through the eternal gates of heaven after having conquered sin and death through the cross and is commanding those gates to lift up their heads, that is to enlarge themselves with a posture of bulging praise because they are to be gaits of exultant praise that welcome a victorious member of the holy triarchy back to heaven to reclaim His glory. Indeed, anyone and anything, even a gate that experiences Jesus' presence, is commanded to assume the posture of thanksgiving, which is the substructure of praise: *"Enter into his gates with thanksgiving…"* (Psalm 100:4, KJV). So, too, should the believer assume that posture of triumphant praise: *"In everything, give thanks; for this is the will of God in Christ Jesus concerning you"* (1 Thessalonians 5:18, ESV).

Operation Invention & God's Legal Trademark of the Church

"And do not bring sorrow to God's Holy Spirit by the way you live. Remember, He has identified you as His own..."

EPHESIANS 4:30 (NLT)

God is devoid of any limitations, and He is full of the capacity for creative extension. His nature of divine creativity was seen in the genesis of the world. God created both the legal system in which He operates, as well as the human beings who are managed by it. As such, He has all direct, indirect, and discretionary rights to His creation, including those known in the American legal system as patent and trademark rights. Starting with the patent right, it is a form of "intellectual property" right that is granted by the United States federal government and gives its owner—the inventor—a legal right to exclude others from making, using or selling its invention, generally for a limited period of twenty years.[67] Because God is an "intelligent designer," and I also submit an intellectual deviser, humankind is His intellectual property: *"So God created human beings in his own image... then God looked over all he had made, and he saw that it was very good!..."* (Genesis 1:27, 31; NLT). For our purposes, pay close attention to the following phrase: "If the [invented] device or process is novel, useful and nonobvious."[68] That conditional phrase must be met in order to receive the patent protection. God was a few eternal steps ahead of the government because the process by which He articulated His own intellectual property met this condition. His creative process was certainly novel because no one had ever "invented" a human species before, nor had it been done via the novel process of taking a mold from the earth's dirt, blowing life into its masculine core, and finishing it with a feminine reconstituted rib as an encore. Even by today's standards, when God miraculously fashions a baby in the lifeless womb, it is novelly and wonderfully made; in fact, whenever God designs life, it is a novelty to behold. *"This is what the Sovereign Lord says to these bones... I will put breath in you, and you will come to life"* (Ezekiel 37:5, NIV). I assert that His process of the inventiveness of humankind is certainly useful in that it allows humankind to function on a very high level on the earth. Finally, I would say God's process of design is definitely nonobvious, meaning it is ascertainably different than anything preceding it because obviously, no process of creation of humankind has preceded His: *"Nothing was made that was not made by Him"* (John 1:3, NKJV). Not even Satan has the power to create, for he can only emulate, counterfeit, or distort God's creative process at times. The God of wisdom had the idea of invention first but graciously shared that propensity with us through His imparted wisdom and knowledge: *"I, wisdom, dwell with prudence and find out knowledge of witty inventions"* (Proverbs 8:12, KJV).

"Trademarks may consist of virtually any form of sign, including letters and words, designs, colors, shapes, sounds and scents."[69] A trademark identifies or sets apart one's services from that of another once it is registered. In simple terms, it acts like an intellectual signature that is recognized in commerce or trade. In an awesome way, God uses a trademark vis-a-vis His Christians who are in His recognizable service of fulfilling His Great Commission to witness to souls everywhere (See Matthew 28:18–20). I've observed that God has both a visible and an invisible trademark that identifies that He is the source of that service. The visible symbol is the cross, and the invisible symbol is the blood of the Lamb of God. The visible cross continues to be the distinguishable bedrock symbol of Christianity. It literally led to both a "trade" and a "mark." God asked Jesus to be struck in our place: *"Surely he took up our pain and bore our suffering, yet we considered him punished by God, stricken by him, and afflicted"* (Isaiah 53:4, NIV). Jesus *traded* places with humankind on a rugged cross and was permanently *marked* by a corpus of wounded flesh, under which lay a mercy seat invented out of crossed beams. Similarly, the blood of Christ Jesus has distinguished God as the blood-covenant God of Christians everywhere. So, God has marked His believers with that blood, putting the world and the underworld on notice that His body of believers is hermetically sealed with that blood for His service. *"God has made us what we are, and in our union with Christ Jesus he has created us for a life of good deeds, which he has already prepared for us to do"* (Ephesians 2:10, GNT). In other words, God gets to legally determine our trade use—or how He wants to use us in the kingdom—and with what regularity He uses us within His spiritual kingdom of commerce.

CHAPTER 9

God, Justice, Bloody Murder, and Double Jeopardy

"Learn to do right; seek justice. Defend the oppressed. Take up the cause for the fatherless; plead the case of the widow."

ISAIAH 1:17 (NIV)

"He has told you, O man, what is good; and what does the Lord require of you but to do justice, and to love kindness, and to walk humbly with your God."

MICAH 6:8 (ESV)

Loving Justice, Doing Justice, Appreciating Justice

"The way of peace they do not know; there is no justice in their path... Truth is nowhere to be found, and whoever shuns evil becomes a prey. The LORD *looked and was displeased that there was no justice."*

ISAIAH 59:8,15 (NIV)

Most people have seen the scales of justice illustrated with the "see-saw effect;" somehow, it appears even-keeled if justice is balanced and appears warped if justice is out of balance. God's scales of justice, however, are always balanced because God—the source of justice—is unceasingly moving justice towards us through the pages of the Bible, or alternatively, it is us that He is constantly moving towards justice through those same pages of the Bible. From this perspective, I like to express it this way, *justice is as justice does*. It stands to reason that seeking justice is not simply pursuing injustice; neither is it to engage in a type of active passivism, but seeking justice lends itself to actively eradicating injustice. The course of action cannot be inaction. Jesus bolted out of the egress of glory, crying out against conventions of injustice. He modeled the active pursuit of justice throughout His earthly ministry. Jesus did not live in the grey zone. Importantly, Jesus did not just shun what was wrong; He actually instituted what was right and good. As pointed out earlier, He went about doing good (Acts 10:38); that means Jesus was a proactive law changer. He always differentiated between God's good law and man's broken law.

The Legal Equitableness, Equality & Equableness of God

"He thought it not robbery to be equal with God."

PHILIPPIANS 2:6 (KJV)

The legal concept of equity must sometimes go beyond the *perceived* law to be accomplished. For example, in Family Law, sometimes a court will order a division and distribution of property to spousal parties that may not be equal in percentage—not reflecting a "50/50" outcome on paper—but from the court's computational perspective, is considered equitable or fair to each of them. The point here is that what may not always look fair can be fair. In that same light, as a young adult, looking at the *"Not robbery to be equal with God"* phraseology seemed unfair regarding Jesus. The fact that Jesus could somehow be "robbed" of His riches but not count it as robbery seemed unjust. I've since come to understand the equanimity of the Godhead and also have a revelation of the depth, fairness, and wealth of the phrase. God, in His unprescribed, discretionary judicial sovereignty and modes of judicial rectitude, is always fair. It was *not* a stolen notion for Jesus to view Himself as God's equal, nor was it a fraudulent concept for Him to think of Himself as equal with God because He was, in fact, God. Jesus, therefore knew they were equals, and notwithstanding this equality, He *chose* to lower Himself by divesting Himself of His colossal, super-rich, and ageless glory to arrive on earth as an uncomely man: *"…He had no beauty or majesty to attract us to him…"* (Isaiah 53:2, NIV). Jesus never thought it was thievish for Father, God to call for His divestiture, nor did He regard it as He having experienced theft in the way that He freely departed heaven. God is both equitable and equable in His nature; that is to say, He is both fair (equitable), and He is unchanging (equable) in His character. Psalm 145:17 voices that God is just in all His ways, and the fact that there is no shadow of turning with Him is recorded in James 1:17. I've learned that God is prodigiously just! What these combined verses are saying, as a practical matter, is that God's believers do not serve a "two-faced" God.

The equality of God is biblically shown as the concept of treating those parties the same that are equally situated, which is in large part, the American reach of legal equality: *"Then Peter began to speak: 'I now realize how true it is that God does not show favoritism"* (Acts 10:34, NIV).

It is, however, essential to note that God's equality is different from His favor; although God does not show unfair favoritism, He does show select favor. God's kingdom favor doesn't always look fair in that it can favor His people above those that are not kingdom dwellers: *"The LORD will make you the head, not the tail"* (Deuteronomy 28:13, NIV). Having made that distinction, I view God's equality as thus: We are all equals legally, and, legally equal to all the parts of God. For example, the Bible says that we are the righteousness of God, which is to say, in Christ, we are equal to that part of God's righteousness because He has legally bestowed it upon us through Jesus. We will never be the divine God or wholly God, but we can be the legal

> *We can never be fully God, but we can be full of God.*

whole of all that is God. We can never be fully God, but we can be full of God. *In toto*, we can be like God, in all of His godliness, for He created us in His image and we bear His encoded, "double helix" of authority: *"Jesus answered them, 'Is it not written in your law, I said, you are gods. If he called them gods, to whom the word of God came—and the scriptures cannot be broken…"* (John 10:34-35, ESV). All that is legally His, Jesus legally recovered it for us. Jesus got humankind's authoritative property rights to spiritual intangibles and earthly land back and all of the legal rights, perks, and privileges that come with them. In real estate law, all this out flowing bounty of attached rights is known as the "bundle of rights," and they legally transfer with the land, as well as with intangible property like stocks which I equate here with spiritual investments: *"The earth is the Lord's and the fullness thereof"* (Psalm 24:1, ESV). We now retain all that legal access which Jesus returned to us by virtue of the enabling equality contained in His act of redemption.

Double Jeopardy and Other Constitutional Violations

The Double Jeopardy Clause in the Fifth Amendment to the US Constitution prohibits anyone from being prosecuted twice for substantially the same crime. The relevant part of the Fifth Amendment states: "No person shall …be subject for the same offense to be twice put in jeopardy of life or limb…"[70] More simply, a person can not be subject to double prosecution and to double punishment for basically the same committed crime. Jesus is tried multiple times for the same offense, so I submit His Fifth Amendment rights were violated per our American Constitution and per Israeli law, too: "An individual may not be punished on the basis of self-incriminatory statements… from *Talmudic* times to present, there is universal agreement among sources and authorities in Jewish law accepting a general rule precluding punitive confessions."[71] Ancient Israel's *Talmudic* law, which controlled, among other things, legal criminal procedure, disallowed the retrying of Jesus' case once He had been condemned, but that is exactly what happened. After being condemned unanimously by the Sanhedrin Council, Jesus was still tossed back and forth from trial to trial, enduring them illegally. Jesus should have never been tried over and over again, especially, because the trials of Judge Caiphas and the SanHedrin, as well as that of Judge Herod and Judge Ananias, were all held under Jewish domain. Arguably, Pilate's trial may not have been violative from that angle of Double Jeopardy because He represented a separate, sovereign Roman State; nevertheless, it was violative on other grounds of the Fifth Amendment. Another main reason for the establishment of the Double Jeopardy protection is so that defendants are not forcibly harassed repeatedly under the unwanted glare of a trial's flickering spotlight. Jesus suffered that very harassment as He was repeatedly struck and derided by the guards and participants of each court where He was tried.[72] A second tier of Double Jeopardy protection is against self-incrimination. I assert that when Jesus was repeatedly and confrontationally asked to self-admit on the witness stand regarding the alleged charge of blasphemy, He was intentionally being goaded into self-incrimination, which is prohibited by our constitutional Fifth Amendment. Ancient Israel had a similar law on its books. Under American constitutional law, no defendant can be made to testify against himself; that means every defendant has the irrevocable right *not to* self-admit or self-incriminate. Correspondingly, self-incrimination was also prohibited under the ancient *Talmudic* Law in Jesus' time: "No man can render himself guilty."[73] Importantly, Jesus did give an express incriminating admission of His identity within the SanHedrin trial, which proved to be incriminating on the charge of blasphemy. As noted earlier, Jesus affirmed His identity by inference only—by inferential admission—in the Pilate trial. Putting the barbed interrogation of Annas to the side since it is doubtful that it arose to the level of a trial—as aforementioned also—specifically, the excessive inquisitorial nature of Caiphas and Herod, and the relentless "inquisition" of Pilate before which Jesus appeared numerous times no less than four times were powder kegs of harassment and provocation that were meant to provoke Jesus into incriminating Himself. I submit that any incriminating admissions that were ascertained were in violation of both American and Jewish Double Jeopardy protection. Although the opposition was elated beyond words, to get the "lid-closer" admission to their trials, Jesus by His own cognitive power tossed them that bone of admission: "For dogs have compassed me: the assembly of the wicked have inclosed me: they pierced my hands and feet." *"Beware of dogs. Beware of evil workers…"* (Psalms 22:16, Philippians 3:2; KJV). It may have been their end game, but it was not Jesus' end-all. It may have "looked" like He was putting a staple in His own culpability, but… He had a plan: "For who hath known the mind of God? or who has been His counselor at law."

Jesus was the perfect Son of God and the second Adam; therefore, He was the perfect sacrificial substitute for the atonement of the first Adam. Because He met the legal bar of perfect substitutionary atonement by dying a legally perfect and ordained death, He perfectly absorbed the first Adam's death penalty. No longer guilty, so no longer condemned, humankind in Christ is, therefore, perfectly acquitted in the legal sense and cannot be tried twice for the same crime. No double jeopardy! God echoed this mainstay of Double Jeopardy in Christ's trial, too. In His word, He touted: *"…Christ was offered once to bear the sins of many…"* (Hebrews 9:28, BSB). God's Court was in session during the crucifixion. Jesus was tried on the cross, and resultantly, the trial was finished forever in heaven's court. All of the devil's counter operatives' missions to humankind's victory at the cross failed. God has done everything within the legal makeup and the just legalities of His own law, which are supremely fair and just, to acquit humankind of its sin which bred its jeopardy. The Godhead put together an ironclad divine case for redemption, and so the heavenly court has adjourned forever on that measure.

God, Murder & Blood

"For the joy that lay before him, he endured the cross."

HEBREWS 12:2 (CSB)

Every murder in the Bible is significant to God because of the outlawry of *Ad Hominem* killing in the Ten Commandments. All murder is an abomination to God, but I believe there are two killings in particular that should command our attention because God, Himself, was very vocal about the way in which it came to His attention. The killing of Jesus and the killing of Abel. In both scenarios, the blood was allowed to actually and audibly *speak* on behalf of the deceased. As such, it was given evidentiary preference in God's Court of law. In our American court of law, that blood-statement could be called a "dying declaration" under the Federal Rules of Evidence and, as such, could be exceptionally admissible in a court of law because of its highly probative value and exploratory force in proving the cause or circumstances of death in a criminal trial.[74] Of course, the vocalized statement usually originates from a person rather than the person's blood, but, therein, lies the awesomeness of God's miraculousness! Although what seemed left of Abel was a lifeless corpse, spiritual life—the essence of true life—still existed in the blood: *"For life of the body is in its blood"* (Leviticus 17:11,

NLT). As said, the value of this evidentiary declaration is its use to establish and prove the cause of death or the ambient circumstances around the death. That voiced declaration in Able's case established the identity of the person who caused the death- his brother: *"And the LORD said, 'What have you done? The voice of your brother's blood is crying to me from the ground"* (Genesis 4:10, ESV). I propose that since both Abel's and Jesus' blood fell into the ground's cavity, Abel's blood spilled into the earth while dying and dying Jesus's blood also streamed into the earth while being lowered into the earth's bowels, both bloods emanated the same enabling spiritual animus which audibly reached the Father's ears in His Court: *"And to Jesus… and to the blood of sprinkling, that speaketh better things than that of Abel"* (Hebrews 12:24, KJV). Jesus' blood similarly cried out, and its declaration also established the circumstances surrounding His death: *"On the altar to purify you, making you right with the LORD. It is the blood, given in exchange for a life, that makes purification possible"* (Leviticus 17:11, NLT). Jesus' and Abel's blood talked, and the details were critical. Evidence from the speaker, or here the speaker's blood, was admissible testimony in God's Court. In both instances, innocent blood was shed, and the cry, therefore, would be one for vengeance before God, the righteous Judge. We see this notion exemplified again in Scripture where martyred, bloody souls cry out to be avenged after their innocent blood was shed: *"They cried out with a loud voice, 'O Sovereign Lord, holy and true, how long before you will judge and avenge our blood on those who dwell on the earth'"* (Revelation 6:10, NLT). It is interesting that the right of blood vengeance—"consanguinity"—is first found in the Old Testament under "Blood Redemption Rights" and is the concept that one has the right to avenge or to kill those who have killed a relative. Incorporating this right would, thus, explain Abel's blood cry for vengeance, and further explain that the cry is made directly to God since, spiritually, Abel would have been related to God, and as Scripture declares that Adam was the spiritual "son of God;" that would theoretically make Abel His spiritual grandson. I believe that God's revenge—or war—against sin was peace. When God wanted to raid enmity on earth, He did not send a battalion of soldiers; He sent a babe of peace. Peace exceeds the punishment of judgment alone, which is the vengeance that Abel's brother received. As punishment, he was exiled from the peaceable communion of God. Jesus' blood cried out for "better things," the Bible says, and I believe it was for peace. Both Jesus and Abel were shepherds, one was the shepherd of a flock only, but the other was The Shepherd of Peace. Both offered sacrifices that were accepted by God. Both had their blood spilled; consider the fact that Jesus' blood was spilling on the ground even at the moment He was being murdered, but I believe His blood spoke what He spoke: *"…Forgive them, Father! They don't know what they are doing"* (Luke 23:24, GNT). It was a cry for peace! God took judicial note of Jesus' blood declaration: *"For this is my blood, which confirms the covenant between God and his people. It is poured as a sacrifice to forgive the sins of many"* (Matthew 26:28, NLT). Jesus' cry was a declaration of peace, announcing His government's position: the state of war had ended. When Jesus bore the cross on His seemingly languishing, feeble shoulders up the "Via Dolorosa," in the Spirit realm, He had, in fact, hoisted the government of God on His broad, able shoulders, exuberantly crying, *"Peace be to you!"* (John 20:21, NASB).

> *Pleading the blood of Jesus is submitting a legal pleading!*

What follows is a legal bonanza for the believer! The Bible says Jesus' blood ever speaks, so when a believer pleads His blood, he is speaking what I have coined as "blood-ese." To explain, "Legalese" is the specialized language known within the legal profession and in its courts, and "blood-ese," I propose, is known in God's Court of law and lets Jesus' blood speak for you. To expound, pleading the blood is to assert its spiritual properties as a legal pleading. A legal pleading is a written, formal argument that is submitted to the court, which contains the claims, defenses, allegations, and denials that one is asserting or answering; basically, it is your legal case. It is exhilarating to realize that "pleading the blood of Jesus" is tantamount to a believer submitting a legal pleading—formally asking God's court for something which is predicated on a legal assertion that he has a right to—by virtue of Jesus' atoning blood. In short, they are his blood rights! In law, a pleader is the term given to the party—or person—asserting his pleading, and importantly, a pleader may also be another person who is pleading on behalf of another; thus, Jesus as our "forever intercessor" may plead His blood on our behalf! *"I love your law. Plead my cause"* (Psalm 120:1, ESV). The literal Latin meaning of the word intercessor is " go between," making Jesus the one who *goes* before the high Court of God, *between* the judgment of God and the believer, and enters our pleas, one of which is innocence. A plea of guilt or innocence can be spoken before a court of law. What is crucial is the understanding that once a pleading—verbal or written—is correctly and procedurally submitted to a court, it is in demand of a response. The court must engage. In 2 Corinthians 10:5, the Bible admonishes a believer to cast down vain thoughts and imaginations or what amounts to legally empty arguments, but we are encouraged to do the opposite in God's Court by lifting up legally effective arguments boldly before His throne of judgment: *"The LORD has heard my pleading, The LORD receives my prayer"* (Psalm 6:9–10, NASB).

An extraordinary question must be explored. How was it that God Almighty could be killed in the first place? *"Jesus began to explain to his disciples that he must go to Jerusalem and suffer many things at the hands of the elders, the chief priests and the teachers of the law, and that he must be killed and on the third day be raised to life"* (Matthew 16:21, NIV). Jesus was the summation of the law, so really, the purveyors of the law could not destroy Jesus because the creation could not destroy its creator; it is *out-matched*. The plotters of His death could no more successfully defeat Him by their falsified claims of His breaking laws, any more than evil could extinguish evil because Jesus was *unmatched*. The legalists and distortionists of Jesus' divinely created law were powerless to destroy Him because they were *under-matched*. His killing was unimaginable, or certainly one might argue His *murder* was unimaginable; murder is defined as the unlawful taking of a life that is thought out beforehand with an intent to kill or to harm the body very seriously (with malice aforethought). Murderous, it was, because God-the-Son was not really put to death lawfully, and Jesus' trial and His linked sentencing did not conform to the legalities of the day: "Every Sanhedrin that executes twice is called a murderous court."[75]

He illegally experienced great bodily harm and subsequent death as the penalty for "breaking" the Jewish law, although He broke no law, and it was premeditatively welcomed by the Jewish leaders. Beforehand, they surely wanted Him executed by exceedingly harmful, body-cruel, romanesque style, which Isaiah had prophesied over three-thousand years before (See Isaiah 53). The net result is this—God was executed. Man executed God—how does *that* happen? The answer lies in Jesus' mouth. On His way to be handed over to His executioners, God-the-Son uttered seven words: *"Hereafter, I will not talk much with you"* (John 14:30, KJV). God incarnate, the Prince of Breath, the Author of Life, could only be killed by restricting life-splashing words from pouring from His mouth. The one who proclaimed He was the *Life*, *Way*, and Truth, and who staunchly declared He was the resurrection and the *life*, *had* to be silent (*See* John 11:25).

"I am the resurrection and the life." After all, in the pages of Genesis, He self-demonstrates that He is the life-giving person of the Godhead when He is released as fragments of life called words from the Father's mouth. In Apostle John's book, He is seen as the *Word* from the very beginning. When Jesus spoke, He took more than vocabularic license; He took creative license for the verbally miraculous. If therefore, Jesus had not harnessed His words, death could not have come anywhere near *life*. This actuality is borne out in the gospel when His captors attempted to take Him by force. The Jewish guards asked if He were Jesus, and He replied, *"I am"* (John 18:5, NIV). When Jesus unstrapped His words, His weakling captors were thrown to the ground like rag dolls. Jesus literally had to "stop speaking much" just to give the guards a chance to arrest him. We see this limited speech again on the cross. Jesus speaks very little on the cross; in fact, only seven sentences throughout His six-hour ordeal. Regardless of the excruciating pain He suffered on the cross, Jesus decidedly *yielded* to the heinous death because He only needed to eject two words to be freed from death. Whether *"I AM"* or two other words He used earlier with Lazarus, "come forth," they would have been two words too much; so Jesus, showing a restrained ferocity, purposely parsed His words in order to accommodate death, indeed to succumb to death: *"For the joy that was set before Him, He endured the cross"* (Hebrews 12:2, ESV). The Resurrection and The Life, the one who could call Himself forward from the tomb on Friday evening in an eyelash-closing second after His expired body hit the grave, but remained patiently entombed, had the capacity to keep Himself on the cross to pacify death. The Bible teaches that the power of life and death is in the tongue (See Proverbs 18:21). Well, Jesus proved it monumentally as God in flesh, and mostly silent; for if the bespectacled God on timber had spoken more than He did, if the cross-ridden Jesus had uttered a smidgen of His life-dancing thoughts with His typical open-ended zest, it would have been impossible for Him to die!

Jesus Takes the Witness Stand!: The Mistrial that Never Was Declared

"The world cannot hate you; but hateth me, because I testify of it, that the works thereof are evil."

JOHN 7:7 (KJV)

Jesus never received a fair trial, and His trial should have been declared a mistrial, as previously mentioned. If Jesus had received a fair trial, perhaps His trial may have proceeded a little bit like this: Jesus takes the witness stand. Defense's Direct Examination is conducted by co-counsel Gamaliel, a sage and jurist of the Sanhedrin tribunal, and Nicodemus, a recent convert and prominent member of the San-Hedrin tribunal. Prosecution's Cross Examination is conducted by an orthodox, pharisaic Senior Member of the Sanhedrin. A Newly Elevated Sanhedrin Tribunal Judge is Presiding.

> Prosecution: Do you swear to tell the truth, the whole truth, and nothing but the truth? (*Laughter in the courtroom*).
>
> Judge: Order in the Court! (*Judge is gesturing with gavel*).
>
> Jesus: In other words, do I promise to talk about myself, tell everything about myself, and talk only about myself and nothing else? (*Laughter in the courtroom*).
>
> Judge: Order in the Court! If there are any more such outbursts, I will have this court cleared!
>
> Prosecution: Objection, your Honor, the witness is mocking the jurisdiction of the court to evince sworn testimony.
>
> Defense: May it please the court, your Honor. May I have a moment with my client? I'm sure He will abide by

this most distinguished and revered court's requirements *(Counsel quickly confers with Jesus).*

Jesus: On my oath, I promise to tell the truth, all of the truth, and only the truth—*Of course* (Jesus is seen peacefully smiling).

Defense: Who are you?

Jesus: I am the Son of God.

Defense: Where does God live?

Jesus: In the seventh heaven. It is a place that is anchored by God's throne and is lined with exquisite compounds of majestic mansions.

Prosecution: Objection! That is a statement of opinion. Moreover, the defendant is not credentialed by our traditional rabbinic establishment. He has abnormally and uniquely obtained His theological proclivities and awareness from an outside source which is foreign to us and, therefore, can not seek to provide expert testimony to this tribunal nor lecture this exalted body on affairs and descriptions that not even we can learnedly attest to.

Defense: I withdraw the question, your Honor.

Defense: Why are you on earth and not in heaven if you are the Son of God?

Jesus: I am here under direct orders to save humankind from the hellish fallout of their morbid fall and to salvage their bleak and dismal relationship with the Father because it's been smashed to smithereens!

Defense: What did you do after you first became aware of the fall of humankind?

Jesus: I carried out the Father's remedial plan of redemption.

Defense: Did you do it right away?

Jesus: Yes and no.

Prosecution: Objection! Your Honor, please instruct the witness to answer the question definitively, yes or no!

Defense: Your Honor, this is not an insular witness, but an eyewitness who has a vast wealth of information and is answering the question, and if allowed to finish, will share information that has a great probative bearing on this case.

Judge: Overruled. I would like to hear what the witness has to say. You may continue.

Defense: Jesus, tell the court in your own words what happened.

Jesus: I carried out the plan of redemption immediately, before the fall of humankind ever occurred, but waited to manifest it later. You see, in heaven where I come from, there is no time, so there is no classification of right away. The only moment that time is relevant is when I step into time on the earth because that is a human measurement. It became necessary for me to step into this *chrono*s labeling of definite time because of humanity's spiritual hardship. To explain, through one man's primordial act of negligence in supervision, mixed with inattentiveness to his bride, followed by a lack of willful disobedience to the Father's instructions, primordial native humankind handed over his bale of spiritual and natural authority to a winding, masquerading, bedeviled serpent. Seeing that great dereliction of faith, at that very hour, the Father initiated "Operation Redemption," which had already been set in place before the earth's formation for this very act of pre-known sin. The Father stilled time, and I stepped into this *kairos* moment of graced time to fix man and his morass, to correct what would become a pandemic blunder.

Defense: How did the Father know that this plan would be needed?

Jesus: Human beings become perplexed, but there are no enigmas in heaven because the Father foresees and knows all things, including the peccable, illegal attack which the Devil-agitator attempted to plot against His throne; but the Father foiled that wicked, monopolistic plan. The Father also knew that the Devil, having lost his positional favor, would then turn his focus to plot the overthrow of his successor of favor in the earth—the Father's beloved humankind.

Prosecution: I object! I sorely object! The defendant is rambling and not making any sense. How could a human being be the successor of an angelic being? Also, this testimony is irrelevant to the heart of this case because the demonic is not on trial here. Jesus is. Your honor, I ask that the aforesaid testimony be stricken from the record.

Judge: Overruled. But counsel, direct your witness to stay within the line of questioning which you have posed. You may proceed.

Defense: Thank you, your Honor. Now, tell the court in your own words what divine history you witnessed regarding the Father's plan?

Jesus: Part of the Father's plan was that I enlighten man as well as this myopic body. Truly, Adam was the Devil's successor in every way before both of their falls. Lucifer, that was his pre-fall name, was Adam's predecessor to God's favor. He bore the light of God through rays of splendor and was called "son of the morning." His body shone with the light of day. Even his name meant light. His intricate, symphonic body was fabricated to worship God. In a matched manner, Adam was God's later fabrication and was royally clothed in God's glorious blades of light. He could let his light shine and was an appointed child of the dawn because God set up a standing appointment to personally commune with him daily in the cool of every dawning day. He, similarly, was fashioned for God's praise and worshipful noise of joy. Adam, like the devil, was initially immortal, having been created to live forever with his God. Up to his old trickery, the devil managed to usurp Adams' authority by appealing to Adams' wife and beguiling her to tempt her husband to disobey God. In doing so, Adam, thereby, gave away his place and authority of rule over the earth, all of its riches, and all of His legal protections. As a result, the earth became sick, as did man's body and soul. It was a sickness unto spiritual death. Man had been subverted and was now a spiritually dying, miserable, and defenseless rogue.

Prosecution: So continuing this fascinating anecdote of yours, if the demonic *were* represented here in this court, might his tale go something like this? "Man yielded the members of his body to me in so far as he did my bidding in the Garden of Eden. He used his body's limbs to fetch the fruit and to partake of it, which gives me the right to forever invade it and make it sick." Something like that… I imagine?

Jesus: No! The Devil will no longer have that right (Jesus now looking directly at the Judge with a piercing stare). Your Honor, not very long from now, I will choose to sacrifice my body for his body. I will give my outstretched limbs on a tree for his sinning limbs around a tree. I will aimfully pay the cost of his aimless, rash actions. I will ransom my body for his! My body was riddled with thirty-nine wounds a little while ago so that his healing would never be a riddle, but a clear atoned for right! (Jesus wincing as He leans back on the witness stand).

Defense: Is this sin, sickness, and death that you speak of all a part of the foreseen fall that you alluded to earlier as part of your divine mission, and does that fall make your being here of the absolute, utmost urgency?

Prosecution: Objection! Counsel is leading the witness!

Judge: Sustained. Counsel will refrain from leading the witness.

Defense: I will rephrase the question, your Honor. Jesus, why does what you've described to the court involve your being here on the earth?

Jesus: My imminent appearance was crucial. Emergent care was critical. Upon entering the earth's *orbit,* my entryway became the doorway to humankind regaining dominance over sin that was endemic to the first Adam and which eventually contaminated the whole world. If I could be blunt, Adam made a mess. I left heaven to fix his mess.

Defense: Could you fix this mess if you were not the Son of God?

Jesus: No. No one could fix this dire mess without divinity and exactitude. No one but the Son of God… I am.

Prosecution: Objection, your Honor! This is preposterous! The witness is adding personal pronouns to his testimony!

Judge: Sustained. Counsel, you have been warned to direct the witness to stay on course. Proceed.

Defense: Yes, your Honor. I have only one final question. How do you propose to fix that mess?

Jesus: I will hand over my temple and die for everyone, including you, and even the prosecution who has been but an unwitting pawn in the devil's great scheme of his soulish demise.

Prosecution: OBJECTION! OBJECTION! OBJECTION, YOUR HONOR! I DEMAND A RULING ON MY OBJECTION! OBJECTION!

In a wonder, Jesus cured the blunder! *"You pore over the Scriptures because you presume that by them you possess eternal life. These are the very words that testify about Me"* (John 5:39, BSB).

CHAPTER 10

Legally Perfect: The Power of One, The Fire of Two

> *"Nor did he enter heaven to offer himself again and again, the way the high priest enters the Most Holy Place every year with blood that is not his own… but he has appeared once for all…"*
>
> HEBREWS 9:25–26 (NIV)

To be sure, the realism of the cross is that there was certainly only one atonement on high where Jesus entered into the heavenly Holy of the Holies and delivered His atoning blood sacrifice. I propose in tandem that before He reached heaven at the appointed time with the appointed sacrifice, He had an appointment on earth with God at the tomb. The tomb and the cross resulted in two fiery consumptions. *"Thy will be done on earth as it is in heaven"* (Matthew 6:10, NKJV).

What gave God legal access to consume Jesus' sacrifice there on the cross? What gave God legal entry into Jesus' tomb to raise Him from the dead? What happened on the cross? What happened in the tomb? The basic response is, God was there. Yes! What, however, is the legal frame of reference for God being at both of those places since God does everything legally perfect and perfectly legal? As shown above, the covenant provided the legal basis for the atonement. It, additionally, was legally perfect because God's plan and action hinged on details that were both perfectly set in motion and that had been perfectly blue-printed many millennia before. To answer the above,

I submit that the cross was really a high-powered, God-ordained altar, so God had legal access to retrieve His sacrifice. Consider that wood was present, the divine Lamb lay slain, so the incumbent shedding of blood was present also, and very essential, two men were present on each side of Jesus. Note that this exact altar configuration was seen in the foreshadowing of Jesus' crucifixion when Abraham attempted to sacrifice Isaac, and there too, Abraham's sacrifice was consumed. Recall that Abraham had set out with Isaac, who represented the sacrifice, with wood in tow and with two male servants beside him. This scenario mimics the precision of Jesus' atonement on the cross; Jesus' death on the unsympathetic cross caused a full-blown emission of both the consuming wrath and the exalted power of God as evidenced by earth's rumbling groan and ambient darkness when the Light of the World died. The preliminary tumult of His death was followed by the triumphant splitting of the age-old, grand curtain of the Second Temple, which by far was an act of acknowledgment of the sacrificial consumption of the Christ. God had come to legally get His sacrifice!

> *God had legal entry into the tomb of Jesus.*

What gave God legal entry into Jesus' tomb to raise Him from the dead? During the time of Moses, God specifically detailed the making of the Ark of the Covenant which contained a mercy seat atop. Because things are done on earth, as it is in heaven, the depictions and dimensions of the mercy seat of the earthly temple were based on the one that existed in heaven. I propose that God legally entered the tomb of Jesus, post-death, to make His presence known, post-haste, at what became an untraditional type of mercy seat on which lay the Savior, Christ.

"If I go up to heaven you are there; if I go down to the grave, you are there" (Psalm 139:8, NLT). The legal premise for God resusci-

tating Jesus from the dead lay on a distinctly fashioned Ark of the "Covenant," which makes sense in light of the fact that God and Jesus had a *covenant* as expounded upon above. How appropriate was it that God's display of resurrection power toward Jesus reached its highpoint around their *covenantal* namesake. There, the presence of God—the Holy Spirit—trod in the tomb and hovered above the "Seat of Christ" where His body rested, causing an emission of God's power and righteous wrath which was manifested by His snatching the eternal luminary out of the windowless, dark grave. God's power was directed toward extricating Jesus, and His angry consumption was directed toward silencing the presumptive refrain of the grave. In other words, God legally finished what He started on the cross.

What was the legal framework that had been laid for this Part II? It was the framework that God had detailed with Moses which came into fruition; it was a transfer of God's legal entry into the tomb: To explain, God had instructed Moses to build the Ark of the Covenant with a mercy seat on top and to have the high priest sacrifice a purified, acceptable offering on the mercy seat. The mercy seat consisted of gilt gold and was flanked by a male angel on each side. Scripture records that at Jesus' resurrection, Mary Magdalene, a female follower—turned evangelist—spread the Gospel that Jesus was risen after she saw two male angels on each side of His head and feet in His tomb (See John 20:2, 12). I propose that this layout suggests that the tomb's slabbed resting place on which Jesus' bloody sacrificial body had been perched, exposed it as a fashioned mercy seat where God's presence legally strode in. It is especially noteworthy that Jesus' body still would have been very bloody because He had died on the Sabbath, and as a result, had been rushed into the tomb before sundown, without time for proper burial cleansing (See Luke 23:54–56; John 19:42). The mercy seat, therefore, would have contained Jesus' high priestly blood sprinkled about, thereby making it a true mercy seat where God's presence was known to reside following the high priest sprinkling the blood of an atoning sacrifice. Because God's presence dwelt above the Ark of the Covenant, that day where Jesus lay would serve as the meeting place at the gravesite. Leviticus 16:2 (ESV), therefore, was the enabling law for God's legal entrance: *"Tell Aaron…not to come at any time into the Holy Place inside the veil, before the mercy seat that is on the ark, so that he may not die, for I will appear in the cloud over the mercy seat."* In one of the most dynamic miracles of the Bible, Jesus was both the *offered* sacrifice and the *offeror* of the sacrifice; He was the lamb and the high priest—the *Kohen Gadol*—all at the same time: *"…Christ who through the eternal Spirit offered himself without blemish to God"* (Hebrews 9:14, NIV). True to the dictates of the relevant Pentateuch law, Jesus legally met every instructive element that God had given Moses for the Ark's mercy seat offering, and God's presence was legally initiated for its consumption.

Building on the theme of a likely mercy seat contained within the tomb of Jesus, and digging even deeper, is my notion that alternatively, Jesus' body, *itself*, typified the Ark of the Holy of Holies and served as a Holy Ark that was tucked inside the consecrated tomb. The death chamber was transformed into a sacred chamber. The new and unused tomb proved to be a consecrated inner sanctum in that it had been set apart and never used-much like the colt which had never been sat upon that Jesus rode on into Jerusalem. Consider that, consistent with the practices of the day, it is projected that a burial cave housed Jesus' body upon a ledge of customary limestone. Since the borrowed tomb belonged to a wealthy follower of Jesus, Joseph of Arithmathea, one can deduce that it was substantially fancier than most, maybe aggrandizing, and possibly gold-laden since, according to acclaimed historian Josephus, it was the convention of the affluent and royals of that day to have extravagant, garden tomb burials. I posit this description for two reasons. Moses was directed to overlay the Ark in gold; since God leaves nothing to chance and decidedly there was gold at Jesus' birth, there very well may have been some gold in like manner that was present at Jesus' death to legally constitute an Ark of the Covenant replica there. Reviewing the contents of the Ark, there was manna, the commanded law, Aaron's priestly rod, and its gold outer shell. Consider that Jesus was the Manna that came down from heaven and that He was the walking volume of the Ten Commandments, for He said He came in the volume of the commanded book, and He was the Good Shepherd with a rod and staff that comforted. Finally, He was the High Priest after the order of Melchizedek, which nearly completed all the compelling components of the Ark of the Covenant portraiture; only a gold overlay would need to be present to legally constitute an Ark of the Covenant replica there. I firmly believe that there was indeed a gold overlay present, and if not on the burial bed, then definitely present in some other fashion; in fact, there *is* an allusion to gold that is found in Scripture which indirectly describes the body of Jesus as gold! I almost missed it, but in glaring technicolor, Exodus 16:33 (ENGBRE) shouts: *"And Moses said to Aaron, Take a golden pot and cast into it one full homer of manna and thou shall lay it up before God."* Well, Jesus is the Manna of heaven, and His vessel body is the container, so His body must have appeared gold-overlaid when the Father looked down from heaven into the tomb. All the elements of the covenantal Ark were there, and God invaded that tomb with His awesome presence! These spiritual constituents were important because as such, Jesus personified all of the contents that the physical Ark contained and provided the legal construct for God's presence to rest on Him, raising Him from the dead: Ephesians 1:19-21 (NLT) *"According to the work of His great might that is worked in Christ when he raised Him from the dead."*

    I maintain that the Ark silhouette was not coincidental; it was a godly instrumentality of choice. The jolting, resurrecting presence and power of God was, therefore, legally justified to be present and to raise Jesus from the dead.

A Wedding Covenant:
The Bride and the Lamb

"Come, I will show you the wife, the Lamb's bride."

REVELATION 21:9 (WEB)

For every girl and every woman who wants to be a bride, this will be *your* day!

God used a three-act agenda to dramatically recreate the Passover on the cross; that's why Jesus *had* to die on the Passover. He was that Passover lamb. It was a glowing bridal portrayal of what was to come; Jesus closed the door to the destroyer by becoming the door of atonement for, literally, the love of *His* life. Praise the Lord! Praise the Lamb! From the beginning of ages, the Lamb set out to set His bride free. Jesus was often heard throughout His earthly three-year ministry saying, " My time has not yet come." Really, that expression seems to have meant more than just a chronological reference to the ticking clock of His entry into Jerusalem to be slain. My thought is that it was a reference to a particular moment of love. There would have been a specific moment when the walking Word, Jesus, would have merged with the scrolled Word to create the world's greatest love story. At the cross, in Jesus' final honor, the declaration of God's love and the execution of God's love became one. God seems partial to love stories, for the Bible is full of them: Jacob loved Rachel, Hosea loved Gomer, Boaz loved Ruth, Moses loved Zipporah, and God penned: *"For God so loved the world..."* (John 3:16, NIV). At the cross, in Jesus' final honor, which became His epic hour of love, the declaration of God's love and the execution of God's love became one to produce a finished love story in all of its zenith! The drama continues: A lamb for a household becomes a groom for a bride. Inside of a wedding temple not made with hands, the Christ-groom gives Himself for her as a lamb, and the vaulted wedding gift to Christ's bride is her salvation: *"... The Son* of God, the One having loved me and Having given up Himself for me" (Galatians 2:20, BLB).

> God remedies legal separation!

The message of the cross is enshrined in heaven because the presence of the fleeced mammal forever signifies the bloody act of the hallowed lamb of God. His blood luxuriates heaven. Everything God does passes His divine judicial muster because He is a profuse reflection of His perfect divinity. God is the very standard of just love because He's the calculus of justice, the very bar and the barometer of justice, and His love exists in tandem with His justice. Because God is right in all of His ways and can do no less, everything He does passes His divine judicial muster. Why was a "Part 2" necessary to replace God's first euphoric, utopian garden, and why was a "Part 2" necessary to reunite the Groom of heaven with His bride? It was needful because the sin of Adam catapulted humanity into a state of legal separation from God. Remarkably, it was the first case of a "legal separation" in the "Divine Domestic Relations" of heaven; that is, humankind was separated legally from God, whom the Bible calls the Husbandman, but Christ would restore the brideship when He came. In John 15, the Bible sketches the Husbandman God as a type of cultivator of agriculture. Interesting is the fact that "husbandman" contains the word husband within it. "To husband" is to take delight in looking after someone or something prudently. It, thus, follows that omniscient God who knows the end from the beginning activated "Operation Redemption," which is a prudent plan of preparedness to take care of His creation in the face of spiritual hardship. To answer the Part 2 question in the most simplistic of comprehension: Because God delighted in His bride and wanted her back! *"Turn, O backsliding children, saith the Lord; for I am married unto you; and I will take you… to Zion"* (Jeremiah 3:14, KJV). Jesus was tasked to go to the cross and die, but exploring the ubiquitous question of the ages, what really kept Jesus on the cross? Was it the gargantuan nails that held Him there?

The world has long queried that scenario with all types of quantum buzz. To answer the complexity of the question is to indeed query the quixotic because one must first rule out the obvious answer—those humongous, prohibitive nails. It seems a "no brainer" that if a tomb, fortified with a two-ton stone lid, could not brace His lifeless body, then *a fortiori*, surely mere nails could not hold the life-pumping, Almighty Savior there? The answer to the universal question—it was love that affixed Jesus to the cross: life-pulsing, heart-throbbing, sin-disdaining, damnation-canceling, honorable, noble, avenging *love!* How eye-opening is the fact that although Christ's body was "nailed "to the cross during His mosaic of passion, it was actually Christ who *attached* His own unleashed lion-limbed, lamb-like body to a pole! The cross's gored lamb set off the legal exchange of grace to humankind in place of graceless punishment. Jesus' dead body on the cross was more than a lifeless corpse; it was the critical mass that put into motion our redemption. Even after Jesus' death, He was still active in the business of saving souls, descending into hell's cavity to share about His lambship and lordship. In life and even in death, Jesus saves!

His had been a surreal surrender. Although He had seen it in His mind so many times, the *Agnus Dei* (Lamb of God) stretching Himself back before the etchings of the earth, it was still both a strange and familiar allegiance to the scaffolding on which He lay. He reflected in the silence. He had been the perfect lamb on His way to a slaughter-fest. He felt the excruciating pain shooting through His body, but He felt this bubbling up joy. No doubt, it was the unsurpassable joy of girding up to defeat death on the other side of the cross. Regardless of His countless contusions and the mounting malodorous stench which was circulating from His massive amounts of gushing "slaughter blood," Jesus clearly found His soft spot-mindset. Not prone to body-whipping nor to thirty-nine backlashes; nevertheless, He knew it pleased the Father to bruise Him anyway. The blood smelled hideously bad to others, but to God, it was not putrid but perfume-scented and sumptuously aromatic because it was the smell of heaven's blood-lamb. Lying there and not seeing the Father's tender face through the darkness that overlay the land, it was as if all were a terse touch of the back of the Father's hand, a literal "talk to the hand" moment." No longer chin to chin, shoulder to shoulder, no longer enveloped in that platinum embrace of the first order that they had always enjoyed. Given this heightened separation, that urgent question's answer takes on an even deeper essence. It was for love's joy which was plattered before Him, that Jesus would stay there. He gave His visceral all. It was a sweet vinaigrette to Him. It was a sheer cognizable moment of palpable purpose and intestinal passion that brought Christ to the cross; it was sober love that kept Him there because He could feel His bride returning home!

> *"I promised you as a pure bride to one husband—Christ."*
> CORINTHIANS 11:2 (NLT)

Legitimate love has a three-letter name, God. God who answers to no one, is indebted to no one, and derives His existence from no one; therefore, He has the sovereign, proprietous right to love whomever and however He wants to. God legitimized His love through the life and death of Christ but chose to never legislate love itself. Neither did He make the process of love an object of legalism towards humankind. In other words, because He was the proprietor of love, it was practical in His eyes to give it unconditionally, and He gave us a choice to receive it. God justly loved us in that He never commandeered our heart to make it love Him, nor forcibly enacted rules of the heart to make us love Him. He was as gentle as a lamb and delicately gave us the free will to love Him while chivalrously pursuing our hearts, although it cost Him everything He had. God legitimized His love for us, but He never legislated love itself. He never made loving *Him* legalistic or a function of coercion. He did, however, legalize the "cross process" by which He expressed His own love for us. God's love was legitimate—it was real—and He used a legal process of atonement to make it possible to love us, hands-on, for all eternity. His lucent love shone *ad infinitum*, seriously never-ending on the cross. It is, then, not surprising that such a God would justly ask us to love Him. He enacted fair rules of the heart. He gave us free will to love Him, and He freely went after our hearts, although it cost Him everything He had. Such is not the act of someone who was forcibly needy; it was the act of someone who needlessly wanted to show love to His creation. Could it be that God preferred to be ruler maximus of the cosmos with us just because He didn't want to be without us? Could it further be that He was willing to give up His own life for us because living without us was not an option that He gave Himself? Could it be that His sovereignty was bolstered only by the jubilation of His pursuit for our love, more personally, that the pangs of being without you could be assuaged only by the sweetness of being together with *you—you were to die for*. No wonder the lamb-like Christ proclaimed: *"I won't leave you like orphans; I will come back to you"* (John 14:18, BSB). Imagine getting a love letter from the one who loved you with just these five words in it, "You were to die for"…, and He did!

The Lamb of God made it possible for His lovely church to be born on His "deathday," ironically not on His birthday, and He would give her a wedding day. With His dying breath, which was waning because it was hard to breathe on the cross, He had His bride on His stilled mind. The cruel, murderous cross by which He was crucified intentionally worked to reduce His breath, so Jesus literally thought of her with bated breath. Although a marriage covenant was fulfilled that day, there wasn't time for a proper wedding ceremony. For that, Jesus will return. He had to ascend to the Father to deliver proof of His blood, wounds, of course, because legally, as in some remaining American states, you need a blood test before you can obtain a marriage certificate. Jesus had to record the blood-stained marriage license in the vaults of heaven forever. To every legal pause in God's kingdom, the concentric response of the Holy Spirit and the bride in the earth is "Come, Lord Jesus." He will one day come back to get His bride and present her formally to His Father as she stands frocked in a splendid white gown. This grand event will take place in the delightful land of Beulah—meaning marriage and signifying a beautiful, botanical border of heaven. The outdoor ceremony will be followed by a formal wedding reception known as the marriage supper. *"…Blessed are those who are invited to the marriage supper of the lamb"* (Revelation 19:9, BSB; See Isaiah 62:4). To almost every wedding, there is sartorial pageantry—the train of the bride. So, too, it will be with this wedding. Jesus, however, will supply the train: *" …I saw the Lord seated on a throne…and the train of His robe filled the temple"* (Isaiah 6:1, BSB). I am struck by the splendor of it all. I perceive that there is glory in Jesus' bridal train. It is the glory of His temple which He raised back up, for that glory follows Him; in fact, I submit that it is the same glory that followed behind God when He showed Moses His "back glory." Indeed, it is the same glory that was found in the hem of His robe that healed the hemorrhaging woman. Leaving nothing out for this grandiose event, I envision a bridal veil plunged in blue, purple, and scarlet, and embroidered with the same gold cherubim found on the one in the Holy of Holies, but it does not separate the lamb's presence. Just like a groom can lift the veil of the church bride; likewise, Jesus will too: *"But when one turns to the Lord, the veil is lifted"* (2 Corinthians 3:16, ESV; *See* Exodus 26:31). There will be a handpicked tiara for the bride, hand-selected by her groom: *"They will be mine, says the* LORD *of hosts, in that day when I make up my jewels…"* (Malachi 3:17, BSB). Finally, Jesus will supply the special lighting for the occasion—not lamp lighting, but lamb lighting from the *"Light of the World"* (John 8:12, Revelation 22:5–6; NIV). As the great future of the nuptials celebration is awaited to be fulfilled, all that is left to be said presently on the earth is the corporate exclamation of the Holy Spirit and the bride who say, "Maranatha!" (See Revelation 22:20; 1 Corinthians 16:22).

For me, one of the most picturesque images seen in the reel of apostle John's revelation is the image of the even-toed, crimp-haired, baby sheep, dead center of the throne of God. Why is the lamb there? The answer is found within Jesus' last night on earth before His crucifixion. Remember that His Gethsemane prayer took place that night. I wondered why Jesus prayed that He would not have to go through with dying. Surely the constituent of the building blocks of life itself was not afraid of death. No, Jesus was not afraid of death; He was opposed to death. Mortality was not off-putting; separation was! Death separates loved ones, and death would separate Jesus from God, if only for an infinitesimal moment that could be felt for an infinity. It is why in the book of Revelation, Jesus still appears as a lanced, living lamb. The work of the cross, which called for the separation of the Holy and divine unitary fellowship to accomplish it, will reverberate forever in the lamb. Although Jesus is depicted as the coming Judge and conquering King, His work as the dead lamb of God is etched forever in glory. Because of Jesus' lamb-some eternality, life-long fellowship with God is no longer a fugitive. Such is why one of Jesus' greatest triumphs of speech is: *"I will never desert you, nor will I abandon you"* (Hebrews 13:5-6, NASB). In other words, I will never separate myself from you. Covenantly speaking, Jesus will never be the one to walk away from the relationship. Emotionally speaking, He never wants to. Doctrinally speaking, He can never be forced to: *"Nothing shall separate me from the love of God"* (Romans 8:38-39, NLT). Dying didn't really bother Jesus; in all reality, it was the "legal nuisance" of death that annoyed Him. Legal nuisance may seem like a contradiction in terms since a nuisance may be an unlawful interference with a protected right and quality of life, but the term is correct here. Because of the legal consequences of Adamic iniquity, death had *lawfully* wound itself up in the coils of interference with the quiet enjoyment of the Father and Son's togetherness. Since death necessarily involved a substantial separation of the worst kind—the forever kind—Christ vehemently disliked it. Even worse, it would cause a separation of the celestial kind for Him and the Father in order to overcome it. Their relationship had always been configured on the reality of presence. It was never one bereft of inclusion. Severance had not even been in their glossary. Jesus died so that humankind would prevail, not just countervail against death. Death, before Jesus' death, had represented duplicitous inauthenticity—it was the defective counterfeit of life. God's work on His Genesis project had militated against that notion, for man was meant to live authentically forever! Jesus' prevailing meant no more fake, temporal existence, for the worst part about spiritual death was its alienation of man from God, but the best part about Jesus' death is that it brought spiritual and physical communion with God. *"To be absent from the body and to be present with God"* (2 Corinthians 5:8, ESV). God consumed Jesus' sacrifice after He bowed His head and died. That bow reminds us that His death was aligned with worship to the end!

CHAPTER 11

A Bottle of Grace & a Keg of Kindness

"There is now no condemnation to those of us who are in Christ Jesus."

ROMANS 8:1 (NIV)

Good Grace: The Facts of the Gracious Gospel

There is a set of facts about the Gospel of salvation that is irrefutably true.

True: The Gospel is a directed story of pardon and a treatise on gracious love. False: the Gospel's message of grace is swallowed up by the anger of God. True: God's extravagant, agapeic love is balanced with His righteous anger. The Bible certainly shows throughout the Gospel's accounts that God does correct those whom He loves, but God prefers to court His people with a redemptive nod instead of a punitive rod. Each and every time a believer's name is written in the book of life, it is God's nod to the gracious redemption of the cross. Conversely, however, to reject this life-saving sacrifice of Jesus is to reap God's wrath and eternal punishment, which is by legal default, a self-consequential damnation. The Bible says in Romans 6:23 (NIV) *"that the wages of sin is death, but the gift of God is eternal life in Christ Jesus our Lord,"* so every person gets to choose what his paycheck looks like; said differently, one should choose wisely whom to serve because one legally gets what one chooses.

Do You Own What's in Your Prayer Closet? Your Legal Possessory Rights

"Then Caleb ...said, 'We should go up and take possession of the land, for we can certainly do it."

NUMBERS 13:30 (NIV)

This chapter could also be called: *Possessing What God Has For You.* Possession of property means holding property in one's power or the exercise of dominion over a property to the exclusion of others. Simply worded, your possession allows you to have control over something, which nobody else can. The familiar adage "possession is 9/10 of the law" is not really a law but an appropriate expression that refers to a person having "actual" or physical possession of property. What does this mean for the Christian spiritually? It means that if God has manifested a fulfilled prayer request for you, then you possess it physically and have the right to partake of it and defend it with prayer against any and all enemies who do not control it. Similarly, in the Bible, when God caused the Israelites to possess the Promised Land, He gave them the right and the help to defend it against all enemies: The Hittites, Midianites, ...etc." (See Numbers 31; Exodus 23:23).

One may ask, what if the believer is believing spiritually for a prayerful possession, but the complete manifestation has not arrived yet? There, American Property law would define the possession as "constructive" possession which *is still* control or dominion over a property, just without having complete actual—physical—possession. When a possessor holds legal title to a property, that is constructive possession, and even though she may only constructively possesses part of it, the law will deem the possessor to hold possession over *all* of it.[76] In other words, in law, a person with constructive possession stands in the same legal position as a person with actual possession. This possession is important because if a believer has taken hold of something spiritually, even though it has not fully manifested, she can be sure, by lawful possessory right, that she has the right to possess *all*

> *Faith funds your powerful possession.*

of what she is waiting on to be manifested. Crucial is the notion that it is *the believing* that yields both the constructive and the actual possession in the spiritual realm; in other words, faith is the funding that gets you the title (constructive possession) to your answered prayers (actual possession) even before you physically occupy it in full. See it! *"That's why I tell you to have faith that you already received whatever you pray for, and it will be yours"* (Mark 11:24, GW). Faith gets you constructive occupancy under God's property law, with a title, which is proof of ownership and is the guarantor of your ownership. Property law says that if you have a title and constructive possession, the law deems you to have possession of *all* of it. Similarly, God's law deems you to have *full* physical possession of whatever you have constructive possession of by faith, and in time it will be manifested in the earth. Holy Spirit is a guarantor of our right to not only possess the blessings in this life but also guarantees us the blessing of eternal life, which will be manifested in the next life. We own, possess, and have the right as possessors of it all.

Christians have to embrace fighting from a superior position in the Christian hierarchy of God's government because we have been given the title—the rightful ownership to the land of blessings; but too often, we do not know how to gain possession of our territory. In Real Estate law, there is the principle of "adverse possession," which permits an outsider to take the land of the rightful possessor if he manages to possess it and is not stopped. For example, if at first a person is illegally trespassing in an open, conflictive manner, but allowed to continue his activity on the land by the rightful owner who ignores him, eventually it is he who can legally own that owner's land if all requirements are met under the law. The invading Devil, who often illegally intrudes upon our property, benefits by being unopposed and gains possessions because Christians are uninformed of their holdings and rights and do nothing to stop him. Jesus' possession at the cross gave the believer certain possessory rights. There was a literal planting of Jesus' feet because He was crucified on Golgotha's hill, which is interpreted as "skull," and there He planted His feet on the figurative skull in shape, but the literal spiritual head of the Devil. This imagery materializes as the word of God comes to life in the Bible's first Messianic prophecy ever: *"Her son will crush your head. And you will crush his heel"* (Genesis 3:15, NIV). Importantly, it was prophesied that Jesus would crush the Devil's head. The skull was the representation of Satan's deathly identity. Jesus, who is identified as Jehovah Nissi or flag of victory, planted His identity on top of the Devil's identity, similar to a victorious war hero planting his flag on taken territory. Jesus laid claim to the Devil's territory—death and lack. By the death that befell Jesus and His ensuing resurrection, Jesus gave us that same right of possession of territorial life by proclamation: *"I will give you every place on which you set foot..."* (Joshua 1:3, NIV). When Jesus died with His feet successfully on the Devil's head, He trampled Him, and we possess this same footwork to stop him! *"Behold, I give you authority to trample upon serpents, scorpions and all the power of the enemy..."*

Why is taking territory or having possession so important from a spiritual kingdom's point of view? To answer this question, it is helpful to look at a historical picture from a natural perspective. All over the world, accumulating territory has always been at the historical forefront, whether by the common man or by imperial governments, whether through lawful expansion or through unlawful seizures. Consider the French Revolution by *bourgeoisie* and peasants, which caused a bloody overthrow of their monarchy, or the Bolshevik Revolution by the proletariat working class, which brutally overran their monarchy, both occurring because of a people's thirst for possessive entitlements, among which was lands. At the other end of the spectrum, consider the territorial quests of Alexander the Great, where history narrates that this king and military commander cried because he had no more worldly lands to conquer upon finishing his massive conquests. Consider, also, the British Empire of old whose historical tagline was "The Empire on which the sun never sits," namely because its global land possessions defied a single time zone; indeed, one of its flags was always flying in some part of the world where there was daylight. Consider, further, the Japanese Empire, which infamously bombed America's Pearl Harbor in its notorious quest to further its empire. Consider, too, the American Revolution and its pursuit of life, liberty, and property, or its "Manifest Destiny," which became President's Monroe's 19th century initiative of amassing new land territories by expansionism. Finally, consider the Bible's kingdom advancement through the crossing of the Jordan River by Joshua, where the fledgling, inexperienced army of Israelites miraculously invaded and took the Promised Land, beginning with Jericho. Conclusively, an unfiltered history shows that territories succumb to a power greater than themselves; therefore, every conqueror, and the conquered, undeniably had to learn the power of superimposition. Taking territory is important geo-politically and spiritually, too, in order to attain, display, and maintain power. In line with this critical reality, the Bible proclaims that believers are "more than conquerors," and since that is the case, territorial gains and possession should be spiritual normalcy for those in the kingdom of God. Corollary to this idea is Jesus' message about kingdom expansion, where He told a parable about kingdom advancement and multiplication. To paraphrase the parable, three servants were given currency to invest by their absentee master. The servants who multiplied the investment and expanded the master's ownership portfolio were nicely rewarded accordingly, but the servant who did not amass any increase for the master was duly punished. Possession and expansion in the kingdom of God are of main importance (*See* Matthew 25:14–30).

The Will

"He brought out his people with rejoicing, his chosen ones with shouts of joy; he gave them the lands of the nations, and they fell heir to what others had toiled for."

PSALMS 105:43-44 (NIV)

"The highest heavens belong to the Lord...but the earth he has given to mankind."

PSALMS 115:16 (NIV)

It is God's will for His believers to dominate, possess, and enjoy the earth, and the proof of it is in the will that Jesus left. Each member of the body of Christ is an heir of redemption. A will is a legal document that distributes ownership of assigned items to a person(s) by the wishes of the deceased one who left the will—the "testator." This legally binding document transfers or divides these chosen possessions which can be real estate or personal property, all of which are known as the inheritance, which pass to the recipient heir (the person who has been selected to receive them). From heaven, God willed a will and said that He, Himself, was the inheritance. God sent Jesus to carry out His will on earth, and I submit Jesus became the deceased testator and left the church that will: *"Then said I, Lo I come in the volume of the book it is written of me to do thy will"* (Hebrews 10:7, KJV). Since a will legally permits the testator to choose his heirs and to make decisions about how his estate will be distributed and managed after his death, Jesus accordingly chose His heirs and the method for distribution and management of His divine estate. It is exciting that God had heirship in mind for His church all along: *"...Are they not ministering spirits sent forth to minister for them who shall be heirs of salvation?"* (Hebrews 1:14, NIV). The heirs are to be the heirs of God's salvation, the body of Christ is the legal heir and rightful recipient of Jesus' inheritance;

and the eternal estate that is to be freely distributed and managed is redemption, which includes eternal life, the blessing, and the earth, with personal property. Romans 8:17 (NIV) records, *"...if sons of God, then heirs of God."* So to be a

> *Believers are legal-equals in Christ's will.*

son of God is to have become an heir of God, and to be a daughter of God is to have become an heiress of God! The Gospel is a true rags to riches story, for the Bible says that before matriculating into the richness of the family of God, our righteousness amounted to filthy rags, but He became our inheritance: *"I am your inheritance"* (Numbers 18:20). *"All the world is mine and everything in it"* (Psalm 50:12, NLT). Jesus left the church everything that belonged to Him. Jesus is the expression of God's will. God willed that the body of believers would be *"heirs of God, and joint heirs with Christ"* (Romans 8:17, NKJV). Believers are, therefore, legal-equals to Christ Jesus under the will and can inherit all that God has and all that Jesus had by virtue of the right of Sonship. We are seated as clients because Jesus is seated at the right hand of the Father as our eternal advocate, and God presides over the Court of heaven, so we are really seated at the attorney's table with Jesus. Worth noting, in our American court system, the only person who is able to sit at the attorney table which faces the Judge in court is the legal counsel and their clients. Our seating, hence, is in line with our inheritance! *"He prepareth a table before me in the presence of mine enemies"* (Psalm 23:5, KJV).

The will is required to meet certain standards to be a legally valid will. God's will, of course, met the legal threshold of validity because Jesus is the expression of God's will. God transcribed His will through the death of Jesus. Let's take a general look, notwithstanding state-to-state variance.

1. The testator (testatrix, female)—the deceased who made the will—must be eighteen years or older. A contextual reading of the synoptic Gospels pinpoints Jesus to be at least thirty years old; in fact, Jesus candidly answered that question, leaving no doubt whatsoever that He was over the age of eighteen when He replied to the Pharisees who said, *"You are not even fifty and you say '…Before Abraham was I Am'"* (John 8:57-58, NIV). There, Jesus underscored the chronology of being older than the ancient patriarch, Abraham, would certainly verify His being over the age of eighteen!

2. The testator must be of sound mind: have the legal, mental capacity to intentionally create the will with understanding; voluntarily and not under duress; not under intoxication; not have some other mental incapacitation. I am "blown away" by the foresight of God and His application to legal details. God made sure that there would be no question as to Jesus' voluntariness and intentionality on the night which they discussed the proposed will, the night of His betrayal.

   "Father… not My will, but Yours be done" (Luke 22:42, NIV). Jesus knowingly denied His personal will to leave the body of Christ a valid will: *"My food is doing the will of the one who sent me and to complete His work"* (John 4:34, ISV). God also made sure there would be no question of Jesus' mental capacity on the cross. I further propose that God used Jesus' recognition of His dear mom and His lucid capacity to be able to lovingly conduct business for her welfare from the cross, His ability to forgive His detractors, and His boldness to confirm that He had finished His mission, all as verification of His mental capacity to soundly execute the will. Jesus was "with it!"

3. Under American Estate and Wills law, a will must usually be dated to be legally valid. Specifically, it must be signed and dated in presence of two witnesses, meaning it must be attested. Jesus' will was surely dated for the ages as "Good Friday," but was the will executed with His signature? I submit that Jesus penned His signature in bold red. Consider that American colonist John Hancock is remembered for boldly signing the declaration of independence in large print under perilous conditions as both an act of defiance and bravery; although deserving of very honorable mention, Hancock's signature did not contain his martyred blood nor save the world as was the reality with Jesus' sea of flowing, red blood.

At least two witnesses are required to attest to the testator's competence at the time of the signing. In this regard, Jesus' will was adequately witnessed. The Bible shares that there were many witnesses from His inner circle at the foot of the cross, including His mother, Mary, and one of His closest friends, apostle John, both who knew Him well and could legally attest to His cognitive soundness and unaltered state of mind because He actually spoke to the two of them from the cross (John 19:26). Usually, acceptable witnesses to a valid American will would need to be witnesses who are not also beneficiaries of the will—or be "disinterested" witnesses. In one sense, this precondition would be a tall order to fill because the whole world was the spiritual beneficiary of the will. Nevertheless, the state of mind competency could have also been seen as attested to by the disinterested, unbelieving Roman soldier who could be characterized as an unlikely, direct beneficiary *at the time* of the crucifixion—although afterward, he and the whole world were potential beneficiaries (See Psalm 103:1–5). That soldier, whose differing religious and patriotic fidelity typically lay in that of the opposing Ancient Roman empire, could categorically be a disinterested party to a Christian will. Along with other bulging, divine things, he was so impressed outwardly with the competent faculties of Christ and His ability to powerfully communicate under the excruciating process of this crucifixion that he heralded Him as the Son of God. I, therefore, do not think it unreasonable to presume any of the witnesses above would have gladly provided their own signatures as part of the attestation process. There, nevertheless, were two final witnesses who, without a doubt, endorsed their signatures: God and Holy Spirit. They both witnessed Jesus' last wish when He uttered: *"Father into your hands I commit my Spirit"* (Luke 23:46, NIV). *"The Spirit Himself bears witness…"* (Romans 8:16, ESV).

In an actual, true sense, it *was* Jesus' *last will* and *His testament*—the New Testament.

"This is my blood—a testament for you" (See Luke 22:20). It is said in the legal world, "the document is legal and above board." How was this accomplished vis-a-vis the will? And why is it relevant? Hebrews 9:16 (KJV) says, *"For where a testament is, there must first be the death of the testator."* As discussed, that above board box has been checked off. After the testator dies, then the will is to be legally "probated" or proven to the court's satisfaction.[77] As shown above, those boxes, too, satisfy God's Court's requirement. There is, however, one more threshold that must be met before the court. During the probate proceeding, not only is the will's authenticity and validity verified, any and all debts incurred by the estate must be paid. Importantly, these debts are calculated, and payment must be remitted *before* the heirs can partake in

the inheritance that is left to them. Did Jesus' will meet this threshold in God's Court? Jesus was the testator. After dying, Jesus' will was probated in God's Court of law. I submit that Jesus was found to have provided for all of the debts He took on, which were our debts, to be paid because our "sin account" conspicuously read "0" balance. Historically in ancient Judaism, once transactional provisions were fulfilled and a debt wiped out, there was particular wording that typically showed up on the sales receipt- the "bill of lading." It is shown as "*Tetelestai.*" This is the very phrase Jesus hollered on the cross just before He died. There, Jesus gave a "shout out" to us; the testator was declaring beforehand that all debts of the estate, which we would be heir to, were paid in full. Christ Jesus was giving notice to God's Court that His heirs could now take part unobstructedly in their inheritance. Jesus died for the remission of our sins, but He also died to remit the payment for those sins. His death was double payment for both a bloody bill and a bloody release of debt. *"In the case of a will, it is necessary to prove the death of the one who made it, because a will is in force only when someone has died"* (Hebrews 9:16–18, NIV).

Yes, the will could be successfully probated or proven in God's Court of law. First, Jesus' will was signed, satisfying the Statute of Frauds signature and writing requirements; in fact, Jesus signed His name in so much blood that the Bible records it as an unmistakable "shedding of blood;" not a mini, but an oceanic outpouring of blood! Of importance is the fact that legally, a signature or one's "mark" can be any mark that affirms an assent to something. The blood was Jesus' signature mark and served as evidence of His signature. Recalling the old frontier expression, "make your mark," His mark was not diminutive but was a "fountain" pen of affirmation for all the world to see. Jesus marked the cross' palette that was showcasing His last will and testament with splattered blood. The stained cross was His assent to bequeath all of His un-worldly and worldly goods. He left behind a fortune!

The will of Jesus was adequately witnessed. The Bible records there were witnesses at the foot of the cross, including His mother and one of His closest friends, apostle John, both who knew Him well and could legally attest to His cognitive soundness and unaltered state of mind because He actually spoke to the two of them from the cross (John 19:26). Usually, acceptable witnesses to a valid American will would need to be witnesses who are not also beneficiaries of the will or "disinterested" witnesses. In one sense, this precondition would be a tall order to fill because the whole world was the beneficiary of the will. Nevertheless, the state of mind competency could have also been seen as attested to by the disinterested Roman soldier who could be characterized as an unlikely, direct beneficiary *at the time* of the crucifixion—although afterward, he and the whole world were potential beneficiaries. That soldier, whose religious and patriotic fidelity typically lay in that of the opposing Ancient Roman empire, could categorically be a disinterested party to a Christian will. Among other divine things, he was so impressed with the competent faculties of Christ and His ability to communicate under the excruciating process of this crucifixion that he heralded Him as the Son of God. There was one final witness. God also witnessed Jesus' last wish, for it was to Him that Jesus spoke it when He uttered, "Father into your hands I commit my Spirit." In an actual, pragmatic sense, it really was Jesus' last will and testament—*the New Testament.* Absolutely, the legal requisite amount of witnesses, as well as the required thresholds of competency and signatures, were met.

It is so important to reemphasize the forethought of God to meet all iotas of the will's legal requirement, even "in the thick" of His crucifixion plan, When Jesus was offered aged vinegar on the cross to lessen the pain, He declined it, as set forth previously. This essential concept of His decline speaks to a legal element here; His refusal allowed there to be no equivocation as to Jesus' mental powers, that is, His legal state of mind for the purpose of His carrying out His intent to create His will. It was only at the end, after Jesus' demonstration of sound mind, that He took the fermented vinegar. He suffered on the cross without a mind-altering pain killer, and without ambiguity, He knew exactly what He was bequeathing—Himself and all accompanying benefits. The Bible records a gathering of witnesses present, including the disinterested criminal being executed alongside Him, who witnessed up close Jesus' intended act of sacrifice, and that He intended to make him an heir of Paradise. This additional witness—the Roman soldier—vitally serves as a legally "disinterested" witness because at the time of his acknowledgment and attestation of Christ being fully Christ, had no ulterior motive as a beneficiary to Christ's will. As an aside, Scripture points out that a demon-possessed man whom Jesus ministered to was then found "clothed in his right mind" again after encountering Jesus. I submit that it is relevant that the One who demonstratedly restores and keeps the mind would have been fully in control of His own: *"You will keep the mind that is dependent on you in perfect peace, for it is trusting you"* (Isaiah 26:3, CSB).

4. Under our current American legal system, not only must a will be in writing in order to be enforceable under our American legal system, but it needs to be inscribed on something, usually paper, to be valid. God made sure the will was in writing. How? He inspired forty authors to write the contents of His will—both the Old and the New Testament—on paper, notably parchment scrolls which were mainly used at the time—over a period of 1500 years.

5. An Executor is needed to execute the valid will. An executor, or executrix if female, is the person named by the testator who sees to it that the desires of the testator are carried out by executing will's provisions. Similarly, in the spirit realm, God set it up so that Jesus named the Holy Spirit—the Holy personhood of Christ—as the person who would come to execute the will because the Bible says that He knows the *will* of God: *"And the one who searches hearts knows exactly what the Spirit is thinking, because his pleadings for God's people accord with God's will"* (Romans 8:27, CSB). Executors of trusts are common in wills. Trusts are instrumental arrangements under which a trustee or an executor holds property for a beneficiary. God has left to believers trusts of beneficial promises in the spiritual realm that are filled with blessings that can be drawn against, and the Executor of the Trinity—Holy Spirit—will see to it that they are carried out. God meant for the believer to have significant distributions throughout life, *"For no matter how many promises God has made, they are 'Yes' in Christ…"* (2 Corinthians 1:20, NIV).

6. There is also an external reading of the will that usually takes place outside of the courtroom. It is doing that reading of the will that the heirs are informed of their respective treasures which have been left to them by bequest of the testator. For the Christian, it is the reading of God's testaments, both the Old and the New, which fully inform the believer of her acquired treasures, both short and long term.

CHAPTER 12

What's in the Legal Name of Jesus

"Some trust in chariots and horses, but we trust in the name of the LORD *our God. They are brought to their knees and fall…"*

PSALM 20:7-8 (NIV)

Jesus poignantly highlighted the great import of His family name. Conceptually, one of the first things He drew attention to while teaching His disciples to pray was His Father's name: "When you pray, say this:' Father, may your holy name be honored.'" During the last of Jesus' prayers which followed His last supper, Jesus cued the disciples and detailed for them that it was by the power of His Father's name that they would find themselves protected upon His crucifixion and after His earthly departure. He went on to drill the point for His listening inner circle with a revelatory unpacking of a monumental truth that it was by the power of His God-given name that He had been able to keep His disciples from harm to this point (See John 17:11-12). He further explained that it was the Father's name, which He legally bore, that released the saving dynamism that would shelter them from the unsafety of the world. No longer taciturn in front of His disciples, but now more direct and vociferous in light of His imminently approaching death, Jesus prayed to God aloud, all the while repeatedly indicating the value of His own God-imbued name and magnifying God's name. There, I believe Jesus was stressing the importance of the Father's name because of the transitional importance that His very own name was soon to have in the life of the believer. Quickly coming on the horizon would be the convergence of praying in Jesus' name, as the disciples would learn. Why was this name conversion so important? Interestingly, the "Lord's prayer," which was the prayer that Jesus had previously recited when the disciples asked Him to teach them to pray, did not end with the words "in Jesus' name." This was the "pre-cross" model of prayer. Substantially, this omission was due to the fact that Jesus' name had not been glorified yet, and, therefore, had not been legally given to the nations as the divine springboard for all effective prayer. After His resurrection, Jesus' name provided the legal impetus to pray in His name: *"Until now you've not been bold enough to ask the Father for a single thing in my name, but now you can ask...And you can be sure that you'll receive what you ask for..."* (John 16:24, TPT). The bar Jesus set is the barometer by which one's prayers are legally assessed and addressed by heaven. The Bible says: "At the name of Jesus, every knee shall bow and every tongue confess, of things in the earth and under the earth that Jesus is Lord."... *"There is no other name by which men shall be saved"* (Acts 4:12, NIV). Those two enlightening Scriptures point to a double essence and a double efficacy of the name of Jesus. With the urging of His disciples to pray the new way in His name, in a solo reference, Jesus was alluding to Himself as Jesus the *Christ*. There, Jesus conflated the Lordship of His name with the Messianic virtue of His Name. Jesus was self-describing both His spiritual dominion to sovereignly triumph over every enemy of the cross, as well as His anointing to save. After all, the angel had given that pronouncement as well: *"For unto you is born this day in the city of David a Savior, who is Christ the Lord"* (Luke 2:11, NIV). Looking at the compounded name and title of "Jesus Christ," it is actually an assemblage of the complete goal of the Godhead. Scripture says that in *Christ Jesus* dwells the fullness of the Godhead, and we can see that this concept resonates in the name-sharing among the Holy Trinity: *"To us a son is given... and his name shall be called... Mighty God"* (Isaiah 9:6, NIV).

Jesus knew first hand of the sacred and wonder-filled reception that the holiness of the Father's name commands. In His old days of heavenly glory, He had a front-row view of the seraphic grandeur that encircled the throne of the infinitely Holy God as Seraphim cried: *"Holy, holy, holy is the* LORD *Almighty,"* and Jesus saw how, *"At the sound of their voices, the doorposts and thresholds shook and the temple was filled with smoke"* (Revelation 4:8, NIV; Isaiah 6:4, BSB). Indeed, this is the God who I envision riding on the waves of the skies and resting His arms on claps of thunder! Jesus had observed on countless occasions that when humankind gets even a sliver of recognition of the manifested God, the reception is the same—he must bow in some way. Because of the weight of God's quintessentially holy and exalted glory, the flesh is compelled to debase itself under that weight, inevitably bowing to its magnitude. Consider that Ezekiel's vision of God on His throne caused him to humbly fall on his face. Consider, also, that when God appeared to Abraham, he fell down to the ground. Relatedly, Jesus legally shares the Father's name and the associated glory of that name, so He observed His own reception from the power of His magnitudinous presence. When the risen Jesus appeared to Saul, he was involuntarily thrust to the dusty concourse, face down; Saul fell down to the ground. When the post-ascended Jesus appeared to the apostle John at Patmos, John fell down like lifeless flesh. On a side note, that fall was really John's second propulsion to the ground, as his first facedown collapse happened on the Mount of Transfiguration when God's glory appeared side by side with Jesus (See Matthew 17:6). Further, consider that when the pre-risen Jesus uncloaked a shaft of His glory in Gethsemane's garden, the helpless, wobbling soldiers forcibly fell backward in an unplanned gymnast's tilt to the ground (See John 18:7). There is a certain appropriate lowering of oneself in the presence of the most superior God, no matter the mode of the manifestation, be it in front of God the Father, God the Son-pre incarnate, or God the Son-post incarnate. As seen above, exposure to any of these manifestations causes a real reaction, one that can show on the faces of the mortal and the immortal. Recall, for instance, the brow-fallen, shame-faced gaze with which the Israelites hid their faces when they saw God's glory reflected on Moses' human face, or the delicate reverence with which the beatific attendants lower themselves in contactless pose and use their wings as ethereal handkerchiefs to shield their unworthy faces in God's presence. Indeed, demonstrating the fact that there is an obvious superabundance of God's presence in His name are the motionless soldiers who could not stand in Jesus' presence at the demonstration of the unanimity of His and the Father's name. Jesus taught us to pray, *"Our Father who art in heaven. Hallowed be thy name"* (Matthew 6:9, ASV). If we concentrate on the plural verb found in the "who *art* in heaven," I suggest that "art" refers to the multidimensionality, the trinitarianism, and the divine unionism of the Godhead, while at the same time is not dismissive of the venerated singleness of the one Jewish God: *"Hear Oh Israel. The Lord our God, The Lord God is One"* (Mark 12:29; Deuteronomy 6:4, KJV). God is both triune and one; He is sole, but not solitary. This distinction is important because of the proliferation of the personhood and power that is found in the summary of God's name. That refined, supernatural exaltation is also found in the name of Jesus. Although lowly and meek, and having divested Himself of many majestic comforts in coming to earth, Jesus did not possess an impoverished name. On the contrary, His name was one that was treasurably rich. Even though God attired Jesus in flesh, God saw to it that the Word of God was garbed in a composition of letters that legally created a name above all other names. It was one that was fitting and nomenclature-powered…Jesus! God-the-Father legally "christened" God-the-Son at His birth with an enriched name meaning Savior: *"Everyone who calls upon the name of the Lord will be saved"* (Romans 10:13, BSB).

> *God legally owns exclusive rights to His likeness.*

The Legality of Jesus' Name

Legally, God owns the exclusive rights to His own likeness, including His name. He had openly declared who He was from the beginning and so put the whole world on legal notice:

"I am Alpha and Omega, the beginning and the ending" (Revelation 22:13, NLT). As such, according to governing laws of Intellectual Property, God's name, thus, is His to dispense at His will, including legally sharing it. In looking at the name of God, we see that the name of God represents His nature, character, and will, and He legally bears those likenesses in His name; Jesus is God of God or God-the-Son, so God legally shares His name with Him. Colossians 1:15 says that Jesus is the image of the invisible God, so *Hashem* had the power and the legal right to present it because *Hashem*, the Hebraic title for God, actually means… "The Name." Concludingly, *"The"* name had the legal right to present *"A"* name to Jesus (See John 1:18).

To me, this divine comity is supremely highlighted at the garden's face-off during Jesus' arrest. There Jesus shared the eternal *I Am Who I AM* name of God. In doing so, Jesus flashed a smoldering prism of all of God's Old Testament names; it was a superlunary flame that would prove brighter than all the gang of flickering torches that the arresting guards approached Him with. The power of God's Old Testament names transported His defining, covenantal power in an exponential mini-second as Jesus stood on the precipice of ushering in the New Testament! God's glory soaked itself in the spoken *I AM* of *"Yahweh,"* and in the contained undercurrents of *"El Elyon,"* and in the present electricity of *El Shaddai*, and in the preemptive voltage of its *El Roi*, and in the potent musicality of *Adon Olan*. Just hours earlier, Jesus had asked the Father to glorify His sent Son; now the armed *Bread of Life*, the *Day Star* of the *Living Water*, that same "Immanuel," the stilled *"Agnus Dei,"* and the pre-incarnate *Adonai*, all fully loaded with Jesus' glory, was about break out! *"Go down and warn the people, lest they break through to the* LORD *to look, lest the* LORD *break out against them"*

(Exodus 19:21–22, NIV). It was a showdown, and the name of the Lord showed out! *"They shall be delivered who know my name"* (Psalm 91:14, NIV). Jesus was under-impressed with the guards, for His name had rank power, not like that of a five-star commander, but that of a Morning Star commander Jesus earned that authoritative rank after His military victory on the cross, for His tour of duty took place on that cross. The amalgam of heaviness and depth of Jesus' identifying name made His combatants cave downward under the weight of God's eternal glory, which is unbounded by time, or even the ignorance of men; so it did not matter if the guards knew academically who Jesus was, or if they were totally unlearned about the certain magnitude, depth, and eternality of Jesus. In any case, they had to succumb to the mightiness of the name because there is a spiritual and legal compulsion to that name.

What drama really sprang to life that night? What mystery was unswathed? There, the Old Testament lineage of God's name met fire to fire with Jesus' New Testament's name; antiquity surely met posterity. The cognomens of the two Lords, Adon and Adonai, and their glorious dunameis came together as their labels of Theophany and Christophany merged (See Psalm 110:1). It was both theatrical and voluminous to behold because Jesus had come in the bulk of the Book containing His names. The supreme God, the *DEUS ALTISSIMUS,* showed Himself in the true Temple of Jesus Christ and identified Himself as the *I AM* before the "temple" guards, propelling the Spirit of the holy triad to come forth and cause a luminous explosion of threesome power! The three in one came together, and mortal men lost their balance in the face of that glorious triangulation—the Holy Trinity.

God is sentimental about His adopted kids!

God and His Legal Adoption Process

"Go tell the disciples I ascend to my Father and your Father, my God and your God."

JOHN 20:17

God created many more sons and daughters through spiritual adoption after Jesus' glorified death, and He did it through legal, spiritual adoption: *"Therefore, you are no longer strangers and foreigners, but… members of God's household"* (Ephesians 2:19, BSB). Under American law, an adoption is the legal relationship of a parent and child that is judicially created and causes the adopted child to become the legal heir of the adopter-parent.[78] God wanted to give us His name. The Bible says that the believer, the member of God's Holy congregation, has been adopted into the family of God and given an heir's name. I love that it is circular; we hallow His name, and He gives us His hallowed name! "I will write my name upon their hearts" (Jeremiah 31:33, Emphasis mine). Each of our names and identities has been inscribed, effectively tattooed even, on the palm of God's hand, and He penned it with love and a holy pride (*See* Isaiah 49:16. *See*, also, Ephesians 3:14–15). He writes His names on our hearts and writes our names on His hand. How sentimental is our God about His adopted kids!

"And just as my Father has granted me a Kingdom, I now grant you the right to eat and drink at my table in my Kingdom…" (Luke 22:29–30, NLT). *"…It is done…those who are victorious will inherit all this, and I will be their God and they will be my children"* (Revelation 21:7, NIV). Only children of the royal court get to eat at the king's table-not servants nor non-royals.

One of the important transfers that take place in a legal adoption is the transfer of the adopting parents' surname, most commonly the father's name. The name of God-the-Father and all of its inherent properties were laid out in detail, so any adopted child stands to inherit a boon! *"To them he gave the power to become sons and daughters..."* (John 1:12, ESV). The heirs' inheritance encompasses all the immensity of God's kingdom, including the possession of all its blessings, abundancy, and glory: *"And I confer on you a kingdom, just as my Father conferred one on me..."* (Luke 22:29, NIV). The Bible demonstrates that Father God gave His believers the power to become adopted within the permissible purview of God's laws, that is, grafted in sons and daughters soundly through His laws of sowing and reaping. You see, God literally sowed His Son, Jesus, to harvest more sons of God, and that is one of the reasons Jesus called the Father "The Lord of the harvest." Jesus knew God loved to harvest children and souls! (See Matthew 9:38). Within the American adoption system, there is inheritable power in the transfer and assumption of a name. For example, if a child is adopted into a wealthy family then presumably, absent any stipulations or barring legal roadblocks, the child inherits the wealth, status, access, and opportunities that come with that name; in effect, she or he receives a type of utilitarian and transactional power by virtue of the name. Similarly, in God's spiritual kingdom, God has secured for humankind not only a legal adoption into His family but also granted His legal daughters and sons the *"power to get wealth"* (Deuteronomy 8:18, ESV). God not only granted the power of capacity, but also granted several means to get wealth that is associated with His name, including favor, faith-based obedience, industriousness, resourcefulness, investment, and spiritually overtaking the spoils of the wicked: *"The wealth of the wicked is laid up for the righteous"* (Proverbs 13:22, ISV). Whether one is on the side of thought that says the wealth transfer is spiritual in nature only or one that says that the wealth encompasses both spiritual and worldly goods, there is an obvious transfer of wealth associated with God's name.

The name transfer does not appear to end on this side of heaven for the believer, according to the book of Revelation. Once there, the Bible pleasantly reveals that God will hand out new names to every single believer, featured on a white rock (See Revelation 2:17). I believe the handwritten rock is very telling of God's prioritization of the name. I propose that the rocks contain our God-given, legally adopted names, dispensed not on white lined 8x12 paper, but on a white rock because it is God's preferred writing surface; after all, when God wanted to write down something that would last forever, He wrote in rock, as with the hewed out rock of the Ten Commandments. One might ask, why would God want to give all of His children new names? I conjecture this ceremonial naming occurs because God handpicked a name for His begotten Son, and Scripture says that He loves each believer as much as He loves Jesus, so God desires to handpick names for His adopted sons and daughters, too. God loves you as much as Jesus (See John 17:26). This fathomable concept can hardly be denied because God will do for us, the same thing which His Word illustrates that He will do for His Son at the world's end: *"[Jesus] will have written on his thigh, a name no man knows but himself"* (Revelation 19:12). Notice, similarly, Revelation 2:17 (NASB) reports, *"to the one who overcomes… I will give him a white stone, and a new name written on the stone which no one knows except the one who receives it."* God will treat us alike. It is exhilarating to think that we will one day understand what the Father saw in us the moment that we were fearfully and wonderfully made because, undoubtedly, His personal name for us will reflect that. God would often ask early patriarchs and the children of Israel to place stones of remembrances as markers of a significant act or exchange between them and God. Could it be that as we are changed from mortality to immortality, here, too, God-*Avinu* (Daddy God) wants that moment marked with a stone of remembrance as He welcomes all of His children home forever with a significant "garden party;" a nouveau Eden event that He had in mind since that one fallen act in the Garden.

> *God really, really does love you!*

People adopt for all sorts of nice reasons, which begs the question, why did God adopt? What did God get out of choosing us? God wanted legal adoption because of relationship, relationship, relationship! God yearned for a close, Immanuel-esque relationship with His children. The Bible records that Jesus sings over God's chosen—us (Zephaniah 3:17). If you have ever witnessed a child cooing or singing over a new baby member to the family, you know it is precious. I believe that excitement is how Jesus sees us when we are born again. Scripture even calls us babies who desire the sincere milk of the word (1 Peter 2:2). I'm sure it is a lullaby of nearness that Jesus sings because He wants such deep friendship, not meager, aloof deportment. God also wants a face-to-face relationship, indeed an unveiled intimacy, which is why He came through the veil of the temple to get to us! God has written a narrative for each heart and reads it to us in His own author's voice. The tenor of the voice can deviate, the cadence can vary, the rhythm can sway differently, but the message remains the same: "I love you. I want to be with you." The God-sized cavity found in each of us connects with that message because it is viscerally true. His message of familyship and friendship is exemplified when Christ knocks and asks, "Will you let me in? Can we be family? Can we be friends?" It may be unthinkable that He wanted to woo us and court us with endearing affection, but He did: *"…With loving kindness have I drawn you"* (Jeremiah 31:3, WEB). God provided a legal element to friendship which He fully satisfies.

The Legal Parameters of Love: Making a Case for the Father's Love

"Give all your worries and cares to God, for he cares about you" (1 Peter 5:7, NLT). Even though God paid the ultimate cost in proving His devotion to humankind by dying on a tortuous, loveless, man-made structure, totally proving that we were worth His paradisal love, yet there lingers in the human psyche that all-pervasive question, does

God really love me? The answer is yes, a million blood drops, yes! The same question has been asked in many life vignettes: David asked it while his enemies were in hot pursuit; Job asked it with his body clinging to sores; Peter asked it in the middle of a raging tempest. Suited differently by each inquirer, but the question remains the same, and God, undoubtedly, is still answering it: I loved you so much that I gave *Me*. You can't fake true love, and you can't inculcate true passion; God never did, but in order to understand it and receive it, one has to use non-fleeting faith. Faith is spiritual, and God is a Spirit, so in order to delve into the fathoms of His world, the supernatural, we need the supernatural instrument and the spiritual marker of faith that He left us by which to access Him. He tells us in His Word, however, that our faith is only as good as our love—His love. It is then that you can receive His love, and the answer—I love you and I care about you—becomes resoundingly clear. One arrives at that love by lingering in God's presence, by basking in His holiness, and by sitting in the afterglow of Holy Spirit's deposit of love.

It is then that the gravitas of Cavalry becomes a reality—that God meant what He said and said what He meant when He showed you that He loved you. *"Great is the LORD! He is most worthy of praise! No one can measure His greatness"* (Psalm 145:3, NLT).

Illegal Religiosity Collides with the Legal Supernatural

It was illegal for Jesus to administer healing to the Syrophoenician woman's daughter. He did.

It was illegal for Jesus to take a drink from the Samaritan woman at the well, illegal at the most and unethical at the least. He did.

It was illegal for Jesus to heal a Samaritan leper on the Sabbath. He did.

It was illegal for Jesus to heal a lame man who was crippled from birth. He did.

It was illegal for Jesus to touch an unclean woman with a flow of blood issuing from her, but it was *legal* for her to draw it out of Him by faith. Jesus redirected her miracle by attributing it to her faith. There is a legal supernatural that trumps natural encumbrances. In the legal vernacular, they may be referred to as "legal loopholes." I prefer to call them supernatural navigation light holes. God leaves a way to navigate through the waters of legalism; He gives us oars of faith.

Mysteries of God

> *"My goal is this…that they may have the full riches of complete understanding, in order that they may know the mystery of God, namely, Christ, in whom are hidden all the treasures of wisdom and knowledge."*
>
> COLOSSIANS 2:2-3 (NIV)

God is a God of mystery and suspense, and He loves to unveil Himself and His ways to those who earnestly desire Him in full; in fact, His name, Jehovah, means the one who reveals. There are mysteries galore concerning God, so many in fact, that I would never be able to list them all; I propose these fifteen, which were revealed to me as I pivoted from a traditional scale view of the crucifixion to fully grasp the boundless backdrop of the cross and salvation: *"Great is our Lord… His understanding is infinite"* (Psalm 147:5-6, KJV).

1. The Bright and Morning Star is born under a star that He, Himself, hung.
2. No flesh shall see Him and live, so He lived in flesh that they might see Him.
3. The Good Shepherd is transformed into a lamb.
4. The cosmic King condescends to bottom-rung servanthood.

5. The Glorious One is degraded.
6. The indomitable Lion is trampled upon.
7. The Sinless One is no longer sin-free.
8. The Word of God is speechless on the cross.
9. The Peace Giver holds His peace.
10. The Healer of wounds succumbs to bruises.
11. The Fountain of Life is thirsty.
12. The Sword of the Spirit is impaled by a spear
13. The Father kills His own Son so that others can live.
14. The Gift of God is wrapped in grave clothes.
15. Lord at His birth rises from a tomb to be Lord over all.

Because of the illimitable vastness of God, I am constantly astounded by the epiphanies He loves to share with His own. Compared to the huge entrees of vision that we will have around His throne, these fifteen are only appetizers. May we, as His beloved, ever grow in our spiritual hunger to feast on who He is, in spite of the fact that grasping His great truths is sometimes a little like steering a tiny kayak alongside one who is navigating an ocean liner. It's humbling! It's knee-bending! Humankind, nonetheless, craves to unpack the mysteries of God because He ordained this privilege for His own: *"You should think of us as servants, who have been put in charge of God's secret truths"* (1 Corinthians 4:1, GNT). May we know Him in the totality of who He is with our three windows of comprehension: our minds, hearts, and souls, and may we equally know Him through the three windows of His make-up: Father, Son, and Holy Spirit.

CHAPTER 13

The Warrior: A Legal-Prone God

"'The LORD is a man of war.' 'Look down upon my sorrows and rescue me, for I have not forgotten your law. Argue my case; Take my side!'"

PSALM 119:153 (NLT)

The law is an adversarial discipline. The pursuit of law occurs in a legal firmament that is paced with adversarial contention and argumentation. The above Scriptures are illustrative of the fact that God is legally-prone and has an adversarial nature: *"I will contend with those who contend with you"* (Isaiah 49:25, NIV). Because the Lord God, who is called a Man of War, beat down the curse of sin and stared down death, believers benefit by never having to face the enemy alone. Because retreatism was not an option for God-the-Son who battled in our place, there are some battles where the only thing required is to stand still and see the face of God instead of the enemy's face: *"Moses answered, 'Don't be afraid! Stand your ground, and you will see what the LORD will do to save you today, you will never see these Egyptians again"* (Exodus 14:13, GNT). Steadying our eyes on eternity, we want to see the man who died for us, but the greater reality is that the Savior, Christ Jesus, wants to see the individual face of the one whom He died for. The Bible encourages us to encourage one another to feed on that pragmatism, that although we see things dimly now, there is a day coming when we will see Jesus eyebrow to eyebrow! (See 1 Corinthians 13:12). We will know Him then fully as He is and as our warrior, and He will know us as His eternal beloved that He went to war for. God does not hide His adversarial side: *"I will be an enemy to your enemies and I will oppose those who oppose you"* (Exodus 23:22, NKJV). The pugnacious nature of the Holy Trinity is seen throughout the Word of God. "The Corporation Salvation," or "Team God"—neologisms, which I constructed to refer to the Father, Son, and Holy Spirit corporately—is active in waging war: *"Now thanks be to God who always leads us in triumph in Christ…"* (2 Corinthians 2:14, NKJV). *"I will give him [Jesus] the honors of a victorious soldier, because he exposed himself to death"* (Isaiah 53:12, NLT). The pre-incarnate Jesus identified Himself as a war-like "Captain of the Host," in charge of an intimidating angelic, military force in Joshua's story of friend or foe (See Joshua 5:13). Indicative of the meaning of God's name, *El Shaddai*, is God's leaning toward mightiness and power, for that name means "God Almighty," or "Overpowerer." The Hebrew etymol of *El Shaddai* is *Sadad*, meaning "destroyer," or *Shadad*, meaning to devastate, and *Sad*, meaning mighty breasted or strong chested God. I offer that God's chest is armored in the precious metal of love. Why the love-clad armor? Because there is nothing stronger and greater than God's love according to the word of God: *"Three will last forever… and the greatest of all is love"* (1 Corinthians 13:13). Why was such a radical adversarial process legally needed for humankind in the first place? God's creation, whom He created to be perfect and to live a peaceful life forever, instead yielded voluntarily to contentious sin, and in turn, created a perfect storm of impending doom and war with death. A bold, militaristic remedy, therefore, became legally necessary in that humankind was immersed in two wars, one with death and one with a Holy God. In steps, a bellicose God, furnishing a complete military angelic escort for Jesus to the cross. The very *Yahweh Sabaoath*, meaning "LORD of Warfare," and whom the Bible depicts as the "Wager of War," and "LORD God of Heaven's Armies," invaded Calvary (Exodus 15:3) (1 Samuel 1:3) (Amos 4:13).

The Creator, however, does something extraordinary. Instead of spilling the blood of His creation as punishment because His holiness was at war with humankind, He spilled His own blood to pardon them and to defeat death with whom they warred. What an extraordinary act. The warrior God did not fight His people, notwithstanding their disobedient uprising. Contrastingly, in the face of secular rebellion, history shows a governing British monarchy firing on its own subjects at the famed American Revolutionary battles of Lexington and Concord. Similarly, African dictatorships, Latin American juntas, Russian oligarchies, Asian autocracies, and other authoritarian regimes have used their governing powers to exact civil vengeance on their own people. The government of God is not like any other government that we have seen in history. The Bible explains: "And the government shall be on his shoulder." I believe that Jesus took fallen man on His back and slung Him over His shoulder and said, "I got this!"

"The kingdom of the heavens is taken by violence and the violent seize it."

MATTHEW 11:12 (BLB)

Jesus: Author of Adversarial Redemption

"Be wise as serpents and harmless as doves."

MATTHEW 10:16 (NKJV)

How could Jesus be both an accommodating adversary and a peaceful warrior? The juxtaposition of the two sets seems counter-appropriate. There is not a grain of doubt that Jesus was a fierce representative of the Divine and was not to be mocked. A close, granular look, however, shows that His sacred boldness was moderated and was equal to His holy restraint on earth. Jesus was an all War God and all peace-loving Savior. When mankind found itself spiritually inert, an enmity-ridden creation at odds with God, and languishing in its sin, God, Himself, actively atoned for the sin of mankind. God-the-Son rescued humankind from His own damming, spiritual inertia: *"We esteemed him stricken, and the chastisement of our peace was upon Him"* (Isaiah 53:4–5, ESV). The grace-filled love God has for His beloved is heartening and amazing.

Although Jesus pursued His "deliverance agenda" regarding Zion zealously, He did not do it to invite adversity. In contrast, some people whom He healed, He asked to keep quiet about it, presumably, so as not to prematurely unravel controversy before His destined station to the cross. In line with His own teaching of dove gentleness and snake-like wisdom, it is clear that Jesus' methodology was not one *necessarily* in pursuit of the adversarial. Jesus preferred a focus on His advent, not His adversity, and preferred to have an unpolluted dialogue, not a concocted diatribe. He was interested in victory, not vitriol. Yes, Jesus was peace-abiding, not given to tirades, but He also didn't shy away from being the warrior advocate. Pugnacious as a lion, He brought a sword to the fight—His words: *"Take…the sword of the Spirit which is the word of God"* (Ephesians 6:17, WNT). It is both war-stirring and war-calming that the God who calls Himself *El Shaddai,* the strong-chested, breast-plated God who is more than enough, wore His battle regalia to garner my peace. In Isaiah 59:17, God's righteousness is His breastplate, and His helmet is lined with His salvation. God's royal, martial raiment bears more than just insignia of war; it conjures up an image of an armored-chested God who is battle-ready…but on a peace-keeping mission, too. *"So Gideon built an altar to the Lord there and called it the Lord is Peace…"* (Judges 6:24, NIV). It is no wonder when God raised Christ from the dead, the first words that were brimming over from His mouth were, "Peace unto you," and some of the last words He was excited to say before departing this earth were, "My peace I leave with you."

Jesus, the Legal Advocate: Criminality in Need of a Defense

I've heard it said, even sung, "Jesus is my Lawyer." That statement is biblically true. It could also be said, Jesus is my "Counselor," or Jesus is my "Court Advocate." The Bible places the moniker of Counselor and the appellation of Advocate on Jesus regarding His performance as Counselor of law and as Legal Advocate to the body of Christ: *"And He will be called… Wonderful Counselor…"* (Isaiah 9:6, NIV). The Hebrew translation for Wonderful Counselor refers to Jesus as the "Miracle Counselor"—Pele-Yoez. The term is fitting because when Jesus pleads our cases before Judge God, miracles abound. *"Lord, you have pleaded my soul's cause. You have redeemed my life"* (Lamentations 3:58, NASB). Jesus is the Divine Advocate General of our souls, for the Bible says we have an Advocate with the Father. How big of a deal is it to have Jesus in the roles of Legal Counselor and Legal Advocate? It is a monumental deal because in America's legal system, if a defendant cannot afford an attorney in court, the judge may appoint legal counsel for him. An appointed legal counsel is usually a public defender or possibly a private practitioner who volunteers his counsel. Relatedly, Isaiah 33:22 says that God is a judge, so our Divine Judge appointed Jesus to be the Volunteer Defender of bereft humanity. The crime was sin, and humankind was so spiritually bankrupt that it could not afford the cost of an adequate legal defense; Jesus then advocated on its behalf: *"The Spirit of the Lord will rest on him-the Spirit of wisdom and of understanding, the Spirit of counsel and of might…"* (Isaiah 11:12, KJV). *"Lord, you are my lawyer! Plead my case! For you have redeemed my life"* (Lamentations 3:58, NLT).

Criminality on the Cross:
Will the Real Jesus Please Stand Up?

Another jaw-dropping mystery appears: How is it that the same Advocate who defended humankind with its criminal offenses now finds *Himself* in need of a criminal defense?

The famous scene involved Jesus and two other notable convicts. What stands out is that it also involved *the lex, the rex, and the crux*—the law, the king, and the cross. There, Mary peered at her memorable baby dangling in frozen form on a vicious cross, hanging between two thieves no less. Jesus was a giver, not a robber; in fact, this is how He felt about it: *"...I hate robbery and injustice"* (Isaiah 61:8, CSB). Even according to His alleged "crime" of blasphemy, it did not include robbery. How atrocious to be hanging there in *that* company because He was slated as an irreverent, heretical speaker, but not a robber. Although Jesus was equal to God, He didn't think it was unjust to lower Himself from His quintessentially lofty status to enmesh Himself in man's base flesh. The fact that He did not view this self-subordination as Him being robbed of His divine status convincingly showed that He was not even predisposed to thoughts of robbery. Certainly, when He abdicated His divine placement in the heavenlies with God, He was literally and voluntarily disrobed of His majesty, but exacerbating that voluntary demotion even further was the derision of being involuntarily disrobed for the cross by His Roman taunters. What proved to be further debasing was the custom of the Roman government to release one criminal on the Passover, and the obvious choice would have been Jesus Christ of Nazareth, who was the real innocent one in the criminal morass of two robbers. One criminal was also a reputed murderer-seditionist. Looking in from the outside through the eyes of modernity, I think it would have been appropriate to intone a popular line at that very moment: Will the real innocent one stand up? Of course, Jesus would have stood out, but God obviously had an alternative plan for that moment. Insultingly, another bearing the name of

Jesus was released, Jesus Barabbas. It was a dark moment when Jesus Barabbas—who was not a stand-up guy by any remote means—was released, especially since his name is the Aramaic patronymic means Jesus, "son of father" (*bar abba*). This moment comes to its full light when in comparison, Jesus Barrabas—"son of father"—was ironically released as a free man while the genuine "Son of God," the real Jesus—the Holy one—died a criminal's death. This titular comparison confirms for me that God is involved in every detail of humankind's salvation, even in all that appears to be sour minutiae, because, there, the "Son of God" took the brutal fall instead of a cold-blooded brute. He did it in order for humankind to be called "*sons*" (and daughters) "*of the Father*" (See Matthew 27:16). On the third day, there would be a legal reckoning with the titles. On that "Gettin' Up Morning," in allegiance to His *true* Son, God legally disrupted the grave and showed who the *real* Jesus was!

The Legal Agility of Christ the Lawyer: The Law v. the Lawyers

"'I have kept your laws since I was a boy,' the young man said."

MARK 10:20 (NIV)

The Sanhedrin Council was composed of many men of the law who thought as this man had. The Council certainly had laws since it was the highest-ranking Jewish religio-legal—as I brand it—council of its time, but were its elitist members seeking the full counsel of God regarding those laws? I submit, no, they were not: *"Blessed is the person who does not walk in the counsel of the wicked…but his delight is in the Law of the LORD"* (Psalm 1:1–2, NASB). There is a difference between the factualness of law and a sloppy application thereof. I view Jesus' legal opponents, those of the SanHedrin, the Pharisees, and the Sadducees, as being too focused on churchism instead of salvationism, on politics instead of penance, and on religiosity and grandiosity instead of Jesus' luminosity and virtuosity. They, therefore, were faulty in their application of God's law. Jesus constantly said, *"You have a law,' 'but I say…' (or) 'You have heard it said…but I say'"* (Matthew 5:27-28, NIV). *"You have heard that it was said to the people long ago…but I tell you"* (Matthew 5:21, NIV), (or) *"I give you a new law…"* (John 13:34, CSB). *"That law is 'love each other…'"* (John 13:34, NLT). The bright, apolitical, and truthful legal agility of Christ, the lawyer, is seen by His "swordology," which was His sharpened words that delivered slicing blows to the falsity and legalism of His ideological and spiritual adversaries.

Jesus would die because He gave the law keepers permission to kill Him. They did not *take* His life; He *gave it* as a down payment, a security deposit toward humankind getting its own life back, lawfully. Jesus illustrated this principle again when the teachers of the law lambasted Him for healing on the sabbath. They, in essence, castigated Him for breaking the Sabbath law, His law. Jesus "wrote the book" on the law, and in essence, practiced His specialty on earth. In an act to recalibrate their wrong application/thinking, Jesus asserted the agent of reality, "I am the Sabbath," He said. There, it was a classic case to the highest degree where the teacher schooled the students: *"I have come in the volume of the book it is written of me…"* (Hebrews 10:7, NKJV). The so-called teachers of the law had dissected its truth but failed to commune with "The Truth" Himself. The verbal brawls between Jesus and the Pharisees or Sadducees were constant failed attempts of legal ensnarement. They continually sought the means to mushroom charges against Jesus by attacking Him through legal discussions of the Mosaic laws. They levied their attacks always misfired. These were surface attacks, but brewing below the surface remained a widely spiritual reason for their attacks: *"For a wide door for effective work has opened to me, and there are many adversaries"* (1 Corinthians 16:9,

ESV). Laws are a necessary basis for trials, and although the factually inerrant compliance with the law by the young man and others like him were commendable, the error was applying inapplicable laws to Jesus. Jesus was an innocent man: *"Tempted in every way...yet without sin"* (Hebrews 4:15, NIV). Those Jewish leaders fully relied on laws, but had they fully consulted the counsel of God, they would have seen that the one who healed with signs and wonders was the highly anticipated Messiah on which they were waiting. True, anyone who would dare make himself to be the Son of God was indeed culpable...*unless* He *was* the Son of God.

Jesus, the Greatest Attorney Who Ever...Died

"Woe to you lawyers! For you have taken away the key of knowledge..."

LUKE 11:52 (ESV)

Since they prided themselves on being keepers of the law, Jesus said, *"If you reject even the least important command in the Law and teach others to do the same, you will be the least important person in the kingdom of heaven"* (Matthew 5:19, CEV). By pointing to their own possession of their "newly tweaked and subjectively stoked" law and comparing it with God's pristine law, Jesus was calling out the Pharisees on "their own" doctored laws. He had noticed it about twenty-one years ago at age twelve.

Jesus, who was the law-bringer, frowned on what had devolved into their law of mostly doctrinal fabrications, which, ironically, got its original mold from Jesus, the Law-Maker. Scripture recorded that even as a juvenile, the "lawmen" had marveled at Jesus' exceptionalism and His pursuant command of the laws. The walking word had wielded the written word with an abundance of supernatural ease. In American cultural-ese, one could say, Jesus was "comfortable in His own verbal skin" and "was at ease in His own element," for He was certainly "operating out of His own wheelhouse." By comparison, Jesus made His critics' sharpest thinking look like a globular mess. Jesus was very shrewd in stirring the primordial pot of His genesis. Effectively, He was making His belittlers face where He came from and face who He was, that He existed even before their newly cobbled, self-produced legalistic system.

Another example of Jesus' astounding lawyerly skills is seen in His adult years with staunch proponents of the law. There were pharisaic scribes who were inflexible practitioners and teachers of the codified law of Moses—to the point of being rigidly draconian in their fanatical application of it. Jesus was also in constant conflict with the expert theological doctors of the law, who were more specialized in their adaptation of the Mosaic law. Both of these factions gave the positive term "law-abiding" a bad name, and both wanted to ensnare Him. Trying to tamp down on Jesus' stalwart legal and ministerial authority to do miracles, they strategically asked Jesus by whose authority did He conduct them? As tactical as they were, they were mistakenly smug in their cleverness, for they had reasoned that if Jesus admitted His acts fell under the authority and the auspices of God, they would have the proof of "blasphemy" which they sought so connivingly. Jesus shrewdly gave a legal answer that equaled the strength of a legal reply that can be given, for instance, in some types of United States federal investment settlement cases: "I neither admit nor deny." It is not surprising that Jesus' was righteously and rightfully guardful because He apparently knew it was not the correct time to reveal the origin of His divine authority, so He parried and said, *"Let me ask you a question first…did John's authority to baptize come from heaven or was it merely human? They finally replied that they didn't know. And Jesus responded, 'then I won't tell you by what authority I do these things'"* (Luke 20:3–8). There, Jesus neither said His authority was of God nor said it was not;

He neither admitted nor denied. His answer was precisely sterling in demonstrating His legal agility as a lawyer!

> *The feat of the cross was…miraculous exceptionalism.*

The Mystery of a Mysterious God

As a teen, I remember hearing the following expression: *"God moves in mysterious ways, and His wonders are to be performed."* From that statement, I was supposed to glean that no one can understand the mysteries of a mysterious God, but that inference is only partially correct. The Bible says that it is God's glory to conceal a matter and our honor to search for it (Proverbs 25:2). While God does perform wonders, the mysteries of God are seek-worthy, and many can be found out; in fact, God encourages us to find them out: *"Call unto me…and I will show you things you've never heard or seen…"* (Jeremiah 33:3, KJV). He constantly leaves nuggets of concealed fodder for us to extract and enjoy. *"Oh taste and see that the LORD is good"* is one of His rally cries (Psalm 34:8, NHEB). The cross and the appended resurrection were more than unexplained phenomena! The feat of the cross and resurrection was deliberate, miraculous exceptionalism; it was an exposition of the Father's heart. If you want to know how fulsome God's love was for humankind, one needs to look no further than the savagery of the cross. Jesus was an unrecognizable mass of a man, mainly because He had been the product of flesh-splitting cat o'nine whips, barbed crowns, and full face, frontal mugging. Following the assault and battery to His visage was the fitting of His hands with irregular, gargantuan nails that bore through the flesh of His wrists, and His hobbled ankles felt the horrific pain, too. Out of this heinous treatment, however, exuded the rubric of God's passion. The mystery of the cross is both the headliner and the discoverable proof of God's love.

The cross is both an enigmatic symbol as well as a plain symbol of God's love; it is ripe with profundity as well as transparency. The cross can be both polished and raw in the same breath when spilling over with messages about God. God was both an onlooker as well as the action figure on the cross. The cross underscored God's ability to be ubiquitous. That is, God was seated in the heavens while at the same time dying on the cross. God has dual existence—God of God. The pleasant surprise is that God granted this proclivity to humankind, too. Specifically, God has made it possible for the believer to have dual citizenship or to belong to a dual citizenry; in other words, we are both inhabitants of the earth and of heaven at the same time. The Bible explains the spiritual citizenry like this: *"We are seated in heavenly places in Christ Jesus"* (Ephesians 2:6, NIV).

The sub-mystery of the great mystery of the cross is how God could be both delighted and repulsed at the same time. With each contusion Jesus amassed on His chafed bloody back, God ticked off two boxes: Iniquity and Healing. It was as if God rejoiced in His own word-inspired proclamation to Prophet Isaiah: *"He was bruised for our iniquities"* (Isaiah 53:5, KJV). Notwithstanding His complete disgust with the quotient of sin, it seems God was absolutely giddy over the ripped-up back of His Son, not because He delighted in the torture He received, but because it spawned healing for a kingdom. Irrespective of the contusions on Jesus and the malodorous stench of the copious amounts of blood that He shed, for a slaughter took place on the cross and not a trickling of blood because Jesus lost a massive amount of blood. Isaiah prophesied Jesus was like a lamb to a slaughter. Sure, the blood smelled bad, but the odor delighted God because it was the smell of the sacrificial lamb of the atonement process which God, Himself, had instituted. What God smelled was the sweet fragrance of a blood-ridden sacrifice. In the midst of the most horrendous sorrow, which Jesus had expressed just hours before, was the double delight of the trinity.

The Legal Pardon of God: Waymaker

"What is man that thou You remember him?"

PSALM 8:4 (NIV)

Jesus made it possible for the lawbreaker to approach the lawgiver. Throughout the Bible, we constantly see lawbreakers. What is a lawbreaker? I think of a lawbreaker in three ways. A lawbreaker is one who has transgressed—or has crossed over the marked boundary of God's law. Alternatively, it is one who has fallen short of reaching the high bar of God's law, or it can be one who is slightly off the mark of hitting the bullseye of God's law. Because of Jesus, there is good news for every lawbreaker. The confetti message of the cross is that the lawgiver has forgiven the lawbreaker because the Way-Maker has made a way in His wasteland. With the birth of the Christ child, the longevity of sin's domination over the lawbreaker was about to come to an end, and its defeat was only a cross away. *Operation Legal Pardon* was about to be launched. God, the highest executive of the universe, could, in fact, issue an executive pardon. Under our American legal system, an executive pardon is executive forgiveness of a criminal offense. A pardon from God was not a random thought but involved a magnitude of legal application. God issued a pardon of forgiveness by proactively getting involved in the affairs of humankind with a purposeful plan to free it from sin's death grip and to negate his punishment. Without it, surely man was headed to an irrevocable death row, but God was thinking of him. Jesus was bludgeoned in our place, and the Bible articulates that the world thought He was being punished for something He had done wrong. His punishment canceled our punishment: *"Put on the new man which was created according to*

> *The confetti message of the cross is forgiveness.*

God, in true righteousness and holiness" (Ephesians 4:24, NKJV). The pardon was issued from God in His official capacity as Executive and Sovereign of all. It was a Pardon *De Jure,* in other words, a pardon as a matter of God's law: *"Let him return unto the Lord, for He will abundantly pardon"* (Isaiah 55:7, KJV).

God was not through, however, and went beyond a pardon. In law, "expungement" is the process by which a criminal record is effectively erased by being destroyed or sealed from a state or federal record. God caused Calvary to act as a divine, colossal eraser of humankind's criminal activity; therefore, all records of all wrong and all criminal engagement have been erased by virtue of Jesus Christ's crucifixion. Jesus Christ silenced our accuser and wiped out all references to humankind's criminal activity of sin against God. What is remarkable and worth noting is that God could have issued a Sovereign Executive pardon *only,* which is forgiveness and which He had the latitude to do, but within His extended sense of justice, He *insisted* on a legal expungement. Along with the pardon. Yes, He issued a pardon but went further than that—why? God wanted to free humankind from sin *and* sin's reputation. He wanted a judicial solution similar to what our American judicial system accomplishes with an expungement order-an erasure; there, the Judge orders all relevant recording parties to treat the crime as if it had *never* occurred. God gave humankind a new reputation, something a pardon alone could not achieve. "Behold, I make all things new." A pardon would have excused humankind for his wrongdoing and exempted it from prosecution but would have still left a stained record behind. God issued an "all things new," "way maker special order." He knew that a pardon alone would not have erased the record of man's initial wrongdoing, and that was the optimally just result that God wanted for every convert: *"As far as the east is from the west… I will remember your sins no more"* (Psalm 103:12, NIV). This judicial route and erasure show the powerful efficacy of the blood covering of Jesus to cover a multitude of sins, and it flashes God's demonstrable, caring, and loving divinity for His humanity!

> *A believer's trial should not be tortuous but revelatory.*

Why God Allowed Jesus to Go to Trial: Why God Allows the Believer's Trial

"Try my reins and my heart that you have put your law in."

PSALM 26:2-3 (KJV)

The Faith trial is not meant to be tortuous but is meant to reveal our heart's faith. It is completely revelatory and evidentiary of what our faith levels and our heart tendencies are (See Hebrew 8:10). It makes sense that God allowed His Son to go through the legal process that was set up. Why? I believe God permitted Jesus to go on trial to reveal the heart of God and the heart of Jesus, as mentioned previously. For that same pragmatic reason, believers must go through trials, too. In the natural court system, when a person goes through a trial, exhibits of behavior and events can be entered into evidence. Similarly, what we exhibit during a trial can be utilized to measure our faith and to render a verdict about us *"When I am tried, I shall come forth as pure gold"* (Job 23:10, ESV). So once the trial is over, and the evidence of our faith is in, God's verdict of vindication from doubt would be tantamount to gold. Obviously, if there's lack of evidence of faith, or if there's mounting evidence of waning faith which convicts, then we have got some work to do.

What a great mystery because God allowed Himself to be put on trial in the form of His Son, to be beaten without a cause and to be dealt deathblows without any wrongdoing. Who does that? Only a God who so fully and so unfathomably loves His creation. Jesus' trial was necessary to show God's redemptive nature—that He was willing to go to any length to redeem us. The trial of the cross revealed Jesus' vast love and *friendship* as the second person of the Godhead. He is the friendship arm of the Trinity, and God is the sovereign arm. Jesus did something very interesting as the defense attorney in the trial of humankind before Judge God. Usually, in a dire case when there are no relevant character witnesses for the defendant, nor any that are up to par, or perhaps where there is mounting incriminating evidence against the defendant, which seems insurmountable to the point of losing the case, it is feasible for the defense to call the accused to the witness stand as a voluntary witness in a desperate juncture like that. Such a strategy, however, is customarily an absolute last and undesirable option because of the high risk of self-incrimination, but it is an essential opening for the defendant to his story. Another way that a defendant might mitigate a bleak sentencing outcome in another last-ditch effort is to throw himself on the mercy of the court. What is so astronomically interesting about this particular legal maneuver is that it is usually *the client* who tells his story on the stand, and it is *the client* who throws himself on the mercy of the court, with the legal representation of counsel or without it sometimes. Despite the horrific instrumentality of the crucifixion process itself, the mean Roman guards, or the atrocious behavior of envious Jewish leaders, they were all unwittingly part of God's agency of preordination. They were all agents of God's plan to rescue the world. Jesus' alleged ruination was engulfed in a powerful journey to the cross that would become a desirable linchpin in the life of every believer to come: *"For judgment is without mercy to the one who has shown no mercy"* (James 2:13, NKJV). In the trial of humankind, however, it is *Jesus* who tells our story of redemption on the cross, and it is *Jesus* who throws Himself on the mercy seat of God for the accused! In short, the blood went to court! After telling our story at the cross, Jesus delivered His blood that drained from His body to God's heavenly mercy seat for our violations of God's criminal code of sin. Thanks to Jesus, mercy prevailed. *That* merciful act from the one who was shown no mercy at Calvary is the cross's golden nugget! Story over!

Silence Is Ruby

> *"The LORD roars from Zion and raises His voice from Jerusalem."*
>
> AMOS 1:2 (BSB)

We've heard the expression, "Silence is golden," but those who were present at Calvary's crucifixion witnessed that silence is ruby. The rich, dark, ruby hue of Jesus' blood poured from His body in His silence. Jesus was indeed silent, but He was not wordless. The roar of His silence was deafening! Although His mouth didn't verbalize anything most of the time while on the cross, that didn't matter because Jesus is the Word of God, and it is impossible to muzzle the impact of the Word of God. Jesus delivered a great part of His oration with His body, and it could have filled libraries: *"There are so many things that Jesus did… that even the world itself could not contain the books that would be written"* (John 21:25, KJV). On that cross, Jesus opined about the love of God. It was a divine filibuster against death for six long hours as Jesus staved off His departure to argue His atonement for the freedom of humankind's soul. The Word of God engaged in a *"fait accompli:"* *"My WORD shall not return unto me void, but will accomplish everything it was sent to do"* (Isaiah 55:11, KJV). God had sent the Word of God to defeat the cross, and He accomplished the cross.

The expression, "wearing one's heart on one's sleeve," falls short of depicting the passion that Jesus displayed on the cross. It is more apt to say that Jesus wore His heart on His hands, for when Jesus died with outstretched hands on the cross, He left heartprints! It was His spiritual heart that freed humankind on that cross, and it was His physical heart that was medically altered in the process, as discussed above.

Such was the magnanimity of His heart for humanity; Jesus genuinely died of a broken heart on the cross, and the donor-Christ donated a piece of it to every man, woman, and child who receives Him. God's love for humankind was undeniable as Jesus interposed His body between the wrath of God and humankind, making Himself a true, divine "bodyguard:" "...*You have given men a body to offer*" (Hebrews 10:5, NIV). The immortal God dying on the cross for us, sheathed in mortal flesh, was more than a demonstration of mere sovereign hubris, and His dying for a lost love is more than a bromide; it was an incontrovertible passion of the purest and highest order. In a very literal and spiritual sense, a heart transplant took place; there, Jesus gave up His heart for ours.

CHAPTER 14

God's Judgeship

"...To God, the Judge of all..."

HEBREWS 12:23 (NIV)

There is a legal enterprise that God has set in motion, and He is the Judge of it all. There are both visible and invisible courts under God's influence and within God's sophisticated system. He amazingly rules the earth and participates in the judgment of our lives and our deaths. God's heavenly judiciary consists of His Holy Alliance—the Divine Trinity: Holy Spirit judges other spirits; Jesus judges the world upon His return; God, the just Judge, judges all. Within His discretionary powers of shared judgment, God involves an interactive, legal conglomerate of believers that, along with Him, can judge the fruit of others, and one day will even judge angels: *"Or do you not know that the saints will judge… the angels"* (1 Corinthians 6:2–3, BSB).

A Judge Throws the Book

To "throw the book" at someone means to impose the maximum possible penalties for all possible charges toward a convicted criminal that are allowable and applicable to his crime(s).

The usual courtroom jargon, "the Judge threw the book at him," is quite common to hear. Said differently, that expression can refer to sentencing from a judge that appeared statutorily merciless or which fell within the harshest permissible tier of regulatory guidelines found in controlling "judicial books." I find that the concept of "throwing the book" is really bible-esque, as it is literally found in the Bible. The judicious Moses was a *shofet*, a ruler-judge, and an early template of Israel's eventual judges (Exodus 18:13). Upon coming down from the "mountain of God" and witnessing the shocking lawlessness in the camp below, the enraged Moses physically threw the "books of law," or tablets of the God-given law, in righteous and livid protest of the offenders of that law. Such was a defining moment that invoked God's quick and unmerciful judgment which resulted in the guilty participants being harshly wiped out. It seems that our American judiciary may have taken a page out of this intra-biblical account with its now popularized terminology: "He threw the book."

BEMA Judgment

The *BEMA* Seat Judgment, or the Judgement of Christ as it is also known, will be a big affair. It is going to happen! *"For we must appear before the judgment seat of Christ, so that each of us may receive what is due us for things done while in the body, whether good or bad"* (2 Corinthians 5:10, NIV). The etymology of the word Bema, is found in the Greek and means "raised platform" or in Hebrew, "high place." In Ancient Greece, the Bema involved what I label as "court calisthenics" because it was centered around a trial regarding the competitive performance of athletes where representatives of opposing sides argued their cases before a raised judge and jockeyed heavily for the favor of the judge's ruling regarding their athletes' performances. It was an all-out legal joust, a true "courtside" event. It is believed that King Herod, in order to parallel Grecian construction, built a judgment seat where he was a spectator of athletic contests.[79] The Bema Seat judgment is just one of two final, heavenly judgments which the Bible depicts through the eyes of Apostle Paul. The Bema Seat judgment involves the Christ-professing, saved believer, in contrast to another judgment, the Great White Throne judgment, which pertains to the unredeemed unbeliever. Both involve future eschatological forums, but they could not be more dissimilar. The believer's judgment is to occur at the Bema judgment and will be composed of a type of award ceremony for God's saints. Similar to the concept which Paul undoubtedly observed during his stay in Greece, for the participants will stand before the exalted Almighty who sits "raised" on His judgment throne: *"And every man shall receive his own reward according to his own labour"* (1 Corinthians 3:13–14); *"Every man's work shall be made manifest, for the day shall declare it, because it shall be revealed by fire, and the fire shall try every man's work of what sort it is. If any man's work abides which he hath built thereupon, he shall receive a reward…"* (1 Corinthians 3:13–14, KJV). The unbeliever's judgment, however, will take place at the Great White Throne and will comprise a ceremony of infliction of penalties: *"Whoever believes in Him is not condemned, but whoever does not believe stands condemned already"* (John 3:18, NIV).

Specifically at the BEMA, because each Christ-believer 's name will have been found in the Lamb's book of eternal life, rewards will be disbursed respectively at the Bema Seat: *"Listen, says Jesus, 'I am coming soon! I will bring my rewards with me, to give to each one according to what he has done"* (Revelation 22:12, GNT). It appears that the only legal argument that will be entertained at the Bema before the high and lifted Holy One is the argumentation by Jesus as a legal advocate, explaining how well His church athletically performed in faith—how they ran well on the concourse of life by putting their faith in Him and finished the race of faith. The judgment, therefore, will be a benedictory "Well Done!" and praises for the virtuous works done by the believer while on earth.

The Crowning

"An athlete is not crowned unless he competes according to rules."

2 TIMOTHY 2:5 (ESV)

In ancient Greece, during the *Isthmian* games, the victorious athletes competed in honor of a false deity for a temporal wreath and were openly crowned as victors following their performances and the judge's determination of their accomplishments.[80] A beautiful part of God's Bema ceremony is that saints will be rewarded with eternal crowns in honor of Jesus at the end of their life accomplishments and will have the opportunity to cast those crowns at the feet of the Lamb who made it possible for them to receive them: *"And everyone who competes for the prize is temperate in all things. Now they do it to obtain a perishable crown, but we for an imperishable crown"* (1 Corinthians 9:25, NKJV). The casting of the crowns is more than *pro forma because* this pleasant exertion *actually serves* two significant purposes. Firstly, it causes the believer to acknowledge that the Lord of the Crown is immeasurably more important than receiving the crown itself, and that is why we will gleefully part with the treasured crown. Secondly, I suggest that the casting of the crowns also represents the valuation of God's currency. That is, only crowns which are given by the Lord of the Crown are commensurate in value with the Crown, and therefore, are worthy enough to be presented to the Crown. It is sobering to emotionally ingest that although heaven's treasury is replete with inestimable gold and wealth, the invaluable contents of its coffers were not even enough to put a down payment on our souls. It took the high-priced, costly life and the affluent blood of Jesus to re-purchase them. For that very reason, believers will eagerly crown Jesus "Lord" at the ceremony. We will be the diamonds and rubies in His crown: *"In that day, they shall be mine when I make up my jewels"* (Malachi 3:17, ESV). Jesus, on behalf of "The Crown," will conduct a two-tier court examination because there are legal rules for every heavenly athlete to adhere to:

> *It means very little to me that you or any human court should cross-examine me. I don't even ask myself questions… Therefore, don't judge anything before the appointed time. Wait until the Lord comes. He will also bring to light what*

> *is hidden in the dark and reveal people's motives. Then each person will receive praise from God.*
>
> 1 CORINTHIANS 4:3-5 (GW)

The Lord will examine the counsel of the heart, which are mental motives, and the acts of life, which are earthly deeds. In law, the motive or guilty mindset (the *"mens rea"*) coupled with the liable or guilty act (the *"actus reus"*) are usually considered together in determining criminal liability, or the lack thereof.[81] Jesus, too, will determine if there are shortcomings in the believers' motives of works. Works don't determine salvation, but they will be recognized or alternatively discarded as loss: *"If any man's work shall be burned, he shall suffer loss, but he himself shall be saved; yet so as by fire"* (1 Corinthians 3:15, KJV). Interesting is the reality that the believer could experience loss at that ceremony, not loss of God's eternal presence because the believer is saved, but loss by disqualification and forfeiture of potential rewards for works that were done with a motive that was less than full virtuous. God's primary focus is always on the heart! *"I am the one who searches out the thoughts and intentions of every person. And I will give to each of you whatever you deserve"* (Revelation 2:23, NLT). Believers will be praised by Jesus when their acts and motive converge in purity for the works of the Lord. *"He who judges me is the Lord"* (1 Corinthians 4:4, NKJV)

In life and in death, Jesus saves! *"For if by one man's offence death reigned by one; much more they which receive abundance of grace and of the gift of righteousness shall reign in life by one, Jesus Christ"* (Romans 5:17, KJV). There, even in the afterlife, a believer's standing will be honored, and he can legitimately approach the Bema Seat of God without peril of eternal death: *"So a book of remembrance was written before Him For all those who fear the Lord and meditate on His name"* (Malachi 3:16, NKJV). Inherent within this concept of after-life salvation begs a mysterious extraction because embedded within the Bema model is another one of God's enfolded triumphs of mystery. Essentially, the rewards, which are received are merit-worthy in nature only because of God's unmerited grace; that is, the believer would have never deserved them at all, but for the undeserving grace of God which caused him to overcome and be award-worthy. One has accessibility, and not terminality, before God only because of Jesus' mitigator's role in expelling sin's original, un-celebratory penalty toward humanity. Because of His mediatorial role, it was agreed that humankind's sin was atoned for by Christ, the perfect propitiation, and its life was exchanged for that of the substituted scapegoat. Because of His attorney-advocate role, Jesus submitted His blood into evidence so that God's eternal progeny could escape a damning conviction and now celebrate its crowns. Jesus went out on a spiritual limb for us! For all these crowning reasons, Let's Celebrate the Lord! *"A scroll of remembrance was written in his presence concerning those who feared the* LORD *and honored his name. 'They will be mine,' says the* LORD *almighty. 'In the day when I makeup my treasured possession. I will spare them...'"* (Malachi 3:16–17, ESV).

Establishing Jesus' Judgeship

"For it is time to seek the LORD, *'till He comes.'"*

HOSEA 10:12 (NIV)

It is mention-worthy that Jesus will one day, at His Father's direction, return with Holy fire to judge the world: *"See, the* LORD *is coming with fire..."* (Isaiah 66:15, NIV). Jesus, although a qualifying judge in the image of His Father, held back executing divine judgment while on the earth: *"For I did not come to judge the world but to save the world"* (John 12:47, ESV).

And save, Jesus did! A great pronouncement and execution of God's judgment took place during the trial of man's soul and resulted in a guilty verdict; however, not against man, but against man's surrogate, Jesus. God's begotten Son—not God's created son—was found guilty. Such was the judgment of God, and the unfathomable twist of justice was fashioned from the cradle to the cross. It was no fluke, no accident, nor happenstance that man was perfectly justified and legally exonerated of condemnatory sin by the Lamb's blood; it was a convergence of the preordained. Jesus, however, reserves that judicial right to judge for His return; *"…The Lord will judge His people"* (Hebrews 10:30, NIV). Jesus had been adjudged guilty before the annals of time in order to legally tender payment for Adam's bill of sin. To reject the consummation of the cross is to start the clock on one's own unfavorable judgment. To reject the consummation of the cross is to curry unending damnation. It is a decision that each practicing member of humankind must make. It is that judgment which inevitably breeds judgment. Jesus bore the undeserved, eternal judgment for humankind, and now He will correspondingly judge legally what humankind deserves eternally. This is the judgment of Jesus. He will finish what God started: *"In the day when God shall judge the secrets of men by Jesus Christ"* (Romans 2:16, KJV; Emphasis mine). Jesus will not only take up the position of Judge, He, Himself, will be the standard of justice and recompense by which all are judged: *"Serve the LORD with reverence and rejoice with trembling. Kiss the Son, that He not be angry and you perish on the way. For His wrath may be kindled quickly…how blessed are all who take refuge in Him!"* (Psalm 2:12, NASB). Judas kissed the Son, not with the kiss of homage or friendship, but with the deadly kiss of rejection. It made Jesus angry, but Jesus also hurt because He knew Judas' rejection of Him as the Messiah would cause him to perish as a son of perdition: *"…What are these wounds in thine hands? Then he shall answer, 'Those with which I was wounded in the house of my friends'"* (Zechariah 13:6, KJV).

The Bible says that Jesus' kingdom has no end, and He even told His followers that the kingdom of God is at hand; so, in actuality, Jesus already possessed the kingdom: *"…The kingdom of the world has become the Kingdom of our Lord, and of His Messiah. He will reign forever and ever"* (Revelation 11:15, NIV). The nuanced reveal there is that Jesus came to earth not to get His kingdom back but to get humankind's right back to partake in His kingdom. When Jesus took the keys of death and hell, it was as if He were the mayor of the heavenly New Jerusalem and giving the key to the eternal city's honorees.

Great White Throne Judgment

"It is appointed unto man once to die, but after this the judgment."

HEBREWS 9:27 (KJV)

Garnering a starkly different result is the final judgment for the unrepentant unbeliever who rejected the redemptive offer of salvation. *"And I saw the dead, small and great, stand before God; and the books were opened; and another book was opened, which is the Book of Life: and the dead were judged out of those things which were written in the books, according to their works"* (Revelation 20:12, KJV). Isaiah 30:27 says that we can testify against ourselves, and Job 15:6 alerts us that our own testimony can "put us away:" *"Thine own mouth condemns you, not I: your own lips testify against you."* A frightful judgment is reserved for those unsaved, lost souls: *"For we know him who said, 'it is mine to avenge; I will repay, and again,' The Lord will judge his people"* (Hebrews 10:30, NIV) (See also, 1 Corinthians 3:10–15). One might ask, does love belong in this chapter since tearful damnation is evident? My answer is absolutely. Thematically, three words are both the prologue and epilogue of God's message: "I love you." For God so loved the world, that it was worth killing for; and Jesus loved God so much, that their love-bond was worth Him being killed for it. Rejection, therefore, of this consummate act of love commands what might look like a loveless consequence, but it really is the just aftermath of one's own terse refusal. To reject the consummation of the cross is to reject a damnation-free, eternal life. It is literally rejecting a life-ark that is made available from a loving God. It, in a true sense, is killing your opportunity for an eternal life with God. *"For our transgressions are multiplied before you, and our sins testify against us; for our transgressions are with us, and our iniquities, we know them"* (Isaiah 59:12, BSB). That verse imparts that God gives determinate testimony about us from His book of records: *"'Listen, my people, and I will speak; I will testify against you, Israel; I am God, your God;' 'Oh my people, listen as I speak. Here are my charges against you...'"* (Psalm 50:7, NIV). Like a real court proceeding, the Great Throne judgment will contain charges, testimony, conviction and sentencing. God's testimony against an individual is absolutely dispositive of the outcome. *"...So I will come near to you for judgment. I will be quick to testify..."* (Malachi 3:5, NASB).

> The Great Throne judgment will be like a court proceeding.

The uncoated truth is that it does not have to end badly for anyone: *"He will give eternal life to those who keep on doing good, seeking after the glory and honor and immortality that God offers"* (Romans 2:7, NLT). *"But because you are stubborn and refuse to turn from your sin, you are storing up terrible punishment for yourself. For a day of wrath when God's righteous judgment will be revealed"* (Romans 2:5, NLT) Although God's testimony on its own could condemn an unbeliever, He is not only judicious, but a God of *prima* justice and does things patently righteously: *"God will repay each person according to what they have done"* (Romans 2:6, NIV). God, therefore, will have a transparent display of proof of the unbeliever's guilt. God will hold court one last time and permit an actual, final trial before sentencing an unbeliever to eternal damnation, *legally proving* his or her rejection of salvation and choice of eternal separation from Him. *God's judgeship begs the non-rhetorical question, the all-essential question which must be asked of us all*: Since God is the ultimate Judge of my eternity, how will I prepare for my immortality, and how will I prepare for court? *"But for those who are* self-seeking and who reject the truth and follow evil, there will be wrath and anger" (Romans 2:8, NIV).

Diversity: The Straight and Narrow of It?

"Your love for one another will prove to the world that you are my disciples."

JOHN 13:35 (NLT)

God did not populate planet earth with homogeneity but with diversity. He obviously wanted a creation of variety and one that would be unified by love and have oneness as its core identifier. Oneness is not necessarily mutually existent with sameness. As His first paragon of human creation, God could have made Adam and Eve identical. He did not. It is clear that given the global diversity of people groups upon the earth, God relishes anatomical, ethnic, racial, and anthropological diversity, to name a few. In the story of the Good Samaritan, Jesus elaborated on the virtue of neighborly love and two roads, the road of religious life and the road to diversity." He said, *"All the law and the prophets hang on these two commandments. Love your neighbor as yourself. Love the Lord your God with all your heart and with all your soul and with all your might"* (Deuteronomy 6:5, KJV). Clearly, the Great Commission is a nation-rich command. It says *"Go...disciple people in all nations"* (Matthew 28:19, CEV). To be sure, when heaven's door opened to Apostle John during His visitation from Jesus, we can see a blessed assortment of people from every nation and tribe, so the Samaritan *will* be represented in heaven. There was nothing incidental about God's miscellaneous selections for eternal occupancy in His up-and-coming eternal neighborhood.

> *To love our brother freely is to love God totally.*

Diversity and God's Round Table, Here & in the Hereafter

The Bible is God's expose on His feelings about divine, ring-shaped inclusion. God's laws of love and demonstration of variety are evident throughout the entire Bible. God did not create a uniform creation, not in nature, not in animal beings, nor in human beings. God delights in His majestic touch of creative differentiation. God's Word is very clear on the celebrations He has planned for His millennial-welcome home party. The heavenly congregation is meant to establish an atmosphere of inclusion of both natives and foreigners to the faith as long as they have the common denominator of salvation through Jesus Christ. All present are meant to reflect God's version of circular inclusion, one that would reflect the round table of heaven. There, God's love flows vertically from Him into us, then laterally through one another, and circles back to Him. To love our brother freely is to love God totally. *"Whoever claims to love God yet hates a brother or sister is a liar"* (1 John 4:20, NIV).

CHAPTER 15

The Devil *Is* A Liar! Legally Shut Him Up!

"I am the righteousness of God in Christ Jesus."

2 CORINTHIANS 5:21 (KJV)

The Devil often conducts warrantless searches and illegal seizures against the children of God. Jesus made it clear that the Devil comes for one purpose only, to steal (unlawfully seize), lie, and kill. The Constitution's Fourth Amendment search, seizure, and warrant protections gave rise to the "exclusionary rule," which prevents unlawfully seized evidence from being admissible in a court of law.[82] The exclusionary rule sees to it that a defendant must have been "Mirandized" before being interrogated or whatever confession made or whatever evidence obtained against him is excluded from being used against him in a court of law. The Bible confirms that the Devil has a two-pronged attack; he first searches by seeking whom he can devour, and he then initiates a destructive seizing and consumption campaign, known as devouring. Know this: if the Devil takes or attempts to take what he does not have rightful ownership of, he has illegally seized it. If it has not been authorized by God, then he does not have a warrant of cause to take it, and his seizure is both *unwarranted and warrantless*. At that point, you can be certain that the Devil is then guilty of the crime of theft, which is stealing, and has violated the believer's Constitutional privileges and rights under God's Constitution. The positive news is that God has a lawful remedy against the enemy's devilment in His Word. Like David, at Ziklag, you have the right to enter into the enemy's camp and take back what He stole from you through Godly warfare: *"I have given you power to tread upon serpents and scorpions underfoot, and to trample upon all the power of the enemy"* (Luke 10:19, WNT).

A central idea of the milestone United States Supreme Court case, *Miranda v. Arizona (1966)*, is that any evidence collected against an individual in an adversarial police interrogation cannot be used against him in court if he were not informed of both this constitutional right against self-incrimination—the right not to be a witness against himself—and his constitutional right to an attorney because that interrogation could be flagged as coercive: "You have the right to remain silent. Anything you say can and will be used against you in a court of law. You have a right to an attorney. If you can't afford an attorney, one will be provided for you..."[83] Correspondingly, in the kingdom of God, the Devil, your adversary, has gone about seeking to devour you and collecting things that you have said and done as evidence of your guilt of unrighteousness. The real truth of the matter is he can't use them against you in God's Court because he is the deceiver and a liar, and as such, did not tell you the truth—that you have protective rights against self-condemnation as a child of God. The Devil is good at accusing us and even getting us to incriminate ourselves by agreeing with him. He doesn't want the believer to know he has had a protective safeguard all along—the righteousness of God in Christ. Your Miranda-like right is the mantle of righteousness that God has established for you through His Supreme Court. When the enemy demonstrates the audacity to accuse you and to interrogate you with his accusatory tone, know that you have your God-given right not to incriminate yourself with efforts of self-condemnation and you have the right to an attorney, Jesus. The cautious aspect about an individual's Miranda rights is that a person may have them, but if he does not invoke them vigorously and unambiguously, they do not operate. In other words, an individual must speak up, be clear and unequivocal about requesting an attorney, or the court may be likely to construe a tepid response as an inadequate response. Likewise, a believer should specifically speak up and declare: I have the right to keep silent, and to be still and wait upon the Lord, but if I should choose to speak, be advised, Devil, that anything I say can and will be used against *you*. Clearly, none of your weapons formed against me will prosper, and every tongue raised against me, including yours, I condemn. Truly, I am *not* condemned, for I am the righteousness of God in Christ. And if I want an attorney, my Father in heaven has already appointed my advocate, Jesus, my legal counsel. *"There is therefore now no condemnation for those who are in Christ Jesus"* (Romans 8:1, ESV). The dome of this chapter is to not let the enemy into your spiritual embrace, your mental dwelling, your emotional space, your bodily temple, or your financial lodging with his roguish intent to illegally seize from you. Nor should you allow his condemnatory rhetoric. Whatever he seizes from you, or whatever territorial gain he establishes by unlawfully accusing you, he will use against you to craftily condemn you. Instead, cast every condemnatory thought away: *"We tear down arguments and every presumption set up against the knowledge of God and we take captive every thought to make it obedient to Christ"* (2 Corinthians 10:5, BSB).

Christ Inside the Courtroom: Rules of Evidence

Federal Rules of Evidence govern the admissibility and authentic identification of exhibited pieces of evidence in American courts. Under Federal Rules of Evidence 901(a)(b), a specimen that is to be admitted as "real evidence" must pass the rigor of the "chain of custody" rule, which carefully takes into account the movement and location of the object to be proffered from the time it was obtained to the time of its admissibility in court, as well as the past actions of the persons who had custody of it.[84] One of the purposes of this rule is to account for the object's whereabouts at all times and to preserve its authenticity and purity. Theoretically, I submit that the freshly risen Jesus admonished Mary not to touch Him because of this very legal consideration; that is, He desired to keep the "chain of custody" pristine regarding His body and blood in order to pass God's evidentiary rules of admissibility when He appeared in God's Court: *"Touch no unclean thing…"* (2 Corinthians 6:17, NIV); *"Touch me not, for I am not yet ascended to the Father"* (John 20:17, KJV). Jesus knew that His very blood was to be introduced into evidence as the mitigating factor to procure a different sentence for culpable humankind. Crucially, if Mary had touched Christ outside the tomb before He presented His blood sacrifice, Satan's probable objection to Christ's admission of the blood sacrifice could have been plausibly sustained because of the broken chain of custody. Jesus' all-important blood had to pass the evidence rule to be admitted into evidence and onto the Court's mercy seat. Satan's strategy, in all probability, was to protest the admissibility of Christ's panacean blood by arguing that, as a matter of evidentiary procedure, it violated the chain of custody because the blood arguably had not been preserved in an adequate manner so as to properly guard against extraneous contamination or tainting. That legal argument could have been exceedingly overcome by Jesus' apparent, heightened safeguard of His own blood as seen with Mary; that protestation also would have been likely overruled effectively because of Jesus' timely ascension with His pure, claret-colored plasma. After overcoming any objections, the Lamb of God was free to take His awaited place on the mercy seat, enthroned between two cherubim with that glorious serum that redeemed humankind from a hellish sentence. Jesus' bordeaux-pigmented blood was sprinkled on the mercy seat for the world *in toto* because anyone in the world who has ever sinned, or who will sin takes his part in crucifying Jesus; He died for the whole world.

Hearsay Evidence

In the United States courts of law, the "hearsay" rule operates thusly: A "hearsay" statement is *not* admissible into evidence unless it falls under an evidentiary exception permitted by the Federal Rules of Evidence or by statute. A "hearsay" statement is a statement other than one made by the declarant while testifying at the trial or hearing, offered in evidence to prove the truth of the matter asserted."[85] I like to simplify it this way: "hearsay" refers to someone else's communication that a person *heard* and is now *saying*. In God's Court of law, the hearsay rule operates like this: Jesus communicated—you've *heard* others *say*... but *I say!*

Another tier of "hearsay" that Jesus articulated was—I *hear* what the Father says, and I *say* it: *"I don't speak on my own authority. The Father...commanded me what to say and how to say it"* (John 12:49, NLT). Importantly, the statements of Jesus are always admissible in God's court; He is a first-rate witness: *"I am the True and Faithful Witness"* (Revelation 3:14, CEV).

> *Jesus was both acquitted and condemned with the same testimony.*

The Testimony of JESUS CHRIST

> *"...Wasn't it clearly predicted that the Messiah would have to suffer all these things before entering his glory? Then Jesus took them through the writings of Moses and all the prophets, explaining from all the scriptures the things concerning himself."*
>
> LUKE 24:27 (NIV)

It's a colorful mystery. Jesus was both condemned and acquitted with the same testimony—His testimony. Jesus was condemned to the cross, but acquitted unto resurrection. Did Jesus take the witness stand? Yes and No. During His trials, did Jesus speak? Yes and No. In His trial before high priest Caiphas and King Herod, Jesus did not speak, but during His trial with the SanHedrin and Pilate, He gave testimony as if speaking from the witness stand. Jesus was never shy about testifying; in fact, the Bible says that His *"testimony… is the Spirit of Prophesy"* (Revelation 19:10, NHEB).

My elucidation of this Scripture follows. Since trial testimony is a form of telling your story under oath, the testimony of Christ is His telling His truthful story about Himself prophetically. That story can unroll directly from His own mouth or can be an indirect story that His Father delivers to the prophets about Him. In front of the Sanhedrin court, Jesus' testimony consisted of a prophetic explanation of how His future victory would occur after His physical demise: *"What is the testimony that these men are bringing against you?…Are you the Messiah?… Jesus said, I Am. And you will see the Son of Man coming in the clouds…"* (Mark 14:60-62, ESV). When Jesus testifies, it is comparable to court sworn testimony in the sense that it has heightened reliability. Jesus is God—the actuated *Word*. *"…Even if everyone else is a liar, God is true"* (Romans 3:4, NLT).

Before His death, Jesus gave testimony of Himself at His trial, and after His death on the isle of Patmos, He also testified to the apostle John: *"I am the Alpha and the Omega, says the Lord God"* (Revelation 1:8, ASV). Does it matter for potency's sake that some of Jesus' testimony was contemporaneous with the earthly trial during His tenure on earth, but some of His testimony occurred several decades later on the aisle of Patmos, after His trial and heavenly ascension? I would argue no, it does not matter for three reasons. Firstly, Jesus' testimony is everlasting and, as such, has present, retroactive, and future power and efficacy; *"Forever, Oh Lord, your word is settled in heaven"* (Psalm 119:89, KJV). Indeed, one of Jesus' names is "the Everlasting God"

(Isaiah 40:28, NIV). Secondly, Hebrews 13:8 says Jesus is *"the same yesterday, today and forever,"* therefore, making His word effective, influential, and truthful not only on the day of His trial but forever. Thirdly, Jesus testified that He is a *"true and faithful witness"* (Revelation 1:5, KJV). The reliability and power of Jesus' ongoing testimony are supported by American court procedure where a witness who has been sworn in to tell the truth may depart for a period of time and then return to the court to give additional testimony without having to be resworn in, only needing a reminder that He is still under oath for that testimony to be acceptable. There, the court affords faith in that witness' testimony, and it is effectively regarded. Lastly, another way of thinking about the longevity and security of Jesus' testimony is that Jesus is called the Word of God, who upholds all things by the *Word* of His power (See Revelation 12:11). Interestingly, God upheld Jesus' resurrection by the *Power of His Word*, one word, arise! Above, men's trial may have yielded a guilty verdict toward Jesus, but in the end, God upheld Jesus' innocence which was determined before the foundation of the world because of the power of those testimonial words: *"You will be proved right in what you say, and you will win your case in court"* (Romans 3:4, NLT).

How is it that God accepted Jesus' acquittal testimony of who He *is*, *was*, and *is* to be, when the earthly rulers did not? The answer is—God is prodigiously just! God sets His courtroom justice, and He follows it. He actually binds Himself to it; in fact, God is so bound to justice and so intent on keeping His own sense of justice by His own Word that God once swore by Himself to keep it (Hebrew 6:13). That self-swearing was not an antic of superfluity or some bombastic, prideful expression of a showy God, but it was the pure, just fall-out of a God overflowing with justice and purity in all His ways. God can be no less, for God not only renders, but also oversees and dispenses justice; He *is* justice. God is strictly just to no fault: *"A God of faithfulness, without injustice"* (Deuteronomy 32:4, BSB).

What should we, as Christians, be testifying about? Here are some suggestions:

1. Acts 10:42 (KJV)—*"And he commanded us to preach unto the people, and to testify that it is he who was ordained of God [to be] the Judge of quick and dead."*
2. Acts 20:24 (KJV)—*"I might finish my course with joy, and the ministry, which I have received of the Lord Jesus, to testify the gospel of the grace of God."*
3. Revelations 22:16 (NIV) *"I, Jesus, have sent mine angel to testify unto these things in the churches. I am the root and the offspring of David, the bright and morning star."*
4. First John 14:14 (KJV) *"And we have seen and do testify that the Father sent the Son [to be] the Savior of the world."*
5. Revelation 12:11 (NIV) *"And they triumphed over [Satan] by the blood of the Lamb and the word of their testimony."*

The last Scripture about testimony is one of my favorites, mainly because God impressed upon me that this Scripture is powered by two amped-up truths! There are *two* modes of testimony in this one statement. The first is the most perceptible—that our words are testimony—and the reason our words have overcoming productivity is that when we testify the Word of God, we are testifying of His power! The second treasured testimony found in that Scripture is a bit more latent but is surely present; it is the fact that, as discussed previously, the blood of Jesus has testimonial presence, persuasion, and power! When we validly apply the blood of Jesus to any situation, His testimony bears witness to the advancing truth that He is *Lord* of that situation!

A final note about Jesus' testimony. Jesus testified to the Devil. Jesus did it brilliantly by splitting His oral testimony with the written word; He would orally reproduce the written Word. There is an expression that is sometimes used in court when a piece of evidence is introduced in a trial, "Let the record show," or "For the record." This expression can be used by an attorney to maximize the importance of keeping a written record of the introduced evidence, and it also can be used to dramatically pivot the jury's—or judges'—attention to that piece of evidence. Jesus masterfully employs this expression when testifying to the Devil by saying, "It is written." In other words, He is saying, "Let the Record show that Heaven has already recorded this! So pay close attention!"

Witness-Corroboration

"We receive the testimony of men, the testimony of God is greater, for this is the testimony of God that he has borne concerning his Son."

1 JOHN 5:9 (ESV)

Within our American court system, where there are two witnesses who confirm or support a testimony, it is known as witness corroboration. Jesus and the Father's native system of witness corroboration already pre-existed. Jesus and the Father corroborated one another's testimony of being what I associate as the "beginning of the beginning" by witnessing each other creating the universe and creating man. In so doing, the Father could bear witness to Jesus' creator identity; without Jesus, nothing was made (John 1:3). There was also a second witness who was there and witnessed the genesis acts of Jesus and could corroborate His identity, the Holy Spirit. *"For there are three that bear witness in Heaven: The Father the Word, and the Holy Spirit"* (1 John 5:7, NKJV). On a side note, I believe it is because of the divine bond of this holy trilogy—this sacred threesome—which God loves so much that God calls for the presence of two or three witnesses as He enters a space. It is as though it is a continuation of His multiplied presence. This propinquity of togetherness evidently delights the Lord when two or more believers (witnesses) host His presence within themselves, amplifying His presence and identity when coming together: *"He that believeth on the Son of God hath the witness in himself"* (1 John 5:10, KJV).

Under Jewish law, credible trial testimony was corroborated by two witnesses also.

Jesus' testimony that He was the Son of God should have been accepted as corroborated testimony because it *was* corroborated by two witnesses: To begin, when Jesus began His earthly ministry, it was God who publicly said, *"This is my Son whom I love; with him I am well pleased"* (Matthew 3:17, NIV). For a second time, just before Jesus was about to end His earthly ministry, it was God again who said, *"This is my Son whom I love, Listen to Him!"* (Mark 9:7, NIV). Jesus also had one more divine witness—Holy Spirit, for Jesus said Holy Spirit would bear witness of Him: *"But when the comforter comes, whom I will send unto you from the Father, [even] the Spirit of truth, which proceedeth from the Father, he shall testify of me"* (John 15:26, KJV). Those are divine, gold bullion witnesses! You don't get any better than that for a star lineup of corroborating witnesses: *"At dawn [Jesus] appeared in the temple courts...When Jesus spoke again to the people He said, 'If I were to testify on my own behalf, my testimony would be valid because I know where I come from and where I am going"* (John 8:14, NLT). *"I stand with the Father...in your own law it is written that the testimony of two witnesses is true. I am one who testifies for myself; my other witness is the Father, who sent me"* (John 8:17-18, NIV). *"But someone else is also testifying about me, and I assure you that everything he says about me is true. In fact, you sent investigators to listen to John the baptist, and his testimony about me was true"* (John 5:32-33, NLT). That Scripture makes it obvious that Jesus' cousin, John The Baptist, corroborated Jesus' identity as well.

Acquittal Evidence Here: The Blood Goes to Court

The gored holes in Jesus' hands were every bit evidentiary in nature. They could have been "Exhibit H" in God's Court of law. They had the highest of probative weight because His hands not only represented His mortal wounds but even more accurately, wounds of spiritual combat against enemies of the cross, which would be on display forever. Further, Jesus' hands were evidence of His having been at the scene of a crime. Jesus was tried as a convict on a cross!

His "crime" read above His tomb. It was irregular, to say the least. Usually, a criminal has been engaged in a crime that preceded his trial. There, the only true crime scene at which Jesus had been present occurred *after* His sentencing, when He was on the cross. That crime had occurred *against* Him. God, in His infinite glory, would weigh the evidence of Christ's involvement as He deliberated on the sentencing of humankind. A different deliberation than the one on earth would take place in the hallowed halls of glory.

The Deliberation: Had Jesus fulfilled the God-given, heavenly statute for sacrificial atonement?

The law required that:

1. A spotless lamb had to be sacrificed. *Check*
2. The lamb must be of the male gender. *Check*
3. The sacrifice must occur on the Sabbath. *Check*
4. The sacrifice must occur outside of town. *Check*
5. A bloodied lamb, for *lots* of blood had to be sacrificed. *Check*
6. The sacrifice could only be made by a high priest. *Check*

The Court's Decision: Jesus *had* fulfilled all that was required under God's law. The Bible says that Jesus is the *"end of the law"* (Romans 10:4, ESV). In other words, as the oracle of God, out of Jesus' mouth does the law of God speak, and when Jesus speaks, that's the end of it! He finished it when He spoke it: *"It is finished"* (John 19:30, NIV). Man's acquittal was all summed up in Jesus' evidentiary speech of the crucifixion.

CHAPTER 16

Good Grace and Good Law

"So we praise God for the glorious grace he has poured out on us who belong to his dear Son."

EPHESIANS 1:6 (NLT)

"Happy are those whose lives are faultless who live according to the law of the LORD."

PSALM 119:1 (GNT)

The above two Scriptures together sound like a contradiction in thought, but they really are in harmony with each other. Consider also these two verses together: *"By grace through faith, we are saved"* (Ephesians 2:8, CSB). *"Open my eyes to see the wonderful truths in your law"* (Psalm 119:18, NLT). Jesus did not come to quash God's law, but he did come to candidly upend man's bad law. The Bible says through the apostle Paul that God's law is good: *"...I agree that the law is good"* (Romans 7:16, NIV. *See* Romans 8:2); *"He that keepeth the law, happy is he"* (Proverbs 29:18, KJV). The centrality of God's goodness is seen in His creation, in His workmanship, and in His laws. God left us good law by which to marshall victories on the earth. God also gave good law, especially the Ten commandments,

> *Jesus did not quash God's law, but upended man's bad law.*

that highlighted the target of righteousness that was often missed, which is what "to sin" literally means—to miss the target. The law, however, was deemed good by God because it did a good thing since it was God's chosen way to reveal man's fallibility. It was good law given by a good God, and therefore, His law would retain its good traits forever because of the absoluteness and goodness of God inherently. Put simply, because God is good, He cannot produce anything bad. God did not spurn His law, for God is His very Word, and because His law reflects that Word, God is His very law. Enter Jesus upon the earth but finds Himself surrounded by self-righteous men—Pharisees and Sadducees—who guard an inflated law which no longer resembles the substantiality of God's law; it is their revised, bad law. The following description of Jesus is worth ruminating on some more: *"Jesus is the end of law"* (Romans 10:4). Definitely, Jesus is the end of the law, but what does that mean? The Bible mentions that Jesus is the oracle of God, indicating out of His mouth does the law of God now speak, and also mentions that Jesus is the Alpha and the Omega of everything, the law also, so it means He started it, and He finished it. It is all summed up in Him! When Jesus said in Hebrews 10:7 (ESV), *"... Behold, I have come in the scroll of the book, it is written of me to do your will O God,"* it means He is the synthesis of the law. This materiality is the building block of Jesus' self-proclamation. Jesus put it this way: *"I have not come not to abolish—end—the law, but to fulfill it"* (Matthew 5:17). Bright flashbulb here—Jesus is "the end" of the law, but He did not come "to end" the law. Jesus did not come to consume the law; He came to subsume the law, that is, to absorb the law. He came to make a good thing better. The law shadowed Jesus, it was *not Jesus, but it looked just like Him; that is why He cou*ld easily step into it-or fulfill it. In actuality, the law continued because Jesus took the law unto Himself and personified it and made hitting its target attainable. The true sequiter is this: Jesus did not come to make believers miserable; He came to deliver us from being miserable. We are not meant to be miserable chaperones of the law or legal nursemaids, but just law-abiding citizens of heaven, like we are asked to be on earth. God just wants us to be aficionados and followers of all of His Word, some of which are actual laws (including old covenant and new covenant law), some are commendations, some are anecdotes, some are admonitions, some are "pep talks," some are promises, and some are pledges of love. God does not endorse being legalistic, but He is not opposed to being legal. God's legal mercies and His legal approach to love, salvation, freedoms, and boundaries are good and are for our good. God is for us! Jesus was the paradigm shift from the frustration and bondage of attempting the impossible under the law. Jesus was the enabler of a new enthusiasm to commune with God and to partake of His laws as the walking representation of abiding by God's fresh concept of grace-overlaid law; and He would do it in that ambulatory fashion of spreading God's Word, and His goodness, as He walked about in the flesh: *Jesus, the only begotten of the Father, full of grace and truth, Teaching them to do all that the Father has commanded*" (John 1:14, NKJV). God's laws which are impregnated into the heart establish an enthusiasm, an orderly practice, and an ability to walk on a highway which God calls holiness, and it comes with a Holy grant of freedom. *"Whosoever looketh into the perfect law of liberty... shall be blessed"* (James 1:25, KJV). How refreshing that God's law is liberating!

GRACE: The Facts of the Gospel

"And I perform grace to thousands of generations of my friends and to those keeping my commandments."

DEUTERONOMY 5:10 (ABPE).

Fact: Jesus, the person of *grace*, gave up His life on a cross for the whole world. A fact is something held out to be true. It is also something that is empirically verifiable and not just theoretical. The Gospel is factual, and the facts of the gospel shine in two succinct statements.

What is true: The Gospel is a directed story of pardon and a treatise on love. What is true: The grace of the Gospel is not swallowed up by a punitive rod. God puts clemency and consequence in balance. Rather than an exclusive punitive rod, God prefers to court His people with a redemptive nod. Both salvation and damnation are arrived at through self-consequential choices. Every time a believer's name is written in the book of eternal life because of his affirmative choice toward Jesus' salvation, that classification is God's merciful nod to the redemptive work of the cross. Conversely, each time an unbeliever exercises the choice to reject Jesus' sacrifice on the cross, that is consequential reaping of eternal separation from God, which by self-default, is punitive self-damnation. *Indeed, our salvation is grace-bottled, but although it is free, it is costly because it cost God's Son a decision to die sacrificially, and therefore, it demands a decision to live.* Preferably, Jesus' work is finished so that our end can be replenished!

"And the Word was made flesh...full of grace and truth."
JOHN 1:14 (NIV)

The Work of the Cross

What does that phrase "the work of the cross" mean in its best orientation? God's best work is frankly seen within the "work of the cross," and I've often thought that term is both accurate and fitting because Jesus really did "work" on the cross. My own checklist follows. I assert that Jesus experienced labored breathing on the cross. Being suspended in the air, He would have had to push Himself up from the lead-like, stabbing spikes, which anchored His feet, just to catch His breath. He would have had to muster all of His fleeting breath and strength to throw His voice and audibly call out His pardon of humankind to the Father. In those sequences of events alone, Jesus definitely "worked" on the cross; in fact, Jesus was in action and labor mode the entire way to the cross, including carrying His cross and falling beneath the weight of the cross. All these things were laborious. The cross was *not* some glamour-ridden event where Jesus was reclining comfortably on plush wood, in an ergonomically upright position, until He took His leave of absence from this world! No, He labored to even focus in the midst of excruciating, throbbing head pain and probable trauma, both of which may have been induced by the spiny thorns that were violently jabbing His forehead. According to Scripture, His face was extremely disfigured, so He probably labored to naturally lift a swollen tongue to speak. He undoubtedly also labored to talk due to probable dehydration and the severe loss of His blood stemming from His prior, brutal back beating. Moreover, He likely labored to lift His bulging eye lid to look at the thief speaking to Him on the cross. In spite of His contused head, He meagerly hauled up what was left of His head to swallow God's cup of wine-wrath. In all likelihood, Jesus labored to stay conscious in spite of His profuse wounds so that He could commit His Spirit to God at the perfect timing. There is no doubt about it; conquering the cross took work! Carpeted in blood, clothless, and likely in mortal shock, Jesus labored to be obedient to the feat of winning His last battle. In a phrase, Jesus "worked up a blood sweat" for us.

CHAPTER 17

Theology of Law

"Do you know the laws of the heavens?"

JOB 38:33 (NIV)

How beneficial that God's Holy law, His Holy Word, is freeing! Only God could make something that is restrictive in appearance but liberating in its application. What is law?

Before answering that question, it is important to ask why God seems to like law? God *is* justice because He is the sum total of all of His attributes, and one of His attributes is His self-described affinity for just administration of law: *"I the Lord love justice"* (Isaiah 61:8, ESV). *As such, God has a strong affinity for the law.*

What is law? Most commonly, in the legal field, American law is *a system of rules and standards* with federal, state, civil, and criminal procedures as to how courts conduct their affairs. The system includes how they secure or safeguard, possibly even promote, the rights of individuals and the way they arrive at, interpret, and enforce their decisions. The rules span our three legislative, judicial, and executive branches. Law is a sliceable concept; although very comprehensive, its sum can be carved in many ways—as judicial precedents, legislative statutes, executive or administrative measures, to name a few. Theologically, these above concepts of law overlap with God's legal system, with some additional bridgework in between. It is perceivable that God's legal system is: His legal sovereignty, His Legal supernatural intervention, and His legal supernatural imposition. The coming together of these legal interconnections and theology is quite serious, but lightheartedly, I identify it like the famous recipe when chocolate came together with peanut butter—the perfect mix! I submit that the Bible is a holy mix of God's authoritative statutes, administrative ordinances, executive pronouncements, judicial action, and miracles, all of which are law-immersed. I perceive that, at its core, the gospel is a jurisprudential story. It is God injecting Himself and His legal authority into the sunken plight of humankind; thus, the theology of law is: The narrative of lost humankind, interwoven with the greater metanarrative of its miraculous, legal rescue by God. To use a modern colloquialism—or just to verbally stack this—"The theology of law is a God thing!" It's God always doing dynamic things to save us. It's unstoppable God being unstoppable for our good. God practices mixed law; that is, He operates the laws of physics, gravity, etc., and simultaneously operates within His legal system as well. He intersperses His divine laws among His natural laws to etch His intellect on His creation. He "gets" that we need Him!

Natural laws exist under the scientific concept of law that says a law is absolute; in other words, the properties of that law always work. For example, under the law of gravity, the gravitational force of the earth will always pull an airborne object toward its center, downward. In parallel, under God's law of love, the absolute property of His love is that it will always be unchangeable. What is interesting is that in God's practice of sovereign law, He can subordinate His natural laws to His supernatural laws, which He also created. Said differently, God can operate outside of them such as when Jesus supernaturally ascended into the heavens; there, He literally defied the law of gravity, proving there is no natural law that can prevail against God's supernatural law: "...*Against such there is no law*" (Galatians 5:23, KJV).

The Law of Faith

"If we are faithless, He remains faithful...for He cannot deny Himself."

2 TIMOTHY 2:13 (NIV)

God is law observant, but He is also above the law because He's greater than the law which He created; He can lawfully suspend it, utilize it, exist beyond it, or make Himself bound by it. He can enforce it, even when holding Himself accountable to it on behalf of His creation: God makes violable law but is never in violation of the law, and He is eternally inviolate—"squeaky clean." Put another way, God enacted laws that are breakable but never broke one Himself. He is law-keeping and inherently incapable of breaking His laws. God is faithful to His laws, and He is faithful to us because of His eternal perfection, purity, and holiness...He has got to be Himself. Turning our focus to faith, God embossed it with His law.

The way to activate any and all of God's laws is done by faith. Faith is a binary substance because it is both a catalyst as well as a cataclysmic force; faith can move things into existence, or the same faith can cause things to be erased, moving them out of the way. According to the natural laws of physics, anything that is moving or that has momentum is a force, so faith is a force. Underlining this forcefulness, Scriptures say that the kingdom of heaven takes things by force: *"The Kingdom of heaven suffers violence, but the violent take it by force"* (Matthew 11:12, NKJV). There, the force is the force of faith. God has established spiritual laws by which he operates in the spirit realm, just like he established earthly laws by which man operates in the earth. The existential God, who has an existential governance, created existent matter. That is, the all existing God who has always existed and will always exist, created all matter, and that matter is subject to

Him; so He uses matter to accomplish His will because it is subject to His laws on the earth.

One example of this existential dominance to accomplish His will is found in the biblical story of the donkey and Balaam. The donkey consisted of matter, as all living things do according to the laws of physics, and God opened this matter's mouth to accomplish His will; He made the donkey talk to express the looming approach of an invisible, angelic guillotine facing Balaam. Another example of how God uses matter to accomplish His multi-fold purpose in the earth is when He caused the sun to stand at attention while Joshua "crushed" his Jerochoic battle, or when He caused the Red Sea to become wave-free flooring so that His Israeli kingdom could cross over it. These vignettes all displayed how God caused natural matter to succumb to His will and how God caused His natural laws to operate in tandem with His spiritual laws. The Bible demonstrates that we understand the natural and then apply it spiritually: *"The spiritual did not come first, but the natural, and after that the spiritual"* (1 Corinthians 15:46, NIV). One of the greatest hurdles for a believer is trying to traverse a world that God made without completely understanding the way God's laws govern His world. Humankind was meant to circumnavigate this global existence while partnering with God's intersection of His supernatural and natural laws. Not doing this is very much like buying a product and using it without the necessity and the benefit of the manufacturer's instructions for that use.

Law of Faith & Healing

"He sent His word and Healed them…"

PSALM 107:20 (NKJV)

The woman who wanted to disappear in the crowd was one of the most conspicuously seen "wallflowers" which the Bible has ever recorded.

She snuck around the back of Jesus to ensure she would remain incognito, but her protrusion of faith singled her out. Although her method of presentation was a bit unorthodox, she had a legal case, and she was making a legal claim. I noticed that by touching the hem of Jesus' garment, she was figuratively asserting her rights as a daughter of Abraham, for in doing so, she was literally touching cannons of divine law. Entwined in that knotted, fringed hem of Jesus' tallit—prayer shawl—were her court exhibits, all 613 of them. They each represented the 613 Jewish Old Testament Mitzvot (commandments), some with promises for her, like Deuteronomy 10:20 (KJV): *"Serve the Lord and He shall take sickness away from the midst of thee."* They were her declaratory rights to her independence, to her being set free. In fact, she kept rehearsing her oral argument, muttering it under her breath, hearing it all the way to Jesus: *"If I can but touch the hem of his garment, I shall be made whole"* (Matthew 9:21, ESV). The law of faith is premised on the antecedent of auditory exposure—an individual must hear the word of God before faith can move. The Bible teaches that faith comes after one hears the word of God (See Romans 10:17). The hurting woman knew that attached to her faith-engulfed words was her legal ticket to her recovery. She had not come to court unprepared; her brief was uncharacteristically brief. All she needed was one passage from the Old Covenant: "The Sun of righteousness will rise with healing in his wings." *She had faith that the Jesus of the New Covenant was also the Lord of the Old Testament. She was right.* A close inspection of the traditional Jewish *tallit* that Jesus would have worn as a rabbi would reveal a wing-like spread to it when the arms are outstretched, and from its corner hems would dangling royal threads, the *tzitzit*, which were those en-coiled, promissory covenants which her case legally rested on. The woman was healed by Jesus and prevailed in her claim. To this woman, I imagine the risen Jesus was truly her *Sonrise*.

The Law of Faith II

"But you dear friends, by building yourselves up in your most holy faith and praying in the Holy Spirit, keep yourselves in God's love as you wait for the mercy of our Lord Jesus Christ to bring you to eternal life."

JUDE 1:20-21 (NIV)

Operating faith creates things! Operating faith moves things! Operating faith changes things!

Sure, the Bible says that only the tiny measure of a mustard seed of faith is needed, but cautiously, there is no room for frugality of faith. Even a quantum of faith is not puny faith. There is something good to be said about releasing a small but strongly grounded faith rather than guarding a clenched, teetering faith that's unstable and preventative in the long run. Jesus applauded lasting faith when He saw it. The key is to have at least the requisite small amount of faith, boldly use it, and don't let it go! The Bible says to "Hold Fast" to your profession of faith, which means to secure it repeatedly from the winds of life and the vicissitudes of the world.

"Oh ye of little faith" was more than a rebuke from Jesus for too small faith based on the fact that the only required quantum of faith is that of a mustard seed which is grossly small, rather it was a helpful warning to *keep* your faith, to maintain it at all costs.

According to the Word of God, faith has a verifiable force. The Word of God says in Matthew 11:12 (ESV), *"the violent take it by force,"* which means faith has a rush to it or a violent agitation about it. God's people were meant to be a kingdom of shakers and takers! Perpetual faith is cataclysmic and creates desired ends, and is a disrupter of unwanted outcomes because the law of faith is linked to dynamism. There was darkness on the face of the earth when God said, "Let there be light," so faith shook, and all of the above maxims of momentum went into being, and darkness had to surrender to the light! The earthly light was manifested out of the spiritual realm because Creator God is Spirit; therefore, all spiritual laws happen in the Spirit first and then are manifested naturally since all spiritual laws emanate from a spiritual God. Stock up on your faith because you will need it to brace your hope. Beware, you can't have hope without faith. Faith is the subfloor of hope. In other words, ask yourself, what does one stand on during a crisis moment? One must stand on faith because it is the pedestal of hope; it is the actual sublevel of one's hope: *"Faith is the substance of things hoped for and the evidence of things unseen"* (Hebrews 11:1, KJV). Completing this picture, Christ is the hope of glory. So in order to get this hope, you must believe in Christ (Colossians 1:27). The world prizes logic; however, the illogical concept of believing in a Jesus you cannot see yields evidence which you can see. Believing *is* seeing! God loves to prove Himself to those who have chosen to embark on the initiative of faith. Sometimes to receive a faith-filled miracle, one must overcome the battle of Logos v. Logic.

Logos V. Logic: Collision with the Law of Faith

"In the beginning was the word… and the word was God."

JOHN 1:1 (NIV)

The American branch of law is inexorably linked to logic. Most attorneys are either logicians or are aspiring logicians since the study of law lends itself to logic. Logic is good and has its place in God's kingdom, too. In Greek, Logos means Word, and God is the *Word*; therefore, God is the Logos. Logic is reasoning. Side by side, Logos has a spiritual connotation, while logic has a nonspiritual connotation, and though seldom twin partners in the Bible, Logos, and logic are not incompatible. Both Logos and logic are legitimate and recurring schools of thought in the Bible, and while they may seem at odds with each other, they are surprisingly congruent at times; but when they are combatants in the believer's battleground of thought, Logos should always supersede logic: *"Human beings cannot live on bread alone, but need every word that God speaks"* (Matthew 4:4, GNT). Certainly, God welcomes believers to reason with Him, for He says, *"I, the LORD, invite you to come and talk it over…Your sins are scarlet red but they will be whiter than snow or wool"* (Isaiah 1:18, CEV). There are levels of engagement with God, and He directs them all; that course of immersion is what serving the Lord "with the whole heart, soul and mind" is all about (Matthew 22:37). God loves for us to intellectually shadow Him with our minds, but notice that the mind is the last of the receptacles listed there to serve the Lord, which makes logical sense because it is usually the last to engage in the salvation experience. I gauge the order as the heart believing first, the soul willing to surrender second, and the mind embracing a cognitive understanding of the death and resurrection of Jesus. All receptacles are necessary, however.

God also loves order, and logic is a vehicle of orderly thought found in the mind. God's ways are not always immediately apparent, but His divine ways always produce His perfect will, and they always make perfect, rational sense to Him, so there *can* be logic in the logos. It is, however, because of our limited perspective that God invites us to trust and believe Him with one's heart, not one's limited, logical capacity. The Logos God communicates to the heart because that's where He inscribed His name. The heart is where the *Word* deposits His words. By God's design, the heart is not only the receptacle of God's Word; it is also the repository for faith. God wired the heart to be receptive to faith, and when faith and the Word of God combine, a spiritual bonfire miraculously happens: *"For with the heart man believes unto salvation"* (Romans 10:10, KJV). Spiritually, weak logic often accompanies strong faith, and to get a miracle by the law of faith, it may be necessary to disable unspiritual logic and embrace the Logos by faith to build spiritual muscle. This type of collision calls for a life choice. A person can live limitedly with logic, but no individual can live fully nor fully live without the Logos. Jesus emphatically simplified it this way: *"Let this mind be in you which was also in Christ Jesus"* (Philippians 2:5, BSB). To commune with the Logos God, we must be spiritually minded by having our full spiritual receptors open: "God is a Spirit, and they that worship Him must worship Him in spirit…"

Law of Love: Lawyer to Lawyer

"If you really keep the royal law found in scripture 'Love your neighbor as yourself,' you are doing right."

JAMES 2:8 (KJV)

The gospel is summed up in one legal argument—love. In the Bible, Jesus talked about the bodacious emotion of love in an epic way. Jesus presented love as not being just a leading emotion but rather as a veritable law, taking first and second place in the monumental ranks of the Ten Commandments. *"…You must love the Lord your God with all your heart, all your soul, all your mind, and all your strength. The second is s equally important: Love your neighbor as yourself. No other commandment is greater than these"* (Mark 12:30–31, NLT). In the parabolic lesson in Luke 10:25–37, Jesus is approached by an ill-meaning lawyer who quizzes Him about the mapquest to eternal life. Jesus dons His lawyer's hat to teach the lawyer a lesson, lawyer to lawyer. He shares the engaging details of the Good Samaritan parable. There, a man was robbed and left for dead on the side of a road. Both the socially esteemed Levite and the venerable priest passed the victim by, but it is the culturally denigrated Samaritan who lovingly aided the man. Jesus asks the lawyer to identify which of the three men acted neighborly. By the way, the Pharisees called Jesus a Samaritan as an insult once! Eventually, Jesus prompted the lawyer to the right answer, and he finally concluded that the Samaritan who showed love to his neighbor was the good neighbor. In all probability, this Jewish attorney would have been haughtily reared to hate the "odious" Samaritans whom they regarded as societal misfits and spiritual "half-breeds." Jesus seized this teachable moment to expound on the second greatest law of all, to love one's fellow man, completely and without caveat. What a lesson in the law of love for all of us! God's unconditional *agape* love is poured into the heart by the Holy Spirit (Romans 5:5). The complexity of the cross is simplified. God's law of love mandates loving one another laterally which Holy Spirit vertically enables us to do—making the shape of the cross. Love is as love does: *"Whoever claims to love God yet hates a brother or sister is a liar"* (1 John 4:20, NIV).

The Law of the Mind

In his Pauline letter to the Roman converts, the apostle Paul details a war between the spirit and the flesh and indicates that the law of the mind is part of a spiritual endowment that has a spiritual essence. Paul tells his *protege*, Timothy, that God has not given His body of believers a "spirit" of fear," but has given us a spirit of a *"sound mind"* (See *2* Timothy 1:7). Paul also says to let the mind of Christ be in us (Philippians 2:5). Taken to its logical nexus, the combined verses can be broken down to read: Let the spiritually sound mind of Christ be in us. The law of the mind, therefore, is that the believer's mind should be analogous to the mind of Christ. There should be a comparable likeness of our minds to Christ. How is this achieved? If we link those verses in conjunction with Paul's popular war-centric verse, we get the answer. We permit the mind of Christ in us by *Putting on the helmet of salvation* (Ephesians 6:17) and maintaining it through soaking in God's Word and through fellowship with Holy Spirit. Applied here, the order of thought would be that the Christian soldier is to array herself with the helmet of salvation which represents the spiritual, sound, and lawful mind of Christ. She, then, is to stand sure-footed with selfless love and power, which are features of that verse to Timothy. The believer should also ready herself in the spirit realm for the battlefield of the mind with the strategic advantage of knowing God's Word and His enabling power.

Law of Divine Healing

Why the spit? Why did Jesus use His spit as a healing salve for the eyes of a blind man?

I suggest that Jesus was emphasizing His spiritual DNA. The man was blind from birth, and from birth, Jesus had been sent to heal the sick: "*…God anointed Jesus of Nazareth with the Holy Spirit and with power. Then Jesus went around…healing all who were oppressed by the devil, for God was with Him*" (Acts 10:38, NLT). Legal forensics involving DNA saliva samples are routinely used in courts to establish a person's identity. I propose that Jesus was establishing His identity as the Messianic healer by using His spit which was naturally and divinely composed of His genetic essence. One of the signs of instruction to the Jewish nation for identifying the Messiah in their midst would be His ability to heal the blind. In a well-choreographed, divine display of that identity, Jesus spit and then sent the man to wash his eyes in the pool of *Siloam* whose derived Hebrew meaning is "sent forth." There, I propose, Jesus was emphasizing that He was the true Messiah who had been sent by God.

With the Messianic Christ, as illustrated with the prophet Moses, the "serpent spirit" of sickness was nailed to the tree, signifying it was spiritually de-fanged and had no more authority nor dominion over our bodies and mind. The serpent's head was bruised and stripped of its power to poison the head of the body of Christ. It was its head for our head; Jesus bruised its head so that we could be *"the head, and not the tail"* (Deuteronomy 28:13, NIV). When Jesus was nailed to the tree, sickness no longer was meant to be a powerful image in the mind because, at the cross, Jesus rendered it fangless and powerless to strike at whim. The blood of the lamb is meant to bring healing to the believer. Why the blood? Because it was Jesus' blood that provided the antidote to the killer, sin. Sin poisoned mankind, dating back to the Adamic fall. The man died spiritually as a result of it. Jesus' blood was the antidote, even as the blood of a shepherd's lamb in ancient Israel's history provided an antidote for a shepherd's lamb, which had been bitten by ravenous vipers along their trails. In short, if a lamb was bitten by a serpent, then a portion of the snake's venom would be injected into another lamb so that it could build up its immune system and create reactive antibodies that would fight off the poison from the snake. The lamb usually made a full recovery. Likewise, Jesus shed His blood as the Lamb of God for the believer's healing so that a believer could apply Jesus' blood in order to inoculate them against the deathly repercussions of venomous sin and sickness. This was an astounding conquest by Jesus, and It occurs to me that many historical conquerors have insisted on an honorific after their name to denote their conquest. This concept taken to its fullest logical progression, would rightly, then, have Jesus listed as *Jesus The Great*.

Self-Care Law: Laws of the Heart

"The Kingdom of God is... joy in the Holy Ghost."

ROMANS 4:17 (NLT)

How do you take care of yourself? Taking care of ourselves is extremely important for quality of life. The Beatitudes are nine listed blessings that are extracted from Jesus' Sermon on the Mount. I describe them as a type of self-care law. Laws are rules, but they are also a type of classification of how things work. If you discipline yourself to *be* in these *attitudes*, then you are really inviting God to come in and take good care of you. If you train yourself to intentionally bask in these nine maxims of God by practicing awareness of these attitudes continuously, you will encounter the promises that flow out of the laws of the Beatitudes. You can promote self-awareness of these blessings by rehearsing the meaning of each blessing. Purpose to augment your overall outlook by staying in the moment of these Beatitudes, which I refer to as, *God's Laws of Merriment*. I developed this term because the Bible notes that the word of God is health to all your flesh and that he who trusts in his God is happy (See Proverbs 4:20-22, 16:20). I now call these Beatitudes—*Happitudes*—Be this and be happy!

Laws are also established facts that have been derived based on empirical observation; put differently, they are proven, observed actions that have been based on facts. Below, I present my layout of the Beatitudes:

1. *Observation*: People experience grief. *Fact*: God is the God of all comfort. *Law*: "Blessed are they that mourn, for they shall be comforted" (Matthew 5:4, ESV).
2. *Observation*: People despair in a day and age of hopelessness. *Fact:* God is the lifter of the dejected head. *Fact:* God has gone away to prepare a heavenly place for them. *Law:* "Blessed are the poor in spirit, for theirs is the kingdom of heaven/Blessed are those who recognize they are spiritually helpless" (Matthew 5:3, NIV/GW). The kingdom of heaven belongs to them.
3. *Observation:* People experience spiritually bankruptcy without the deposit of the Holy Spirit. *Fact:* God cures every deficiency through His Holy Spirit and His heavenly touch. *Law:* "Blessed are those who recognize they are spiritually helpless" (Matthew 5:3, GW). *The* kingdom of heaven belongs to them.
4. *Observation*: Humble people often chase meekness. *Fact:* God draws near to the humble (Psalm 138:6). *Law:* "Blessed are the meek, for they will inherit the earth" (Matthew 5:5, NIV).

5. *Observation:* People everywhere are looking for satisfaction. *Fact:* God satisfies (Psalm 107:9). *Law:* "Blessed are they that hunger and thirst, for they will be filled" (Matthew 5:6, NIV).

6. *Observation:* People hurt in a merciless society. *Fact:* God's mercy endures forever (1 Chronicles 16:34). *Law:* "Blessed are the merciful, for they will be shown mercy" (Matthew 5:7, NIV).

7. *Observation*: People's hearts are either panting for God or they are failing and falling away from God. *Fact*: God has given to every man a moral light (Luke 21:2; 2 Thessalonians 2:3; John 1:4). *Law:* "Blessed are the pure(clean) in heart, for they will see God" (Matthew 5:8, NIV).

8. *Observation*: People are experiencing record-breaking world conflict and disputations. *Fact:* The Prince of Peace gives an enabling, perfect, and quality peace which the world can not take (John 14:27) *Law:* "Blessed are the peacemakers for they shall be called the children of God" (Matthew 5:9, NIV).

9. *Observation:* People are experiencing real-time persecution for righteousness' sake. *Fact:* The world hated Jesus because He was righteous, and they will hate His seed for the same notable reason. *Law:* "Blessed are they those who are persecuted because of righteousness, for theirs is the kingdom of God" (Matthew 5:10, NIV).

The beatitudes promote self-awareness of the inner windows to the heart. Through Holy Spirit, who guides the believer into all intimate truth about God and about herself, the believer can take self-stock of her spiritual circulatory beauty. If ashes are found along the inventory process of the heart when unlawful things are burned away by the refiner's fire, the positive news is that God gives beauty for ashes, and He makes all things beautiful in His own time (Ecclesiastes 3:11).

Law of Spiritual Warfare

The Bible speaks of angels' tongues and spiritual tongues, holy tongues, and holy utterances.

Some judicial rulings result in a protective order. A protective order can be an order in which a Judge orders the ceasing of a particular activity by one individual in order to protect another individual. *An Ex Parte* protective order is a legal injunction—a restraining order—and is a one-sided or unilateral petition by a petitioner without the defendant's knowledge or presence when it is in the interest of safety. In the spirit realm, this unilateral act of safety can also be done when a believer petitions God through a single party, secret transmission. Notably, the White House employs secure channels for transmission. Speaking in tongues by the believer is a secure channel by which a believer can bypass the usual open, audible, and deciphered transmission of her prayers by her opposer, Satan. The Bible says that the Holy Spirit interprets the bombardment of indecipherable groans and utterances of a believer and prays them back to God through the use of tongues, which results in a cryptic transmission to God, one which Satan can neither understand nor intercept. From a defense perspective, because it is unintelligible to the devil's kingdom, it's similar to what the United States Central Intelligence Agency denotes as a secure channel.

CHAPTER 18

The Christian's Bill of Rights

"Those that are rooted in the house of the LORD shall flourish in the courts of our God."

PSALM 92:13 (KJV)

God, in His beautiful beneficence, established a *Bill of Rights* for the believer and His descendants, and what's more, these divine rights have been conferred on the body of Christ for practical use. In America, it has become popular for hospitals to encourage patients to "know their rights" or for watchdog organizations to encourage consumers to "demand their rights." On a higher level, God wants believers to know their God-given rights, too. Even more, these rights extend to the believer's posterity in what I refer to as "limited perpetuity." In other words, they are forever biblically and legally enforceable but are inheritable up to a limited thousand generations by the believer's seed (Deuteronomy 7:9). Of course, a thousand generations is an extremely long time, and God has empowered the believer that way, but many believers do not know that they can take action by asserting their legal, divine rights in the Court of God, and further can expect victorious results for themselves and their generations to come! "The secret things belong to the LORD our God, but the things which are revealed

> *Believers can assert their divine, legal rights in God's Court.*

and disclosed belong to us and to our children forever, so that we may do all of the words of this law" (Deuteronomy 29:29, NIV).

Divine right has always been a biblical concept. It was seen with the first king of Israel, Saul, whose kingly inauguration actually consisted of an anointing by a prophet, therefore, merging governance with divinity. God refers to Himself as a King: "Thus says the Lord, the King, and Redeemer of Israel, the Lord of Hosts: *I am the first and I am the Last, there is no God but me*" (Isaiah 44:6, NIV). God's Kingdom principles have always included government. Consider that, historically, kings would seal their decrees with a signet ring because the impression from the seal signified their kingly authority and their right to govern. Likewise, God has a symbolic, signet ring with which He also seals. Through His Holy Spirit, God impresses a holy seal on the believer, and by sealing him, signifies the preeminence of God's divine empowerment in that believer's life until the kingly and final return of Jesus: *"And do not make the Holy Spirit sad. The Spirit is God's proof that you belong to him. God gave you the Spirit to show that God will make you free when the final day comes"* (Ephesians 4:30, NIV). Importantly, God left divine rights for the empowered believer to execute today! The *Bill of Rights*, also referred to as the *Declaration of Rights*, is composed of the first ten amendments to the United States Constitution and confers certain legal rights upon the American citizenry. Authored by James Madison, it was added to the Constitution by this country's founding fathers in 1791. The American Constitution is a powerful delineation of important, centralized rights, and its Bill of Rights is the resourceful insistence of the ideals of free-flowing, individual rights. Similarly, God is the founding Father of humanity and He also has a Constitution with ingrained Bill of Rights for His citizenry: "But our citizenship is in heaven" (Philippians 3:20; See Hebrews 12:23). God's *Bill of Rights* contains the foundational encasings of essential Christian legal rights for the governance of His believers' lives, such as their: minds; bodies; properties; religious liberties, interests, relationships; welfare; and warfare. Having a *Bill of Rights* should be a "diner's delight" for the believer and a pragmatic poison for the opposer. This theological conversion of legal principles is not to be shelved with an abstract mindset, but these heart-pumping truths are for real daily application. God did not give these divine concepts for "play play"—they are offensive "fighting pieces" for a winning church! In a manner of speaking, Satan's legal license to practice godly angeology was revoked because of his fall. He, thus, is a renegade and has no authority to practice his devilment in the lives of the vigilant believer. He was accordingly kicked out of heaven, so when the Devil tries to impersonate an angel of light while carrying on his dark, devilish work, the believer has the right to offensively kick him out of his presence just like God did. Jesus' triumph at Calvary stripped Satan's dominion over the earth and over His people. In the end, God's "beat-all," loftier plan was carried out.

The Christian Bill of Rights: My Version

We, the people of God, do accept these sacred, enumerated rights which are ordered and established by God, and we do openly declare them for our use and the use of our seed unto a thousand generations. By God-given authority, by benefit of Holy Spirit, and by faith in the all-powerful name of Jesus, we decree our possession and manifestation of the following covenantal, lawful rights:

1. The legal right to be saved from eternal damnation and the twin right to embrace eternal life. *"If you declare with your mouth, 'Jesus is Lord', and believe in your heart that God raised him from the dead, you will be saved"* (Romans 10:9, NIV). *"Blessed are they that do His commandments that they may have right to the tree of life…"* (Revelation 22:14, KJV).
2. The legal right to forgiveness and freedom from the chains of sin. *"Through the blood of his Son, we are set free*

from our sins. God forgives our failures because of his overflowing kindness" (Ephesians 1:7, ISV). *"You have changed my sadness into a joyful dance; you have taken away my sorrow and surrounded me with joy"* (Psalm 30:11, GNB). *"He brought them out from darkness and the shadow of death, shattering their chains"* (Psalm 107:14, ISV).

3. The legal right to declare war on any and all spiritual enemies, in the earth, under the earth and above the earth. *"Evildoers will bowdown in the presence of the good, and the wicked at the gates of the righteous"* (Proverbs 14:19, NIV). *"No weapon formed against you shall prosper…"* (Isaiah 54:17, BSB). *"Who shall separate us from the love of Christ?… For I am persuaded…nor principalities, nor powers …shall be able to separate us…from the love of God which is in Christ Jesus our Lord"* (Romans 8:35–39, KJV).

4. The legal right to bodily, mental, and soulish healing and wholeness: *"Beloved, I wish above all things that you prosper and be in good health even as your soul prospers"* (3 John 1:2, KJV). *"And the power of the Lord was with Jesus to heal the sick"* (Luke 5:17, NIV). *"And By His wounds you are healed"* (Isaiah 53:5, NIV). *"Thou Oh Lord are a shield… lifter of my head"* (Psalm 111:3, ESV).

5. The legal right to have unburdened provision and heightened, sustainable blessings. *"The blessing of the LORD, it maketh rich, and he addeth no sorrow with it"* (Psalm 10:22, HCSB). *"You are blessed in your coming in, you are blessed in your going out"* (Deuteronomy 28:6, ABPE). *"Blessings crown the head of the righteous"* (Proverbs 10:6, NIV). *"For you, oh Lord, will bless the righteous; With favor you shall surround him as with a shield"* (Psalm 5:12, KJV).

6. The legal right to peace. *"For the kingdom of God is… peace, and joy in the Holy Ghost"* (Romans 14:17, KJV).

"*You keep him in perfect peace whose mind is stayed on you*" (Isaiah 26:3, ESV).

7. The legal right to access the atoning blood of Jesus and its umbrella protections and overcoming power. "*And they overcame him by the blood of the Lamb, and by the word of their testimony…*" (Revelation 12:11, KJV). "*My prayer is that you…protect them from the evil one*" (John 17:15, NIV).

8. The legal right to the superior authority in the name of Jesus. "*…Whatever you ask in my name…I will do it*" (John 14:13, NIV). "*Whatever you bind on earth will be bound in heaven…*" (Matthew 16:19, NIV). "*…I give you power to tread on serpents…and over all the power of the enemy*" (Luke 10:19, KJV). "*Then Jesus came and said to them, 'All authority in heaven and on earth has been given to me'*" (Matthew 28:18, NIV).

9. The legal right to approach Holy God, God the Judge. "*We have confidence to enter the Most Holy place by the blood of Jesus by a new and living way which He opened up for us through the curtain, that is, His body*" (Hebrews 10:19–20, NIV).

10. The legal right to declare household salvation for loved ones, including those who are far away, the prodigal, and the estranged. "*Salvation has come to this home today… For the Son of Man came to save those who ar lost*" (Luke 19:9–10, NLT). "*The promise is for you and your children and for all who are far off*" (Acts 2:39, NIV).

"*You don't have the things you want because you don't pray for them*" (James 4:2, NIV). Remember that the word of God is living, and its law has real-life force. God esteems His Word, and believers must place the same premium on it! Its legal principles are redemptive, and as one applies the legally framed words of God, that application ushers in the complete *Shalom* of God which is His peace, power, provision, deliverance, and everything else you need. The God-centric *Bill of Rights* has a righteous boldness and its confessions of law are easily adaptable to your candid life situations. Overcoming all earthly obstacles and spiritual foes is accomplished by daily declaring the sword-like word of God and by meditating on the offered blood of Jesus-with faith. God honors His Word because His Word is law! In the United States landmark case of *Marbury v. Madison* (1803), the court established in an unanimous decision that the United States Constitution was actual law and more than a collection of tall ideals and giant principles.[86] So, too, has God established that His Word is more than stupendous concepts, but is perfected law: *"The law of the Lord is perfect, converting the soul…"* (Psalm 19:7, ESV).

Know God's law, keep it on the tip of your tongue, and make a practice of going to God's Court and getting what belongs to you! You can flourish in the Court of God because God keeps His covenants with His people, and you have the law on your side. The believer has indomitable joint-seating opportunities in Christ, including sitting in heavenly places, and among those places are seats in the Court of heaven. *"Who will bring any charge against God's elect. God is the one who justifies;" "But we are citizens of heaven, where Jesus Christ lives. And we are eagerly waiting for him to return as our Savior"* (Romans 8:33, ESV) (Philippians 3:20, ESV). We get to have earth-shattering, blood-shed moments of legal victory within the blood-stained judicial halls of glory! *"Thanks be unto God which always causes us to triumph in Christ"* (2 Corinthians 2:24, NLT). What does that triumph mean for the believer? It means having a right standing with God, as a result of being justified from sin and being justified through faith in Christ which allows you the privilege to confidently *stand* before Him in His court. In other words, you are spiritually just now, and having obtained this right legal standing in the spirit realm, that legal stance gives you an entitlement to rights which you can pursue in His Court. Scripture teaches that heaven and earth shall pass away, but God's

Word will forever stand, that is, have standing before Him forever (See Matthew 24:35). It is, therefore, important to stand before God with His authoritative Word. Just as the Constitution guarantees and safeguards the enforcement of your qualifying rights, the believer has certain rights which are enforceable in God's Court of law. The Bible, the word of God, constitutes God's constitutional authority and sets forth these rights. Your legal standing empowers you to come before God's Court for the just enforcement of His Word: *"The LORD gives grace and glory; No good thing does He withhold from those who walk uprightly"* (Psalm 84:11, NASB1995).

For the believer, it's raining rights!

RIGHT: Because you have been justified by your right position in Christ, and because of your remission of sin by the blood of Jesus, the Bible red flares that you can *rightly* come boldly before the celestial bench of God with your petitions, being reunited without the endangerment of being cast away: *"Therefore if any man be in Christ, he is a new creature…be ye reconciled to God. For he hath made him to be sin for us, who knew no sin; that we might be made the righteousness of God in him"* (2 Corinthians 5:17, 21; ESV).

Humankind went the wrong way but now has the "right of way!"

RIGHT: In my labeled legacy case of *Adam vs. Sin's Reach*, where redeemed participants acted upon the Word of God by confessing the Lordship of Christ and received their victory-surging, water-shedding moment of salvation, God's Court decided that their conversion legally granted deliverance from sin's reach over the old Adam and gave them access into God's newness of eternal justice. "While the names have been changed to protect the guilty" *in the above fictitious case, the outcome was very much real. Your redemption is a legal right! Your deliverance is a legal reality!* The word "remission" is linked to "justification and means the deliverance of- or the cancellation of- one's past sin charge or penalty so that punishment is no longer incurred:

For all have sinned, and fall short of the glory of God, being justified freely by his grace through the redemption that is in Christ Jesus, Whom God hath set forth to be a propitiation [as the atoning sacrifice] through faith in his blood, to declare his righteousness for the remission of sins that are past, through the forbearance of God.

ROMANS 3:23-25 (KJV)

Humankind has fallen but has the right to get up!

God's Patriot

"I agree, the law is good."

ROMANS 7:14 (NIV)

How does one come to appreciate the goodness of God through His laws? It occurs through the pattern of loving the one who is both the Lion of Judah and the Lawgiver: *"Judah, my lawgiver"* (Psalm 60:7, ESV). Judah is closely associated with Jesus because the Bible depicts Him as a lionesque descendant of the tribe of Judah: *"Stop weeping! Look, the Lion of the tribe of Judah, the heir to David's throne, has won the victory"* (Revelation 5:5, NIV). The Lion of Judah, whom I affectionately refer to as the "Lion of the Law," evinced law, was immersed in law, and roared with the law: *"The LORD will roar from Zion and raise His voice (thunder) from Jerusalem"* (Joel 3:16, NLT).

Historically, patriotic love for a country first yields a love for its good foundational laws. Patriotism, which is an allegiant identification and passion for one's country, is routinely built on an appreciation for those good foundational laws. To be a patriotic person, usually one must first identify him or herself with that country. There is normally a corresponding passion that then arises between the country and the citizen. Likewise, there must be patriotism for the kingdom of God by its citizenry, too. The love for God's kingdom's laws must start with an identity with the kingdom and its King—the lawgiver. Out of that identity proceeds a passion and love for the king, kingdom, and the King's laws. That patriotic identity is similarly understood and assumed through the laws of God's kingdom, for it is through His Word that the lawgiver, Jesus, expresses Himself, and the passionate attachment is made. If the godly laws in God's Word are no longer observed, then the passion for God's kingdom and the lawgiver will correspondingly decline or grow cold. In the last days before Christ returns, it is critical to keep the embers of lawful, passionate, and godly patriotism burning for Him and His laws: "Evil will spread and cause many to stop loving others" or *"Because lawlessness will increase, the love of many will grow cold"* (Matthew 24:12, ESV). The Matthew passage articulates that in the last days, men's hearts will grow cold in love; that is, their hearts will be frostbitten both towards each other and towards God. There, the Bible forecasts that in the days before Jesus' return, there will be a real frigidity of heart that takes place in society. Whether this occurs through a blatant disregard or a gradual dismissal of God's laws, there will be a rush and a tickle to choose lawlessness rather than a need or a desire to keep God's laws which enjoy a parity with grace; there is equality between the two of them because everything that God disseminates is equal to Him and His character. God is not capable of being lopsided or imbalanced. God's justice is always balanced by the scales of His love with laws and grace, which is kindness and favor. Jesus said, *"If you love me you will keep my commandments"* (John 14:15, NIV). It can seem at odds to equate obeying a command with being free, but Jesus gives us the liberty to love with this paradox—the freedom of restriction. Consider that God justly chastises those whom He loves and that Holy Spirit through which we freely enter God's presence also justly constrains us, the Bible teaches (See 2 Corinthians 5:14). The highest form of liberty, then, is love within a boundary. and anything that unjustly blurs that line is not in line with the greatest of patriotism. *"Stand fast therefore in the Liberty by which Christ has made us free..."* (Galatians 5:1, NIV).

> God set up His own system of remedy and damages.

Legal Compensation: Pay Day in God's Court

"And I [The Lord] will compensate you for the years that the swarming locust has eaten, the creeping locust, the stripping locust, and the gnawing locust..."

JOEL 2:25 (NASB)

"But if [a thief] is found, he must repay seven times..." (Proverbs 6:31, NIV). There are legal damages that a Christian can recover in God's court, which are similar to those of the United States' courts. Under the American judicial system, damages are monetary remedies that are awarded in court to a complainant and are meant to offset the losses a person has suffered because of the illegal conduct of another. I like to put it this way; it is judicial damage control payment. In simple terms, an individual receives an award of money to balance the effects of how he has been damaged. Damages are broken down into three categories: *Compensatory* damages, which compensate for a proven injury or loss; *Restitution* damages which are restorative where the defendant has been unjustly enriched at the plaintiff's expense; *Punitive* damages, which are awarded on top of either of the previous damages and serve to punish the wrongdoer and to discourage similar wrong behavior. God has always been opposed to loss for the believer. In fact, God set up His own system of remedy and damages under Judge

Moses and Apostle Peter, and as a result, there are legal remedies in the spirit realm that believers have access to: *"Cast not your confidence away for it has great recompense of reward"* (Hebrews 10:35, KJV). These remedies resemble the ones within the American legal processes. One such remedy is a "Letter of Demand," which puts a legal demand on someone to do something. An analysis of this letter will follow below, but the Bible has its own process of demand. Peter exclaimed, *"Lord, If it is You…command me to come to You on the water. 'COME,' said Jesus"* (Matthew 14:28-29, KJV; Emphasis supplied). There, Jesus issued a command statement which demanded something of Peter and of his surroundings. Jesus taught His disciples to pray, *"COME thy kingdom, on earth as it is in heaven!"* (Luke 11:2-4, KJV). As one of Jesus' predominant disciples, Peter was presumably there when Jesus taught His disciples to pray, so I believe he remembered and associated the power of the command which he had learned that day during the lesson on the Lord's prayer. Peter observed the power of the command and had caught the meaning of the demand. If Jesus commanded him to come, he knew that nothing and no one could withstand the command of Jesus; in essence, he knew that whatever Jesus commanded was a "done deal," for each spoken command created the spiritual demand or vehicle by which it was transported into the physical realm. Such is how Peter had the faith to walk on the water after Jesus bid him, *come!* The surrounding bottomless waves had to become subject to God's spiritual laws. Jesus' command to Peter demanded that the waves become nautical floaties for Peter's feet. Believers are given that same power to command something in the spirit realm through verbal decree and make a demand on that to manifest in the physical realm. What does it mean to make a demand on God's word? It means to make a withdrawal from the spiritual bank of heaven where Jesus has deposited the free-flowing currency of the church's paid ransom—His blood. It is to make a request with an aggressive faith and to confidently expect to receive it's manifestation because of Christ's shed blood. Confidence derives from two Latin words: *"con"* meaning with and *"fide"* meaning faith, so we receive the fulfillment of the demand with our faith. The Bible, in a clear sense, gives the believer a type of bank prospectus from its pages, part of which acts like a spiritual bank account guide that governs your faith account. When faith presents a withdrawal request or demand, it is legally met with a release of praiseworthy increase, under which falls your kingdom blessings, rights, and privileges: "… *Oh God, let all the people praise thee. Then shall the earth yield her increase; and God, even our own God, shall bless us*" (Psalm 67:5–6).

Turning to the "30 Day Demand Letter," as illustrated under Massachusetts law, this letter of demand is a legal letter that is sent by an aggrieved party who demands that a specific action take place within thirty days or face the threat of a distasteful lawsuit, double or triple damages, and unwanted attorney fees.[87] The demand is in furtherance of rights under the Massachusetts statute, which allows a pre-litigation settlement payment—in money or property—because of unfair or deceptive practices toward an individual who has suffered loss. Germane to the Massachusetts Consumer Protection Act is the thirty-day time limit which the letter reflects, but a legal letter of demand also can encompass other numbers of mandated days by which a besought party must respond to an injured party. Notice with me a similar spirit-realm example of this remedy where the Bible illustrates the same principle of demand as the believer's *One Day Demand Letter*.

For instance, God instructs Moses, who was God's legal ambassador on the earth, to cause the Israelites to give their Egyptian captors a twenty-four-hour notice of demand to hand over valuable property of jewelry and items. I refer to this demand as a spoil-rich demand which they had a right to by virtue of the spoils of battle. God, having spoiled the Israelites enemies, then openly exacted the price of victory: *"Having despoiled the principalities and the powers, he made a show of them openly, triumphing over them in it"* (Colossians 2:15, ASV). "And all this assembly shall know that the LORD saveth… the battle is the LORD's" (1 Samuel 17:47, KJV). The Egyptian captors had aggrieved the Israeli captives by unfairly consuming their labor through the unfair practices of slavery and the exacted demand served as a type of legal remedy. The valuables were equivalent to restitution damages that offset the suffering of their wrongful captivity by which the Egyptians had prospered at their expense: *"Yet if he is caught…he might even have to give the wealth of his house"* (Proverbs 6:31, NIV). They legally qualified for restitution. Moreover, God told Moses to instruct the Israelites to "borrow"—meaning request—gold and silver of the Egyptians. God empowered them to take legal action, for this request was legal in nature because it was also based on God's statutory law where the Bible says that if a thief is caught in his wrongdoing, then he must make punitive restitution by giving back to the wronged person a payment of four times to seven times what that payee lost (See 2 Samuel 12;6; Luke 19:8). In assessing the seven-fold multiplication, it appears that since seven represents completion in the Bible, seven-fold restitution would have symbolized complete restitution; alternatively, thinking about it from an aggregate perspective, punitive treble damages added to four-fold compensatory damages would have also equaled the seven-fold payout and would appear a just computation also under a different model.

Since God is a God of legal recompense, the requested indulgent compensation from the Egyptians is in step with that notion of punitive "payback" or punitive damages, which our American courts allow to exceed the regular award of damages. I conclude that the Egyptians stole labor from the Israelites, were caught, and were unjustly enriched to the detriment of the Israelites. This idea of multiplied compensation by God as Judge is also in line with what American courts call "treble damages," where the court can rule that three times the amount of awarded damages is appropriate, particularly when malice or intentional, spiteful evil was involved. Arguably, in determining the requested damages, God had taken into consideration the acute malice which the Egyptians demonstrated toward the Israelites when they intentionally retaliated against them, out of spite, to make bricks without straw (See Exodus 5:7).

On a final note, I find it interesting that God seems to have finessed inside of Moses's command to Pharaoh His own type of legal demand to "Cease and Desist"—"Let my people go!" Consider that, there, Moses was demanding that Pharoah cease from holding God's people against the will of God and against their wills, that he halt his pagan lordship over them, and that he desist from inducing their forced labor. That legal model could also be seen as God granting injunctive relief where diligent Moses successfully got a court order from God's Court for the release of the Israelites and could be considered an equitable remedy which is given when monetary damages at law are not enough to make the plaintiff whole, and where the plaintiff would suffer irreparable harm if not given. To be sure, the Israelites would definitely face irreparable harm were they not let go. "*...Must believe that I am and a rewarder of those who diligently seek me*" (Hebrew 11:6, KJV).

CHAPTER 19

Satan's "Legal" Defense

"He setteth a table before me in the presence of my enemies."

PSALM 23:5 (KJV)

Satan strode in court, as defiant as he was overconfident, as misguided as he was cocky. He had studied the law for eons, so he spoke with hauteur before God's judicial bench.

"I've already won this case against me. The Man-God is dead! Humankind's greatest star witness, aka chief lawyer, is dead! He cannot take the stand and tell how He came to set humankind free. He can no longer boast that His lineage is straight from God's, that Adam, like He, are both legal sons of God. Legally, without that divine breathing, talking, living eyewitness to my actual criminality, nor any circumstantial evidence of my alleged crime against humanity. It is I who has mastered this lawsuit handily. Yep! In the bag!! I dishonorably move for a dismissal of this case against the accused, your Honor. I don't have to be afraid of any more double-takes of His appearances and no more looking over my shadowy shoulders. He can no longer wield incriminating exhibits against the landscape of a foreseen Calvary at my expense! No more fancy lawyering at the drop of my hooded hat. Nope! That stellar combat lawyer is 'M.I.A.' The cream of the crop has been…cropped! Certainly, no intervening evidence to mitigate the sentencing of humankind in that other case. No more of His detailing the minutiae of how He came to destroy my works. I worked to destroy Him, Hah!, and that is the only indisputable evidence left on the table. No more live records of my ins and outs to be shown—oh, how I hated letting the record show! Hehe, I was the one who showed

Him something! It was prophesied that He was stricken for them, well strike that from the Court's record because only the permeation of death and dead professions exist now. He called Himself the Lamb of God. Well, the Lamb of God is irrefutably no more! Deathly silenced! Deathly vanished! Gone!"

Out of Satan's soliloquy of the moment, one which he no doubt rehearsed over and over to his squad of deformed-willed followers, repeating it more for the drunken escape that his words brought him than the need to rehearse them. He hawkishly reflected: "I saw His army of winged soldiers ordered to a no-flight formation as they watched their exalted Captain restrained and crucified in a no-flight zone. They were told not to engage the enemy, and all they could do was observe our wicked, frenzied jubilation!" Old slithery Slew Foot's inflated pitch became higher as if reliving his whole sordid, frenetic lust for blood and drunken warfare over the body of God's Son! Suddenly, there followed a splinter of stupefied pause. Satan thought he felt the earth move in a quadrant of ground in the Middle East plain. He gave it no care. "Maybe just an atmospheric aftershock of the earth's tilt and the red moon three days ago," he reasoned. *A little earth-quaking, maybe a little rotational righting of its axis,* he thought. "Nothing to worry about- my plans remain uninterrupted. Right on schedule! Bang! I saw the brutally beaten corpse go into the dug-out ground they called a tomb," he recounted to himself like a dog wagging his tail. He spoke up again now. "I and my deliriously satisfied posse of—shall we say 'evil misfits'—witnessed the prophetic whispers of *your* most faithful prophets come to an end. No way," he muttered, "No Messiah breathing! I move for a Dismissal, your honor. Dismissal!" Satan really thought Jesus couldn't save Himself or His "Jesus Nation." In his anti-Christ, warped imagination, he thought he would darkly rule over a nation of lost souls forever. Satan rejoiced that the soul's hope for its valuation died the moment the Hope of Glory collapsed into that grave. All of a sudden, a beam of light so immeasurably brighter than his one dim memory of his own extinguished light that saw an end as he despairingly free-fell in waves of unfiltered speed from heaven appeared and vice-gripped his drooping tentacles as his keys fell! The eyes of The Living Fire seared through all of heaven and hell, with a voice of forceful, surging waters! In a nano of a minuscule moment, Satan and his pitiful band had been disarmed with a bow shot of holiness that rampaged hell's vulnerable foundation. In a classic lawyer to liar moment, Satan and his feeble unmighty whimpered "No!" as the *Word of God* bellowed *"Yes!"* With a dispirited cringe and sunken knees made to bow, and his recalcitrant tongue created to confess that Jesus is Lord, Satan pathetically withdrew his untenable legal motion and grudgingly accepted the badged conquest of his Lord and God. Staring at the shrapnel and the heavenly patrol all around him, he struggled to lift his dejected chin as the Lion of Judah roared four words—*this* is *My* legal hour! After disarming Satan and his principalities, there stood a silence. As quickly as He appeared, Jesus was gone in a victorious ball of light, leading "captivity captive" and assembling gifts of vividity for His offspring—the celebrated procession of the vindicated sons and daughters of God: *"No weapon forged against you will prevail, and you will refute every tongue that accuses you. This is the heritage of the servants of the* LORD, *and this is their vindication"* (Isaiah 54:17, NIV).

The cross-tested God's performance of His unsurpassable power against all "sub-rivals" because God has no true rivals. In order for Satan to be a true rival of God, he would have to be an equal, and he is not: *"That at the name of Jesus every knee shall bow, of those in heaven, and those on earth, and those under the earth, and that every tongue should confess that Jesus Christ is Lord, to the glory of God the Father"* (Philippians 2:10–11, ESV). The cross proved whether God would actualize His power toward Jesus in the tomb, and in doing so, establish Jesus' post-resurrection title as the All-Powerful One. In heightened mystery, Jesus is a

> *Jesus is a type of Bronze Gate.*

type of Bronze Gate of the Old and New Testament. Jesus declared that He was The Gate (See John 10:9), and He is shown bedecked in bronze feet (See Revelation 1:15). The imagery of Jesus as the Bronze Gate is striking, and the deduction is manifold since, in the Bible, gates represent essential seats of authority as well as powerful entryways. Looking at the symbol of the gate, there is a biblical association with the impenetrability of the bronze gate. The metal's strength was uncontested and at the top of its category, and its attainability was readily prevalent in biblical times. The symbolism forecasts the strength of Jesus' seat of authority. Biblically, gates establish dominion and imperial kingdomship; the inability of the gates of hell to conquer God's body of believers was imprinted when Jesus declared: *"The gates of Hades will not prevail against my church"* (Matthew 16:18, BSB).

When Jesus announced that the gates of hell would not overcome His church, He uttered this statement while standing in Caesarea, Phillipi (See Matthew 16:18). At that time, many in the area mistakenly believed that the actual vicinity of this Greco-Roman city was the very gate to Hades, the underworld. It was there that Jesus purposely asked the disciples who they thought He was. Why? Because demarcating the hellish entryway and defining His identity in front of the perceived gateway of Satan would set a precedential way of thinking and establish God's theology of His ultimate power over life and death. When Jesus stood making that declaration against the pagan-celebrated, false gateway to their believed underworld, He was intentional about making a statement in direct reference to His surroundings about the battle of empires. Jesus wanted it clearly understood, right there in front of that pagan, maritime satanic stronghold, that His kingdom would win because it is ensconced between Him—The Gate In Chief—and the glory gates of heaven. So outwardly decisive was He there, that the Lord and future exponent of the hugely successful military victory that was going to take place at Calvary, legally took His postured stand of Lordship against the Devil's kingdom, and in a very literal sense, stacked His kingdom against the defeated forces of hell. It is clear that Jesus effectively pitted His infinitely superior, glorious gates of heaven against the comparatively shambled gates of the overcome one. God performed His power of triumph over the gates of hell and defeated Satan's blood-thirsty and false claim of underworld dominance: *"Neither death nor life, neither angels nor demons...not even the powers of hell can separate us from God's love. No power in the sky above or in the earth below"* (Romans 8:38–39, NLT). Jesus knew with certainty that He would soon leave this finite locale called earth, proclaiming that all authority had been legally given back to Him post-resurrection. Jesus is not only the gate of heaven, but He is also the gatekeeper of heaven. Consider His advice: *"No man comes to the Father except through me"* (John 14:6, NIV). Consider also, *"Strive to enter in at the narrow gate; for many, I say unto you, will seek to enter in, and will not be able"* (Luke 13:24, KJV). It is patently clear that in order to lawfully enter heaven's eternal gates, one must first go through the gate, Himself.

Hide & Seek: Game Over!

> *"...Jesus Christ and him crucified, but we speak God's wisdom in a mystery, the wisdom that has been hidden, which God foreordained before the worlds for our glory, which none of the rulers of this world has known. For had they known it, they wouldn't have crucified the Lord of glory."*
>
> 1 CORINTHIANS 2:7 (WEB)

This is a great mystery that God has gifted the world with—that Jesus' crucifixion was hidden while it was in plain view! I marvel that on the cross, Jesus was both incognito and conspicuous at the same time; although Jesus died in plain sight for the world to see, His crucifixion's fruit was out of view to the one who plotted it because the Devil was taken by surprise when it crested. I submit that the evil one was short-sighted about Jesus' crucifixion because if he had not been, the Bible communicates that he would never have *arranged* for the clandestine crucifixion of The Lord. The Word of God alludes that if he had known that our Salvation was incumbent upon the risen Christ, he would not have gone through with crucifying the Prince of Peace. It looks like the prince of darkness was in the dark about the mysterious efficacy of the work of the cross. Clearly, the effectiveness of the cross was enshrouded, but simultaneously, was on boastful display. On the one hand, God sheathed the work of the cross in Himself, for it appears that God likes to hide things within things and people within people; after all, He hid salvation within a male sheep and hid the church within Himself: *"Truly, you are a God who hides Himself. O God of Israel, Savior!"* (Isaiah 45:15, BSB). Like Jesus, we are both exhibited and legally hidden in God. My answer to the age-old question, "Were you there when they crucified my Lord," is yes! Because I was concealed in God-the-Son's side, I was waiting to be born as part of His church. When He died, and blood and water gushed out of His wound-womb, so too did the church come forth out of that birth canal. *"For you have died, and your life is hidden with Christ in God"* (Colossians 3:3, HCSB). Significantly, in Hebrew, God's name is also El Rachem—The God of Mercy and the Womb.

It may seem like the work of the cross was secretive, especially since Jesus warned people not to tell anyone about some of His miracles, but was its opaqueness really part of a plan? I think not, only partly. The work of the cross was both surreptitious and overt, at first purposely hidden by God and then widely revealed. Ultimately, Jesus was on exhibition for the whole world to see at Calvary. *"Thank you father that you have revealed this to them"* (Matthew 11:25, NIV). The Bible, particularly in the unobscured 53rd chapter of Isaiah, openly predicts the crucifixion of the Savior. The Devil was so aware of this open prophecy that he tried to short circuit the life of Jesus several times before Jesus made it to the cross. Using a "friendly fire" approach from his strategic arsenal, he even enlisted Peter in his battle plan to deter Jesus from His trajectory to the cross: "Satan, get behind me," was Jesus' unfriendly reply to Peter when Peter implored Him not to keep His appointment with Calvary. The Devil, then, sought to destroy the redeemer's path to the cross by churning a

> *The Devil had a bad day on Good Friday.*

plan to throw Jesus off a cliff, but Jesus supernaturally passed through the angry crowd. The Bible portrays in a simple sentence how Jesus miraculously waded through an alert and irate crowd undetected: "...*but Jesus hid himself*" (John 8:59, NASB). Jesus' hiding was another example of being hidden in plain sight. This polarity that the devil demonstrated between an awareness that teetered on the brink of conspiratorial, homicidal mania on the one hand, and being shockingly ignorant of Jesus' forecasted death, on the other hand, was scripturally striking. The devil's ignorance contrasted with his foreknowledge, I conclude, encapsulates the preferential treatment of God's believers: *"Because it has been given to you to know the mysteries of the kingdom of heaven, but to them it has not been given"* (Matthew 13:11, ESV). The Devil just could not figure it out; he failed to see the impact which Jesus' death and absolution of sin's penalty would bring. The chronicled prophecies of the Savior's forthcoming death were announced so much that the enemy tried to kill Jesus, most notably as a newborn, to stop His ascent to the cross. The inference that the Devil and his rulers were clueless to Jesus' impending death and intertwined resurrection is a mystery within itself. One might ask, what caused the Devil's oblivion? Why could the devil not debunk the mystery of the cross? Was the devil spiritually myopic? Was he just "off his spiritual game?" Did the Devil have a bad day on Good Friday? I propose that Jesus' crucifixion and converging resurrection was not apparent to the enemy because he had lost his heart for God: *"You will seek me and find me when you seek me with all of your heart"* (Jeremiah 29:13, NIV). The fall out was manifested in three ways: The Devil could not debunk the cross's mystery in real time because, although he had heard emphatically about the prophesied death and resurrection of Jesus, he only believed it in part: *"Even the demons believe—and tremble with fear"* (James 2:19, BSB). Perhaps he believed that Jesus was the Messiah who would die but never really believed that Christ would be victorious over death. Also, the enemy could not disentangle the great mystery of the cross because he was an arachnidian victim of his own webs of lies; that is, he was a victim of his creation. For example, when he induced Adam and Eve to believe a lie about God, he spun a web of truth in part and falsehood in part, so he could never get past his own lies about the truth of God. He duped himself. Finally, I believe that the divine law of reprobation played a role in the Devil's inability to decipher the mystery of the cross. The Bible illustrates that if one refuses to turn from his wicked sin, then the unrepentant, sinful behavior will not be tolerated endlessly by God, but rather, God will allow him to become a reprobate toward that sin. In other words, he will be controlled by the very wicked thing that he has chosen of his own accord to bow to: *"Whoever sows to please their flesh, from the flesh will reap destruction"* (Galatians 6:8, NIV). It, thus, seems that God would have turned Satan over to the very thing that he chose to deify, unbelief and falsehood. No longer able to distinguish truth from his purported half-truths, the devil appears victimized by his predilection to lies over truth all the time, including when Jesus' death and resurrection was broadcasted in extroverted, pennant fashion for the whole world to see. The third day, therefore, had to be calamitous for the Devil inside the earth when he experienced the rally cry of Jesus from the dead. I suggest that the Devil's morning consisted of a game of mental Tectonic Plating for breakfast as his denial came to an end amidst his switching of the plates of truth and half-truths around. *"Mystery which was hidden from the ages now manifested to His saints"* (Colossians 1:26, NIV).

CHAPTER 20

Making It Legal: The Gospel in a Nutshell

"Filled with the fruit of righteousness that comes through Jesus Christ, to the glory and praise of God."

PHILIPPIANS 1:11 (ESV)

The following synopsis is the gospel in a nutshell, or perhaps, is the gospel wrapped up in a fig leaf. Once upon any eternity, God reached out and coddled the world, His world. Jesus, who is the lovely seed of God, lovingly died on a remorseless cross for you and me, and when He was resurrected, He shot up out of the ground like seeded plants do, becoming the first fruit of the resurrection. Jesus had an embryonic effect on humankind. In a sense, Jesus impregnated the earth, and it had to give rise to the eternal bloom of that seed. Jesus died and was resurrected during the Jewish feast of First Fruits, and so legally fulfilled the dictates of that festival by becoming the first fruit of those who are dead; importantly, His seed sprouted and brought more plants out of the ground, harvesting the body of Christ: *"By this my Father is glorified, that you bear much fruit and so prove to be my disciples"* (John 15:8, ESV). Those who are born again with this new, implanted spiritual fruit-life are termed "in Christ" because they are born after Christ's fruitful seed. They are, as a result, imbued with that same part of Christ Jesus' spiritual DNA which caused Him to spring forth as glorious, resurrected fruit out of the earth: *"You did not choose me, but I chose you and sent you out to produce fruit, the kind of fruit that will last"* (John 15:16, CEV). That God-like DNA—genetic sequencing—causes the believer to progress to maturity and flourish likewise on earth because the believer is the second fruit—or the fruit of the first fruit. "Filled with the fruit of righteousness that comes through Jesus Christ" (Philippians 1:11, NIV). I refer to this fruitful replication as the "Legal Halo Effect of the Cross," that is to say, the most beautiful part of the cross is the resultant glowing effect of God sowing His Son as a seed to legally harvest many sons and daughters according to His law of sowing and reaping: *"For those whom he foreknew he also predestined to be conformed to the image of his Son, in order that he might be the firstborn among many brothers"* (Romans 8:29, ESV). *"But in fact, Christ has been raised from the dead. He is the first of a great harvest of all who have died"* (1 Corinthians 15:20, NLT).

It was no accident that Christ made His decision to die for us in a garden filled with olive fruit trees. The renowned Romano-Jewish historian and Jewish priest, Titus Flavius Josephus, or Yosef ben Matityahu at birth, observed the Savior's execution as piteous.[88]

It was, but it was both piteous and glorious! Seeing Jesus die the way He died on that cross, under the detention of such dire and gruesome savagery, must have been visual anathema, but it was also a visual preponderance of His treatise on love. Humankind was the cherished object of that love! The arc of the gospel is summed up in one legal argument—love. Love is God's legal codification for everything. Love is both the complexity and the legality of the cross simplified. Jesus' blood was a veritable fountain of not waterfalls, but *blood falls* containing within it an echo cavity that resounded loudly with each spill. It was heard all the way to the corridors of eternity, over and over again. Its erupting echo sounding of—it is finished, it is finished, it is finished. Jesus' blood varnished the cross crimson, and it left Cavalry outlined in thriving garnet. God desired to reveal the love which soaked the cross; His touch extended beyond and above competing man-made laws, sects, and traditions that day. Such regulations were present but not confining to an almighty God who stepped into the calendar of time and thrust His legal will forward. The gospel contains the awe-inspiring work of God's nexus of the earthly and the spiritual coming together on the cross. It was a spiritual germination in an earthly space. *"You did not choose me, but I chose you and sent you out to produce fruit, the kind of fruit that will last"* (John 15:16, CEV). Once planted in this massive topsoil, one might ask—how does humankind grow in the fruitfulness of that salvation? It is worth pondering. I propose three steps:

1. In the natural world, a believer is born and grows in his physical body and in his mental senses according to his chromosomal programming, hereditary content, and surrounding environmental values. Not dissimilar, in the spiritual world, he grows spiritually in his spiritual faculties and stature as part of a spiritually-breathed, DNA-coded helix, and by immersing himself in a corporate environment with other valuable believers: *"But we have the mind of Christ"* (1 Corinthians 2:16, NIV). *"Let us not neglect meeting together"* (Hebrews 10:25, BSB).
2. The spiritually-free believer is no longer a slave of unrighteousness but free to live righteously. How does one live righteously? To live righteously is to live godly. *"All that will live godly in Christ…"* (2 Timothy 3:12, KJV), but how exactly does that occur? It straightly means living the way God wants us to live by the example of Christ. Christ died upon a tree, and when He arose, He planted trees: *"Those who are planted in the house of the LORD Shall flourish in the courts of our God"* (Psalm 92:13, NKJV). Salvation is free, but there is a sum total that Jesus says that one must calculate: *"Suppose you want to build a tower, you would sit down first and figure out what it will cost…"* (Luke 14:28, GWT). Righteousness is a towering inheritance with legal abundance and legal boundaries, but God is not trying to trick the believer or frustrate the believer's

intentions; God loves His creation and is not fixated on being mad at them. He left a roadmap to get to

> *God made salvation legal, but you have to make it count.*

Him; Jesus Christ is the Way, so living like Christ lived is the right way to live, and that equals living righteously. Simply follow the mapquest to arrive at the eternal destination—home.

3. Jesus was the Lumen of lambs who lit the way for us to the cross. The cross demands a decision—inaction is not an option; it demands either an affirmation or a denial. The cross is the central figure of salvation and is linked to victory over eternal death. When one acknowledges the cross, affirms his understanding of the finished work of the cross, and decides to believe in Jesus as the Savior of the cross, he receives the entitlement to eternal life: *"… Believe in the Lord Jesus Christ and you and you will be saved, along with everyone in your household"* (Acts 16:31, NLT). God made salvation legal, but you have to make it count. Jesus said, believe, and you will be saved; if not, you will be damned. There is no in-between (Mark 16:16). Here is the visual: Flailing within the sin-infested and damning waters, the one who believes accepts the life preserver from a rescuing Jesus, but the one who refuses automatically accepts the alternative which is perishing without a life preserver. The crucial is in the crush. Jesus'

> *The cross demands a decision; inaction is not an option.*

cross is a universal symbol that is "polar-centric" because either one embraces it or spurns it; one cannot stand on the periphery of a decision. God prefers a decisive and lucid, not an incomplete sleep-sounding, lethargic response to it: *"So because you are lukewarm, and neither hot nor cold, I will spit you out of my mouth"* (Revelation 3:16, NASB1995). The cross represents the wonderful bounty of love, joy, and the real perks of everlasting life. The cross equally represents the virtuous reality of declination, for Jesus said to take up your cross, deny yourself, and be holy. That denial consists of denying unholiness and denying selfishness; holiness is purity and separated maturity, while selfishness is an unmuted and unstrained flesh. God does not demand perfect holiness, for no imperfect humanity can achieve that. God kept it simple; He looks for the commitment and a growing pursuit to be like Him, who is Holy. *"Be holy, because I am holy"* (1 Peter 1:16, NIV). Huge incoming news—God is not looking for the flawless, He is looking for the faithful! *"His lord said to him, 'Well done, good and faithful servant… Enter into the joy of our lord'"* (Matthew 25:23, NKJV).

All Souls Rise

"Bless the Lord, O My soul, and all that is within me, bless his holy Name."

PSALM 103:1 (ESV)

Symbolic of our posture of giving God upright praise, we rise. It is meant to be a worshipful posture by which to bestow worship on its most worthy recipient. Across America, and even across the world, in pews or in lined chairs of places of worship, we rise in adoration to the one who chose to come down. After the mandatory bid to "All Rise" is heard in the courtroom, it is most unusual for a judge to get off his judicial seat, exit his judicial box, and come out to greet or speak to anyone seated in the courtroom. Such an aberration normally would not be considered proper courtroom protocol for a judge. The Bible, nevertheless, demonstrates that God "the just Judge," Judge of the highest degree whose throne is known to be at the greatest point northward, made a crucial, steep descent to inhabit a virgin's womb. To put it succinctly, He exited the throne to greet the human soul. In doing so, He became the narrow-runged ladder for humankind to make its way upward. When a child is born into this world, although the body is alive, the soul is surely stillborn. It was the God-guided, geographical exchange between heaven and earth where the soul realized its worth. This conflation took place on what a hymnist penned was an "Oh Holy Night." The conversion of the soul's worth is only as good as the access it has to the mender of it: *"After the anguish of His soul, He will see the light of life and be satisfied; By His knowledge My righteous Servant will justify many"* (Isaiah 53:11, BSB). On the night of Jesus' birth, men's souls were transported through a *foyer* of peace, one that gave His creation the possibility to all rise before heaven's throne: *"This child is appointed for the fall and rising of many…"* (Luke 2:34, ESV).

Be It Resolved: All Souls Matter

"Let my soul live and it shall praise You."

PSALM 119:175 (NKJV)

The soul coming into its appreciation was like being in a disregarded cave, looking out into the outer sky, grasping the tint of sunlight, peeping at the unexpected, and watching as the opacity gave way to the ostentatious light without measure. Cognizant of its newfound beauty, it surely leapt: *"You turned my sobbing into dancing"* (Psalm 30:11, GW). The longing of the blistered soul to matter, the cogitating over its own salvation was not an option until the Prince of Heaven knelt close to it and redeemed its beggarly state with a kingly ransom. The soul profited in the company of God. In this age of T-shirt-fests, I would relish one that says, "Profitable Soul Here." *"For what profit is it to a man if he gains the whole world, and loses his own soul?"* (Matthew 16:26, NKJV). Jesus' blood was the ransom that paid the bill of extortion for our souls. Straight and simple, it was blood payment! In gripping fashion, Satan held the soul's eternal trajectory hostage: *"But now as God's loving servants, you live in joyous freedom from the power of sin"* (Romans 6:22–23, TPT).

When does the soul matter? When was one of God's greatest decisions on whether a soul has a legal right to exist, re-exist, and be prosperous? To answer these questions, one must consider my relevant term, the "law of extant action"—the law is as the law does. God put this question to rest when He enacted His own executive law regarding the soul with a proclamation, followed by stern action from His throne. Firstly, God seemed to say: Be it resolved that the soul shall bless the Lord at all time (Psalm 34:1). Secondly, be it resolved that the soul shall no longer be cast down (Psalm 43:5). Thirdly, be it resolved that above all things, the soul shall prosper (3 John 1:2). Fourthly, be it resolved this day old things have passed away and have become new (2 Corinthians 5:17). Fifthly, be it resolved that man has shed his benighted soul and has become a living soul. In the garden of Eden, the very presence of God was so close to man that it was only a lip's distance from him; from God's mouth to his, a tributary of breathy life went forth as the *Ruach Ha-Kodesh* of God poured into him like a deep stream: *"And the LORD God…breathed into his nostrils the breath of life, and man became a living soul"* (Genesis 2:7, KJV). In the presence of God is the soul made well. It was this presence that enabled man to not only have a living soul but to live with his soul. Hence, the converse is true, that to be excluded from God is to have an occluded soul, a barren soul, a dead soul, and a lost soul. This reality was summed up so poignantly in Jesus' narration of the prodigal son. There, the father who represented God exclaimed that his son had been dead but was now alive, and simultaneously had been lost, but was now found. The insinuation was that the son's lack of proximity to the father had caused a dead and cloudy soul and, therefore, a lost son. The emphasis on "lost" addressed the deficiency of the soul and was not just a metaphoric reference to the son being directionally challenged and losing his way home, for he obviously knew how to find his way back to his old address; rather, the emphasis on "lost" reinforced the awareness that out of the Maker's presence, the soul suffers spiritual inertia and spiritual death. God did a divine reset; the soul was worth God coming to earth for. *"Why are you cast down, O my soul, and why are you in turmoil within me? Hope in God"* (Psalm 43:5, ESV).

God would forever change the course of the soul's history. God enlivened the womb of a virgin for the eventuality of having a reunion with the reckless soul of humankind. God deposited life in a womb that would eventually bring life to fallen humankind; the Prince of Life then courted the spiraling soul. Through trickery and devilish artifice, Satan had secured the legitimate right to incarcerate humankind's soul. It was contractually detestable, a deal gone left—between informed Adam and unsuspecting Eve—technically just short of voidable, but nevertheless, our souls were condemned forever. The soul was spiritually captive; the captor was sin, and the master was Satan; but, wonder of wonders! Jesus' death mastered the master! *"What can man give in exchange for his soul?"* (Matthew 16:26, BSB). When the Son of Heaven breathed His last breath, humankind was entitled to breathe its first breath in a reborn soul… and that matters! *"Marvelous are your works, And that my soul knows very well"* (Psalm 139:14, BSB).

The goal of this book has been to share veins of thought about God's legal intentions toward humankind. While it is impossible to completely unpack the ingenuity and the inimitable layering of thought that God had in mind as He breathed life into His creation and further breathed His Word to that beloved creation, it is clear that God had a ginormous legal plan to redeem humankind's pinned-down soul from the mat of damnation and to reconcile that beat-up soul to Himself. God's delightful divulgence of His "FEMA" plan to rescue emaciated humankind is well laid out in His Word and revolves around the cross. Albeit it is a privileged and mammoth task to inquire into the mindset of God, God desires fulsome, intimate, spiritual, soulful, and intellectual partnership so that He can share His heartbeat with His believers. It is a thrilling expedition when God draws back that long, thickly lined drapery to give us a peek of His divine thought pattern. He permits us to lunge closer, enabling us to miraculously perceive the immeasurability of His loving heart. He whets our spiritual appetite. He opens our eyes; then, we see that the journey has become the end. We see the real reason for the vastitude of the cross; all He ever wanted was us close to Him. It was all about the encapsulation of His data of love. The journey to be enclosed in Him is both the means and our sumptuous end if we cling to the cross and not abdicate our faith. In the Old Testament, God and His glory departed the earth, east out of the now inglorious temple where it previously abode; this aweful departure is referred to as "Ichabod." In the New Testament, the glory came back swaddled in baby clothes until the glorified, manful temple of Jesus departed the earth enveloped in a cloud with angels proclaiming that God the Son will gloriously perforate earth's molten nucleus once more, aloft a cloud (See Luke 21:27). He left but left enough of His glory behind in the person of His Spirit—Holy Spirit—so that you could find Him. Make His cross legally count for you, won't you?

CHAPTER 21

The First of Noels: Execute the Challenge!

"Ask me for the nations, and every nation on earth will belong to you."

PSALM 2:8 (CEV)

A portraitist's dream was seen on the night of Jesus' coronal birth, where God's flamboyant aerial production of the cherubic-throated coronation became heaven's heavily oiled canvas. "Glory to God in the highest" burst forth from the mighty vocalists (Luke 2:14, NIV). It was a kingly concert of divine heralding, angelic pageantry brushing the divide that separated heaven and earth. That celestial throng "*Noel-ed*" some attentive, lamb-laden attendants. A second annunciatory *Noel* decisively occurred during the resurrection of Jesus when Mary found herself surrounded by two light-coiffed angels who announced the good news of the resurrection of Jesus (John 20:11–28). A third *Noel* realistically followed when two stunning angels, frocked in white, sounded the futuristic return of Jesus: *"…Why do you stand gazing up into heaven, this same Jesus which is taken up from you into heaven, shall so come in like manner as you saw Him go into heaven"* (Acts 1:11, NKJV).

God's redemptive innovativeness included three punctuated announcements about His heavenly Son: Jesus' birth, Jesus' resurrection, and Jesus' return. In broadcasting the announcements, God demonstrated a three-fold maximalism of His redemptive plan: A Savior had to be born *legally* on earth; A Savior had to be resurrected *legally*—once dead on earth; A Savior would have to re-enter earth *legally* for

His second return. Having successfully prepared for all three epochs, it is at once apparent that through His trilogy of *Noels*, God paraded the radical greatness, faithfulness, and hopefulness that heaven's venerated child would bring to the globe. It is there that the New Testament begins; it is the inception point of the Gospel. God's hand was premeditatively showy. He knew beforehand that fallen humankind would need a Savior and had immediately fashioned an ostentatious message and an equally aggressive legal plan of deliverance. In days of Olde, God showcased the "*Noel* System" by which to announce to the world the Good News of Jesus Christ. Bad news had preceded the good news; because of Adam's sin, every man and woman thereafter was born with an inherited rotten, congenital disposition of sin and an inescapable core of naughtiness. Because of Jesus, the Christ, God pulled off a serious "leap frog" over humanity's engrained ancestry of sin. He tented His announcements of that good news against a landscape of grace, faith, and community. The ingenuity of the Creator's sharing of the gospel is prevalent throughout its biblical read. No letter nor lesson—no segway nor season—of the gospel's publication was wasted. *"And this is the victory that has overcome the world—our faith"* (1 John 5:4, ESV); *"For truly I tell you, until heaven and earth disappear, not the smallest letter, not the least stroke of a pen, will by any means disappear from the Law until everything is accomplished"* (Matthew 5:18, NIV). From there, Jesus picked up the "divine baton" for the *Noel* marathon. Jesus "Nailed it!" Now in glory, this paradigmatic architect of our faith and great Carpenter of God's church enlists our services and our "good news" testimonies to further build His church: *"Jesus Christ Himself being the Chief cornerstone, in whom the whole building, being fitted together, grows…"* (Ephesians 2:20–21, NKJV). Jesus literally built the Church on His back at Calvary, and as such, is the bedrock of instructional and revelatory disseminations for spreading His news. We are the celebrated stones that He uses to raise a useful testimony in the world's eyes. Our faith erects a column of adulation to Him, and with it, He makes us part of the divine construction process of building His church here on earth. *"And you are living stones that God is building into his spiritual temple. What's more, you are his holy priests.*

> *God commissions every chosen believer to engage in the world.*

Through the mediation of Jesus Christ, you offer spiritual sacrifices that please God" (1 Peter 2:5, NIV). For sure, rudimentary foundations are found in any earthly church or cathedral. For instance, a gothic cathedral commonly has what's called a "flying buttress," which is the foundational beam that helps to hold the structure up. Metaphorically speaking, our upstanding faith is that flying buttress of adoration that holds the granite house that we build on Christ: *"Anyone who hears these words of mine and obeys them is like a wise person who built a house on solid rock"* (Matthew 7:24, GNT). *"I will build my church and all the powers of hell will not conquer it"* (Matthew 16:18, NLT).

Today, God challenges His followers to transport this same "good news" that Christ is born and that Jesus is still building His church! We are to be global carriers according to the imperative of His law, to be *in* the world, but not of the world: "…You are not of the world, but I have chosen you out of the world" (John 15:19, BSB). In other words, God commissions every chosen believer to engage in the world, not peripherally, but in full throttle, world-interfacing in order to establish the joyous message of Jesus Christ and the voluminous love of God: *"So we are Christ's ambassadors; God is making his [legal] appeal through us. We speak for Christ when we plead, 'Come back to God!'"* (2 Corinthians 5:21, NLT; Emphasis supplied). We have to let the whole world know the simple, powerful Gospel that long ago in a garden, Adam enjoyed God's walking presence day by day, but one day the presence of *Jehovah Shammah*—The Lord who is present and The Lord who is there—was not enough for him; so Adam chose the presence of another. It was a decision gone wrong and the beginning of his sinful downfall. After that, God was born with the name "God With Us" to remind the world that He still wanted to be present, walking every day in our lives. God then died excruciatingly on a cross, but only after leaving a garden that reminded Him of Adam and the days when His presence had been enough. God self-resurrected and went back to heaven, but not before reminding us that He would never withhold His presence if we called Him Lord, and so He double-promised: *"I will not, I will not leave you;"* and so He triple promised: *"I will not, I will not, I will not let you down"* (Hebrews 13:5) (*See* also Septuagint & Expanded NT). Go tell it on the mountain! Go shout it from the top of the ages to all generations, that God wants to be present in our lives forever, and that His presence *can* be enough… It *must* be enough! *"…And from that day on the name of the city shall be,* THE LORD IS THERE" (Ezekiel 48:35, BSB). Accept the challenge! Execute the fourth *Noel*!

"I will fulfill my vows to the Lord in the presence of all his people, in the courts of the house of the Lord" (Psalm 116:18–19, NIV).

AFTERWORD

"The Almighty is beyond our reach; he is exalted in power!"

JOB 37:23 (BSB)

This book is meant to evoke an uncommon representation of God as the lawful Creator who is a deliberate and supremely intelligent legislator and designer. It is meant to delve into the subsurface intellectual attainment about God's law, life, and salvation. It sheds light on the deeper depictions of God and His legal world. Christianity, much to the assertions of antagonists, is not a vacuum for the crutch-minded who never bother to dig deeply for enlightenment. On the contrary, God's blueprint of Christianity welcomes the foraging into God's enigmas and legal ways, for He says, *"Seek and you will find"* (Matthew 7:7, BSB). This book introduces a round picture of the *lex* and the *amor*—the law and the love—of God by sharing some fresh strata of legal truths and their application to the gospel of Jesus, the Christ.

BIBLE VERSIONS

- New International Version (NIV)
- New Living Translation (NLT)
- English Standard Version (ESV)
- Berean Study Bible (BSB)
- Berean Literature Bible (BLB)
- King James Bible (KJV)
- New King James Version (NKJV)
- New American Standard Bible (NASB)
- Amplified Bible (AMP)
- Christian Standard Bible (CSB)
- Holman Christian Standard Bible (HCSB)
- American Standard Bible (ASV)
- Aramaic Bible in Plain English (ABIE)
- Contemporary English Version (CEV)
- Douay-Rheims Bible (DRB)
- Good News Translation (GNT)
- GOD'S WORD Translation (GWT)
- International Standard Version (ISV)
- The New English Translation Bible (NET)
- New Heart Bible (NHEB)
- Weymouth New Testament (WNT)
- World English Bible (WEB)
- Young's Literal Translation (YLT)
- Webster's Bible Translation (WBT)
- Geneva Bible of 1587
- The Vulgate Version
- The Septuagint Version

ABOUT THE AUTHOR

Juanita Sanders Thomas was educated and/or received specialized training at Dartmouth College, Columbia University School of Law, Harvard University, New England Conservatory of Music, Berklee College of Music, Emmanuel Gospel Center, and other notable institutions of academia and the fine arts. Currently enjoying retirement, she embraced both the corporate and public sectors as an attorney of over twenty years before transitioning into expansive ministry outreach. At the precocious age of eight, she recited fifteen-page sermonic poems unassisted and from memory. At the age of sixteen, she launched door-to-door evangelism and community outreach. Additionally, at sixteen, Juanita was chosen as a court mediator, setting a record for one of the youngest mediators in the country. Never losing sight of the connection between the legal and the spiritual, she joined the Christian Legal Society.

Later, Juanita had a God-given, unforgettable dream in which she wore a judicial robe while standing at a minister's podium. Around her flowed loud, forceful, and huge waves that dare not be silenced. Juanita grasped deeply the realization that God was calling her to wade in merging waters of the theocratic revelatory and the systematic legal, and that she needed to be a clarion voice for Him. This book is a product of that vision and several prophecies which followed.

ENDNOTES

1 U.S. Const. Amend. V; U.S. Const. Amend. XlV; The Fourteenth Amendment Clause, *See* www.constitutioncenter.org; Accessed 10, Nov. 2021

2 Fed. R. Civil P. 8 (a).

3 U.S. Const. Amend. X.

4 U.S. Const., art. 1, & 9, Clause 1-2; AEDPA(Antiterrorism and Effective Death Penalty Act) 1996, DTA (Detainee Treatment Act) 2005, MCA (Military Commissions Act) 2006; *Boumediene v. Bush*, 544, U.S. 266 (2008); 28 U.S.C. § 2241-2256. https:www.law.cornell.edu/wex/habeas_corpus; *Sanders v. United States*, 373 U.S.1, 18, 83 S.Ct. 1068, 1070, 10 L. Ed. 2d 148, *See also Delo v. Stokes*, 495 U.S. 320-322, 110 S. Ct. 1880, 109 L. Ed. 2d 325.

5 Jude 1:9

6 Chisholm, Hugh, ed. (1911), "Body-Snatching." Encyclopedia Britannica. 4 (11th Ed.) Cambridge University Press, p. 112.

7 Kidnapping, 18 U.S.C § 1201(a)1

8 W.W. Thornton, A Treatise of the Law relating to Gifts and Advancements 2-3 (1893)

9 Samuel Williston, Contracts & 1.1(4th Ed. 1990)

10 Formal Requirements; Statute of Frauds. U.C.C, § 2-201 (Amended 2003).

11 Ibid.

12 *See* Gregory Koukl, The Story of Reality, p.127, Grand Rapids; Zondervan, 2017; See also, B.P. Grenfell and A. S. Hunt, New Classical Fragments and other Greek and Latin Papyri, pp. 5-13, 22, Oxford: Clarendon Press, 1897; Admin, Tetelestai-Paid in

Full, <preceptaustin.org> updated 28 May, 2018; Accessed 1 Nov., 2021: Tetelestai is Greek for *It is finished* or *paid in full*. In Latin it is "Consummatum est," meaning *it is consummated*. In the Ancient Middle East, promissory notes/debt certificates had Tetelestai written on them once the debt was paid.

13 Hebrews 6:13, The Holy Bible, New International Version (1984). Grand Rapids: Zondervan Publishing House.

14 Shichun Ling, Jacob Kaplan, Colleen M. Berryessa, The Importance of Forensics For Decisions on Criminal Guilt; Science & Justice, Volume 61, Issue 2, March 2021, pp 142–149; Science & Justice 61(2021)142–149; www.justice.gov/olp/forensic-science

15 *See* Forensic Pathology Report on Jesus, www.GodOnThe.net; Iannone, John C. The Mystery of the Shroud of Turin. New York, Alba House 1998 ISBN 0-8189-0804; The Blood and the Shroud. New York, The Free Press, a division of Simon & Schuster, Inc. 1998 ISBN 0-684-85359-0

16 Iannone, *supra*, at 2–4; *See* Forensic Pathology Report on Jesus et al., *supra*.

17 Ibid.

18 Ibid.

19 "On the Physical Death of Jesus Christ," Journal of the American Medical Association, Vol. 255., No. 11. 21 March, 1986. 1459

20 Rev. James Ussher, Annals of the World (1658); hbu.edu Bible Timeline (281) 649-3000; blogos.org. The Fullness of Time. The Timeline between Adam and Jesus. Burt Lockwood (2021)

21 Denise R. Johnson, Reflections on the Bundle of Rights, Vermont Law Review, Vol. 32:247 p.251 (2007)

22 National Geographic Society 2020, "Revolution"; Accessed 18 Oct., 2021, <nationalgeographic.org>; "Revolution" 2021, Accessed 18 Oct., 2021, <law.jrank.org>

23 "Revolt." https:www.mvorganizing.org Accessed 15 Nov., 2021

24 U.S. Const. amend. V.

25 www.biblicalarchaeology.org; "What the Temple Mount Looked Like" _Biblical Archeological Review, November/December 2016; "Relics in Rubble: The Temple Mount Sifting Project" _Biblical Archeological Review, November/December 2016; Katherine M. D. Dunbabin, Mosaics of the Greek and Roman World (Cambridge; Cambridge Univ. press, 1999), pp. 254-264; Josephus, Jewish Antiquities; XV 412, trans. By Ralph Marcus and Allen Wikgren, Loeb Classical Library 489 (Cambridge, MA; Harvard Univ. Press 1943)

26 Ibid

27 Ibid

28 Katz, L. (2010), A Theory of Loopholes, The Journal of Legal Studies, 39 (1), 1–31

29 John 4:20. The Holy Bible, New International Version (1984). Grand Rapids: Zondervan Publishing House

30 Ibid, at 4:9

31 Ibid, at 4:11

32 Ibid, at 4:25

33 Ibid, at 4:12

34 Ibid, at 4:17

35 Ibid, at 4:19

36 Ibid at 4:15

37 Ibid at 4:26

38 Meacham (leBeit Yareh) "Legal-Religious Status of the Jewish Female." Shalvi/Hyman Encyclopedia of Jewish Women. 13 July, 2021; *See* jwa.org; Accessed 11 Nov., 2021

39 Lilly Ledbetter Fair Pay Act, 2009; *Ledbetter v. Goodyear Tire & Co.*, 550 U.S. 618, 127 S.Ct. 2162; 167 L.Ed.2d 982; 2007 U.S. LEXIS 6295; 75 U.S.L.W.4359; Amended the Civil Rights Act of 1964

40 Versa, Opinions of the Supreme Court of Israel, http://versa.cardozo.yu.edu/, 2014

41 *See* Lacus Curtius, Roman Law-Cautio, penelope.uchicago.edu; Vindicta manumission

42 Size of New Jerusalem in Square Miles, www.iris.org.il, 2021

43 *See* Katz, Leo, "A Theory of Loopholes," The Journal of Legal Studies, Vol.39, No.1 Updated 4 June, 2018, Accessed 15 Nov., 2021

44 Jeno SH, Varacallo M., Back, "Latissimus Dorsi" [Updated 11 Aug., 2021].

45 UN General Assembly. "Universal Declaration of Human Rights." United Nations, 217 (lll)A, 1948, Paris, preamble; art.2, *See* https:www.ohchr.org. Accessed 02 Dec., 2021. *See also*, www.un.org., Accessed 19 Oct., 2021

46 *Brown v. Board of Education*, 347 U.S. 483 (1954); "*Brown v. Board of Education of Topeka* (1)." Oyez, www.oyez.org/cases/1940-1955/347us483. Accessed 11 Nov., 2021.

47 2020 Model of Professional Responsibility; *See* ABA CANONS OF PROFESSIONAL RESPONSIBILITY, CANON 7 (1908) Canon 7, A Lawyer Should Represent A Client Zealously Within The Bounds of Law., DR 7 101.

48 *See* Uniform Power of Attorney Act, § 106, UPOAA_2011_final; Accessed 12 Feb., 2021; https:www.uniformlaws.org

49 Numbers 11:16-18; Rabbi Aryeh Kaplan, 1979 "Handbook of Jewish Thought," https://www.aish.com; Accessed 21 Oct., 2021.

50 U.S. Const. Amend. V.

51 *See* Hestrin, Ruth, Israel, Yael, Mshorer, Yaakov, Eitan, Avraham, Inscriptions Reveal: Documents from the time of the Bible, the Mishnah and the Talmud, the Israel Museum, Jerusalem, 1973; The Israel Museum, Publisher: Harry N. Abrams, Inc., 2005; Israeli, Yael, Mevorach, David, Cradle of Christianity, the Israel Museum, 2000 "To the Place of Trumpeting," https://www.ima.org.il, Accessed 21 Oct., 2021.

52 1 Thessalonians 4:16

53 D-T, Torah; American-Israeli Cooperative Enterprise c1998-2021

54 U.S. Const. Amend. Vl, *See Lewis v. United States*, 518 US 322 (1996)

55 Maimonides. "The Sanhedrin and the Penalties within their Jurisdiction." 11.1 *See* Court Sessions, Jewishvirtuallibrary.org; *See* Shira Schoenberg, Ancient Jewish History: The Sanhedrin

56 Ibid

57 Disqualification of Justice, Judge, or Magistrate, 28 U.S.C § 455

58 D-T, Torah

59 *See* Eliahu Harnon, "Criminal Procedure In Israel-Some Comparative Aspects," University of Pennsylvania Law Review, Vol.115:1091; *See also* D-T, Torah

60 U.S. Const. Amend. Vl; U.S. Const. Amend. Vll

61 D-T, Torah

62 Exodus 23:18

63 Mark 14:36; See Otfried Hofius, "Father," NIDNTT 1:614–621

64 John 15:15 (ESV).

65 Amicus Curiae, US Supreme Court Rules 33.1, 34, 37.2, 37.3

66 Definitions.uslegal.com; Accessed 23 Oct., 2021; Handcuffs

67 Patent Act of 1952, 35 USC § 101–103

68 Ibid

69 Frederick M. Abbott. Thomas, Cottier & Francis Gurry, International Property in An Integrated World Economy 8 (2007); Federal Trademark Act 15 USC 1051 et.seq.

70 US Const. Amend. VI.

71 Samuel J. Levine, An introduction to Self-Incrimination in Jewish Law, with Application to the American Legal System: A Psychological and Philosophical Analysis, 28 Loy. L.A. Int'l & Comp. L. Rev., 257, pp 264-265 (2006); CODE OF MAIMONIDES, Laws of Sanhedrin 18:6

72 *See* Mark 14:65, Matthew Isaiah 50:6, *See* Mark 14:65; Luke 22:64; John 19:2)

73 Cornell Law School-Double Jeopardy/Wex/US law/Lll/Legal Information Institute; THE CODE OF MAIMONIDES, BOOK 14; THE BOOK OF JUDGES, Sanhedrin ch. 18, para. 6)

74 "Dying declaration," Fed. R. Evid.804(b)(2)

75 Aaron Schreiber, Jewish Law and Decision-Making: A Study Through Time 29–30

76 Possession. *See National Safe Deposit Co. v. Stead*, 232 U.S, 58,34 S. CT. 209, 58 l. Ed. 504 (1914)

77 *See* Anthony R. Mellows, The Law of Succession 6 (3 ed. 1977) *See* https:www.americanbar.org/probate, Accessed 24 Oct., 2021. When a will is legally probated, the court acts as a supervisor over its administration and execution, specifically according to the testator's wishes.

78 *See Division of Labor Law Enforcement v. Transpacific Transportation Co.* 88 Cal. App. 3 823, 829 (Cal. Ct. pp.1979); https://www.law.cornell.edu/wex/adoption

79 *See* <www.holylandsite.com> Accessed 25 Oct., 2021

80 *See* <www.panhellenicgames.org> Accessed 26 Oct., 2021; Apostle Paul is reputed to have been living in Corinth, Greece at the time of an Isthmus game in 51AD

81 Mens Rea; *See Staples v. United States* 511 US 600, 114 S.Ct. 1793 (1994); *See also* Marshall, Thurgood, and Supreme Court of the United States, U.S. Reports

82 US Const. Amend. IV.

83 *Miranda v. Arizona* 384 U.S. 436 (1966); Const. Amend. IV. U.S. Const. Amend. V; U.S. Const. Amend. VI

84 Chain of Custody, Fed. R. Evid. 901, 902; See C. McCormick, Evidence 527–8 (2d. Ed.) 1972 *Novak v. District of Columbia*, 160 F. 2d 588, 589 (D.C.Cir. 1947).

85 Fed. R. Evid. 801, 803, 805 (Double Hearsay)

86 *Marbury v. Madison*, (5 US 137 1803)—"held the role of the judiciary to interpret what the constitution permits'-the principle of judicial review."

87 M.G.L. § 93(A), Sec.9, Massachusetts Consumer Protection Law; *See Moronta v. Nationstar Mortgage*, LLC, 476 Mass. 1013 (2016)

88 *See* Josephus and Jesus-Apologetics, https://www.namb.net, Published 30 Mar., 2016; Accessed 28 Oct., 2021

CPSIA information can be obtained
at www.ICGtesting.com
Printed in the USA
BVHW031949170622
640071BV00010B/436